Everlasting Gospel Series:

Genesis

Everlasting Gospel Series:

Genesis

Chunsik Park, Ph.D.
Translated by Juhyun Park

도서출판 디자인

Endorsement

Dr. Chunsik Park has produced a magnificent biblical theology of the book of Genesis, concentrating upon the Everlasting Gospel and related themes in the first book of the Bible.

Starting with his landmark doctoral dissertation on "Theology of Judgment in Genesis 6-9" (PhD dissertation, Andrews University, 2005), Dr. Park has devoted much of his scholarly career to researching the marvelous subject of the Everlasting Gospel throughout Scripture, with special focus on the Gospel narratives in the book of Genesis. This book represents a sample of the succulent ripe fruit of that lifetime of diligent study.

Throughout the book he has taken care to be faithful to the foundational biblical principles of interpretation as articulated by the Reformers: Sola Scriptura ("Bible Only"), Solus Christus ("Only Christ"), Sola Fide ("Faith Alone"), Sola Gratia ("Grace Alone"), and Soli Deio Gloria ("Glory to God Alone"). Going far beyond mere proof-texts to support the various themes that relate to the Everlasting Gospel in Genesis, Dr. Park has meticulously and forcefully presented the wider archaeological, linguistic, and/or theological context of each passage dealt with.

In the 21 chapters of the book, after sketching the intricate literary-theological structure of Genesis within the wider context of the Pentateuch, the author provides a profound and comprehensive biblical synthesis of the major themes involved in the Everlasting Gospel of Genesis, divided into five parts: The Great and Merciful God, Humanity, Sin and Judgment, Grace and Salvation, and Beginning and End. Each part is well organized and rich with scintillating theological insights, in-depth word studies, careful documentation in footnotes, analysis of pertinent sub-themes that support the major themes, and cogent connections with later revelations of the themes elsewhere in Scripture.

While Dr. Park's book is a masterpiece of biblical theology, it is written in an accessible style that invites the reader to embrace the everlasting gospel in his/her individual experience. I have personally received a great spiritual blessing from reading this book; it has enhanced my appreciation for the Everlasting Gospel in Genesis and the rest of Scripture, and it has deepened my love for Jesus Christ, the Center of this Everlasting Gospel.

I am honored to be asked to write a recommendation for the book of my esteemed colleague who long ago I was privileged to guide and mentor in his Ph.D. program at Andrews University. Words fail me to adequately describe the wonderful book he has written, but I have done my best to succinctly present the aspects of the book that have been most meaningful to me, and hopefully, to the reader. I highly recommend this book to all who wish to have an increased understanding and experience of the Everlasting Gospel in Genesis (and beyond), and who wish to share this amazing Christ-centered Gospel message with the world.

Richard M. Davidson, Ph.D.

Senior Research Professor of Old Testament
Seventh-day Adventist Theological Seminary, Andrews University

Foreword

Every sacred page of the Bible resounds with the voice of the Almighty, who in his infinite grace yearns to deliver humanity from its fallen state. Through the sacred text, God imparts divine instruction, solace to the weary, and hope that illuminates the path of his beloved creation (Rom. 15:4). All Scripture is the Word of God, inspired by the Holy Spirit. This same Holy Spirit, whose gentle touch graced the prophets of old, descends upon us as we enter into prayer and seek to unlock the profound wisdom within the sacred pages. In humble obedience, we approach the Scriptures, allowing the Spirit to attend to our spiritual needs, guide our earthly pilgrimage, and transform us into vessels worthy of dwelling in God's eternal kingdom.

The eschatological message that prepares us for God's eternal kingdom is referred to as the "everlasting gospel" in Revelation, the last book of the Bible (Rev. 14:6). Once this everlasting gospel has been preached to "those who dwell on the earth—to every nation, tribe, tongue, and people," Jesus Christ will return to reap the harvest of his saints and bring them into the heavenly granary (Rev. 14:14-20). The everlasting gospel has eternal consequences. How vital and urgent it is to understand and accept this message in this age!

What is the everlasting gospel?

This gospel is essentially that all of humanity, which inherited the consequences of sin through the first Adam, may receive eternal life through Jesus Christ, the last Adam. This divine plan of salvation has been part of God's wisdom throughout eternity and was fully unveiled through the incarnation of Jesus Christ. The fulfillment of this redemption was, is being, and will be achieved through the Lord's death, resurrection, ascension, and Second Coming. It is a subject of profound praise, deserving of eternal gratitude and praise from humanity throughout eternity.

Since the dawn of time, beginning with the promise of Jesus Christ as the seed of the woman in Genesis 3:15, God has consistently proclaimed the "good news" of mankind's salvation through various means, including covenants, laws, prophecies, and the sanctuary system. Ultimately, the "good tidings of great joy which will be to all people" was fulfilled through the first coming of Jesus (Luke 2:10. Cf. Isa. 40:9; 52:7; 61:1). The Advent of Jesus Christ is a profound eschatological event. He is the one who appeared "in these last days" and, embodying the Gospel, proclaimed the Good News of the kingdom through his person and ministry to shine the light of salvation on those who were lost deep within the valley of the shadow of death (Heb. 1:2; Matt. 4:16, 17, 23; 9:35). Through his restorative ministry of teaching, preaching, and healing, Jesus restored physical health to the infirm, brought joy to hearts weary from false teachings, and imparted holiness to hearts corrupted by sin. Prior to his crucifixion, Jesus ardently desired that the gospel of the kingdom be preached to the ends of the earth; after his resurrection, He entrusted his disciples with the great command to preach this gospel to all nations (Matt. 24:14; 28:18-20).

The everlasting gospel is the truth revealed by the Holy Spirit throughout the Bible, from Genesis to Revelation. God's revelation of the plan of salvation commenced in Genesis and progressed steadily, shining brighter and brighter as it unfolded throughout the Bible. A comprehensive study of the Scriptures allows us to grasp the plan of redemption; through such a course, readers will find that parts of this plan which were previously understood only in part become as clear as daylight. The essence of true faith lies not in devising or pursuing novel truths through human intellect, but in being faithful children of God who earnestly seek to comprehend his timeless plan of redemption. This plan, meticulously prepared since the dawn of creation, is encapsulated within the Word of God—the Bible.

The everlasting gospel is a crucial truth that needs to be proclaimed in the present age. Throughout history, Satan, the great deceiver, has led people to attack or ignore God's special truths in order to destroy mankind. In each era, the Church has been entrusted with specific truths from God. In these last days preceding the Second Coming of Jesus Christ, the eternal gospel is the crucial message that must be preached to prepare people for salvation (Rev. 14:6-7).

The everlasting gospel encompasses important theological themes including God's desire to save, Christ's Second Coming as the hope of mankind, man as the object of God's love, God's gifts in the form of his covenants and laws, righteousness by faith, and motifs such as judgment-salvation and creation-re-creation that reveal the destiny of individuals and the world. A profound grasp of the theological themes related to the everlasting gospel can help God's people from being deceived by erroneous teachings and false ideologies, and enable them to partake fully in God's abundant grace, which is sufficient to prepare them for the imminent Second Coming of Jesus Christ.

The everlasting gospel is a core truth of the Bible. The Lamb of God, who was sacrificed for sinners from the foundation of the world, is at the heart of the gospel. True Christian doctrine must always be centered on Christ. Any theological subject that fails to reveal the Holy Trinity extending salvation to sinners is like the dry bones that Ezekiel saw in his vision. Christian doctrine is not simply an intellectual exercise but should be a transformative experience. Dead souls must be brought back to life, souls must be reborn and totally transformed to live a life of gratitude and worship of God—all through the power of the Holy Spirit.

The book of Genesis, though classified as a part of the Pentateuch and as a book of the law, consists not of legal provisions but of captivating narratives. The stories of the Creation, Adam and Eve, Cain and Abel, Noah's Flood, the Tower of Babel, Sodom and Gomorrah, Abraham and the other Patriarchs are all found within this book. These stories touch on crucial theological themes such as God, man, sin, judgment, salvation, covenant, righteousness by faith, the remnant, creation, and the end times. These themes are vital to understanding the everlasting gospel.

This book deals with theological topics in Genesis that pertain to the everlasting gospel. These are essential topics for understanding the gospel of Jesus Christ. Of course, these do not make up the whole of the everlasting gospel. God, who is our salvation, is the "all in all" and "Father of all," and Jesus Christ his Son is "all, and in all," and "heir of all"; thus, salvation is not a theme that can be described using just a few subjects (1 Cor. 15:28; Eph. 4:6; Col. 3:11; Heb. 1:2). The Bible is a great ocean of truth. It is the author's hope and prayer that this book will serve as one of many humble vessels that aids the reader as they navigate the sea of God's grace in their journey towards heavenly shores.

This book takes a different approach from many other works that deal with biblical themes. Many theological works cite to various passages of Scripture that support the relevant theme, without fully exploring the context of the cited Scripture. Although this approach can be helpful to understanding the particular theological topic, one sometimes receives the impression that the interpretation is forced. Readers may also end up with a superficial understanding of the biblical passages that are stripped of their context. This book, in contrast, presents the archaeological, linguistic, and theological background of the text, using the original Hebrew Bible (BHS)—thus it seeks to provide a richer and more concrete understanding of the passages that are examined. While the book is rooted in Genesis, it also connects to other parts of the Old and New Testaments. In short, this book is written from a biblical theological standpoint, with an emphasis on biblical text and theological aspects. This book will be helpful to seminary students and pastors, as well as to other believers including those in laypersons' ministry who wish to explore core truths of the Bible and teach the Word based on sound theological positions.

The everlasting gospel can be defined as Jesus Christ. Said He: "You search the Scriptures, for in them you think you have eternal life: and these are they which testify of me" (John 5:39). In other words, the book of Genesis testifies of Jesus Christ. This aspect is covered in more detail in the companion book to this one, Jesus Christ in Genesis. Through the hermeneutical lens provided by the Bible itself, the reader can see Christ as revealed in every chapter of Genesis.

The study of Genesis marks only the initial step in comprehending the depths of the everlasting gospel. As one delves into the entire spectrum of biblical books, from Genesis to Revelation, one encounters a rich tapestry of unique hues, voices, and images, each contributing to the grand narrative of God's plan of salvation. The river of redemption flows like a mighty river over the vast expanse of God's truth. Jesus Christ, our Shepherd, provides his flock with nourishing spiritual sustenance and refreshing living water. It is the author's heartfelt prayer that while reading this book, readers will experience the transformative power of the gospel. Embracing this gospel will ignite a fervent desire to live dedicated lives as disciples of Christ, fervently proclaiming his righteousness and hope to all corners of the earth.

I would like to express my heartfelt gratitude to the individuals who have contributed deeply in my journey to share the everlasting gospel. First and foremost, I extend my deepest thanks to my beloved family. To my wife, Hyunsook, who has been a constant source of love, support, and prayer. Her unwavering encouragement and desire for me to stand firmly as a man of the Word have been a driving force in my ministry. I am grateful for her enduring patience and understanding as she walked alongside me on this path. To my daughter, Juhyun, I am thankful for unwavering support and encouragement in my evangelistic endeavors. Her enthusiasm for sharing the gospel has been a great source of inspiration. My son, Sungjoon, has been a blessed and loving presence in my life. He has consistently reminded me that God is my ultimate hope and has directed my attention to the far corners of the earth, where the need for evangelism is pressing.

I want to express my immense gratitude to Dr. Richard M. Davidson, Dean of the Department of Old Testament at Seventh-day Adventist Theological Seminary, Andrews University in USA. As my advisor and mentor, he prayed for and encouraged me on my academic journey and also provided opportunities for me to teach Old Testament lectures to students from various parts of the world. his mentorship and expertise have enriched my understanding of the Scriptures and have been instrumental in shaping my theological perspective.

Lastly, I want to extend my appreciation to the publisher, Light and Sound, for their professional efforts in bringing the Korean edition of this book to life. Their commitment to excellence has made this endeavor possible.

To all these individuals and countless others who have supported and contributed to my journey of sharing the everlasting gospel, I offer my sincerest thanks. May we continue to be vessels of God's truth, proclaiming his message of hope and redemption to all who would hear.

Chunsik Park, Ph.D.

Contents

PART I
The Theological Structure of the Pentateuch and Genesis

PART II
Great and Merciful God

PART V
Grace and Salvation

Chapter 12 Events and Procedures of Judgment in Genesis / 151

Chapter 13 Salvation / 178

Chapter 14 The Covenant / 190

Chapter 15 The Law and the Sabbath / 207

Chapter 16 Sacrifices and Altars / 220

Chapter 17 The Remnant / 226

PART VI

Beginning and End

Chapter 18 Revelation / 233

Chapter 19 Creation / 244

Chapter 20 Creation and Judgment / 249

Chapter 21 Eschatology / 256

PART I

The Theological Structure of the Pentateuch and Genesis

Chapter 01 The Theological Structure of the Pentateuch

Chapter 02 The Theological Structure of Genesis

Chapter 01 | The Theological Structure of the Pentateuch

1. What is the Pentateuch?

The Bible consists of the New Testament and the Old Testament. The Old Testament was composed primarily in Hebrew, with some portions written in Aramaic, while the New Testament was recorded in Greek. The book of Genesis, which is the focus of our study, is a part of the Old Testament.

The arrangement of the Old Testament varies between Christianity and Judaism. In Christian Bibles, the Old Testament is arranged in the following order: the Pentateuch, the historical books, the Psalms and wisdom literature, and the major and minor prophets. Judaism divides the Old Testament into three sections: the Torah ("Book of the Law"), the *Nevi'im* ("Prophets"), and the *Ketubim* ("Holy Writings"). In accordance with the Jewish classification, Jesus spoke of the Old Testament as "the law of Moses and the Prophets and the Psalms" (Luke 24:44).

The Torah, which constitutes the initial portion of the Bible, is called the Pentateuch (or the five books of Moses, after its reputed author) because it consists of five books: Genesis, Exodus, Leviticus, Numbers, and Deuteronomy.[1] The Pentateuch serves as a crucial foundation for comprehending the rest of the Bible, as many major theological concepts and ideas found throughout the Bible can trace their origins back to the Pentateuch.

Torah means "law." However, it is important to note that while the Pentateuch contains legal elements, its primary content consists of a rich narrative. In addition to its legal aspects, the Pentateuch encompasses stories that hold profound theological significance, including the Creation account, the fall of mankind, the Flood, the Tower of Babel, the story of Israel's patriarchs—Abraham, Isaac, Jacob, and Joseph—and Moses, the Exodus, and the experiences of the Israelites during their journey in the wilderness before entering Canaan.

These stories carry a profound theological intent. They reveal that God, the Creator, is not

1 The English word "Pentateuch" is a combination of the Greek words *penta* (πέντα), meaning "five," and *teuchos* (τεῦχος), which literally means "a case for carrying papyrus rolls" and later came to refer to the scroll itself. Herbert Wolf, *An Introduction to the Old Testament Pentateuch*, 17.

separated from his creation but rather actively intervenes in human history. The Pentateuch showcases God's close and intimate relationship with individuals, nations, and the world as a whole. From the outset, at creation, God blessed mankind and gave the command to "be fruitful and multiply; fill the earth" (Gen. 1:28). However, humanity's fall led to a world fraught with suffering, marked by the threats of disease, death, natural disasters, and war. Nevertheless, God through his plan of redemption seeks to restore to mankind the peace and happiness of the lost Eden. Throughout the narratives of the Pentateuch, we witness God's continuous efforts to save humanity and bring about restoration. The stories of the people in the Pentateuch serve as profound illustrations of God's ongoing work to redeem and reconcile mankind to Himself.

Torah also means "instruction, guidance." Within the Pentateuch, the interplay of stories and laws serves to impart profound insights into God's love for humanity and the proper ways for individuals to live in relation to both God and fellow human beings. Through the study of the Pentateuch, we can uncover the fundamental principles that underlie God's interactions with human beings. This knowledge provides us with a valuable paradigm through which we can interpret the diverse sources and messages found within the Bible, facilitating a deeper understanding of God's love, divine purpose, and ethical guidelines for righteous living.[2]

The Pentateuch is not merely a haphazard assortment of stories and laws. Each book within it is thoughtfully organized with a focus on chronological and theological coherence. By discerning the central content and theological intent of each book, we can apprehend the unity that underlies the entirety of the Pentateuch and recognize the theological themes that flow throughout the Old Testament. Furthermore, a profound comprehension of the Pentateuch serves as a foundation for grasping the main teachings of the New Testament.

The Old Testament period may, based on the history of the Israelite nation, be divided into the following: the pre-patriarchal age, the age of the patriarchs, the Exodus, the settlement of Canaan, the age of judges, the age of the united kingdom, the age of the divided kingdoms, the age of the kingdom of Judah, and the age of exile and return. Among these, the Pentateuch covers the pre-patriarchal age (Gen. 1-11), the age of the patriarchs (Gen. 12-50), and the Mosaic age (Exodus through Deuteronomy).[3] Let us now examine the theological structure of the Pentateuch using this chronological division.

2 David J. A. Clines, *The Theme of the Pentateuch*, 102.

3 Walter C. Kaiser, Jr., 'The Theology of the Old Testament,' *The Expositor's Bible Commentary: Introductory Articles*, 291-305.

2. Historical Classification and Major Themes of the Pentateuch

(1) Pre-Patriarchal Age

The pre-patriarchal age, found in Genesis 1-11, pertains to the early phase of human history before the arrival of the Israel's patriarchs. Genesis 1-11 records the creation, the fall, the Flood, and the tower of Babel, all of which are essentially global events. Theological themes of "creation-uncreation-re-creation" and the "spread of sin and spread of grace" are intricately woven throughout this section.[4] The "creation-uncreation-re-creation" theme highlights the greatness of God, emphasizing his power and authority as the ultimate creator. On the other hand, the theme of "spread of sin and spread of grace" bears witness to God's merciful nature as the savior, extending grace to humanity despite the presence of sin. Both themes underscore the reality that the great creator, exercising absolute sovereignty, offers the gift of grace by working to restore the lost paradise to mankind.

The truth that God the creator is our savior and restorer, is an eternal reality, representing the essence of the everlasting gospel. The core message of the everlasting gospel is embedded like a seed within the narratives of Genesis 1-11. This seed germinates, progressively develops and bears rich fruit against the backdrop of the great controversy between God and Satan. Let us briefly examine the fundamental principles of salvation present within the narratives of the pre-patriarchal age.

1) Blessing

God created man to be the most blessed among all creatures. Made in the image of God, humans received a divine blessing to "be fruitful and multiply; fill the earth" (Gen. 1:27-28). Remarkably, this blessing persisted despite the presence of human sinfulness. During the pre-Flood era, this divine promise found fulfillment as "men began to multiply on the face of the earth" (Gen. 6:1). After the Flood, this blessing was reaffirmed to the new Adam, Noah (Gen. 8:17; 9:1, 7). The genealogies outlined in Genesis 1-11, tracing the descendants of Cain, Adam, Noah's three sons, and the line of Shem after the tower of Babel, serve to demonstrate the continuity of this divine blessing (Gen. 4:16-22; 5:3-32; 10:1-32; 11:10-26). As we progress through the Pentateuch, we find this blessing extending to other parts of the narrative, underscoring the significance of this divine favor in the unfolding history of God's people.

2) Descendants

When Adam sinned, God offered the promise of salvation for humanity, as recorded in Genesis 3:15.

---

4 Clines, 61-79.

This divine promise entailed that salvation would come through the "seed" of the woman, who would triumph over the serpent by bruising its head. The Old Testament tells the story of God's preparing for the birth of Jesus Christ, the seed of the woman, by selecting one race (the Semites) (Gen. 9:26-27); one man (Abraham); one nation (Israel); and one dynasty (king David's line). In the fullness of time, Jesus Christ was born on the earth as a descendant of Abraham and David (Matt. 1:1; Gal. 4:4).

(2) Patriarchal Age

When humanity faced dispersion as a consequence of God's judgment following the Tower of Babel incident, God called Abraham and made a covenant with him in order to save mankind. The Abrahamic Covenant has the following characteristics:

1) Nation

"I will make of thee a great nation" (Gen. 12:2). This promise was fulfilled through the birth of Abraham's sons, Isaac and Ishmael; Isaac's sons, Jacob and Esau; and Jacob's twelve sons. Through them, the various peoples of the Near East emerged. Through the lineage of Abraham, Isaac, and Jacob, the nation of Israel emerged as a central figure in the grand tapestry of redemptive history. Genesis 12-50 tells the story of the patriarchs of the nation of Israel. It shows God preparing a nation destined to stand on the side of the seed of the woman in the great controversy between good and evil.

2) Land (Inheritance)

God promised to give the future nation of Israel the land of Canaan, and promised that its borders would extend "from the river of Egypt to the great river, the River Euphrates" (Gen. 15:18). The fulfillment of this promise is shown later on in the Old Testament: Exodus through Deuteronomy tell the story of the Israelites' exodus from Egypt and journey toward the promised land, while Joshua and Judges deal with their settlement in the land of Canaan. The territorial expansion that God promised took place during the days of David and Solomon.

3) Gospel of Blessing

The promise that Abraham would be a blessing to all nations is an extension of the proto-evangelium (original gospel) encapsulated in Genesis 3:15. The woman's seed would come through the Semites, and specifically, from among the descendants of Abraham. God separated Abraham from the idolatrous land of his ancestors in order to make him the source of the gospel of life—the

Mesopotamians had worshipped more than 400 gods.[5]

(3) Mosaic Age

After the Israelites migrated to Egypt because of the great famine in Jacob's day, they continued to enjoy God's blessing given at the time of creation, to "be fruitful and multiply"; however, they could not fulfil their destiny of becoming the source of blessing for all nations as long as they remained assimilated within Egypt's polytheistic culture, in which as many as 240 gods were worshipped. Thus, in his providence, God raised up Moses to lead the Israelites out of Egypt and to guide them through a transformative period of forty years in wilderness. During this time, Israel had the precious opportunity to encounter God's presence firsthand, and to be transformed into a holy nation and a royal priesthood.

1) God's Presence

In the days of Moses, God intimately walked alongside his people. God looked upon the Israelites who were suffering in Egypt and cared about them (Ex. 2:25). The first commandment in the Jewish version of the Ten Commandments, found in Exodus 20:2, bears witness to this divine relationship: "I am the Lord your God, who brought you out of the land of Egypt, out of the house of bondage." This declaration serves as an official statement indicating God's presence and guiding hand and is reiterated approximately 125 times throughout the Old Testament. While the Exodus itself was a singular historical event, its spiritual significance endured throughout Israel's history. The memory of God's deliverance in the Exodus was cherished and continually invoked in times of distress, offering renewed hope and assurance to God's people whenever they faced adversity.

During the time of Moses, abundant symbols of God's presence manifested in various tangible forms: the thorn bush that remained unconsumed by the fire; Moses' rod that displayed miraculous power; the guiding pillars of cloud and fire; the daily provision of manna; God's appearance on Mount Sinai; the giving of the Ten Commandments and the Law directly from God Himself; and the sacred sanctuary, which served as God's dwelling place. These material symbols were profound representations of God's involvement in the lives of his people.

Through the Sinai Covenant, God established Israel as his *segulla* ("possession"), that is, his treasured possession or special people, uniquely belonging to him (Ex. 19:5).[6] The divine promise outlined

5 Young Jin Kim, Torah – *Introduction to the Pentateuch*, Revised and Expanded edition (Seoul, Handeul Press), 25.

6 John P. Milton, Our Hebrew Christian Heritage, 95.

in Exodus 19:6 reveals two important roles Israel would play in redemptive history through their communion with God: first, a "kingdom of priests," serving as mediator between God and the other nations; and second, a "holy nation," set apart and consecrated to live in obedience to God's commands.

2) Nation of Priests

Just as the priesthood was instituted to benefit the people, so Israel, as a kingdom of priests, was to exist for the benefit of all nations. They were to be a source of blessing by faithfully keeping God's law, heeding the voice of his prophets, and being faithful in their covenant relationship with God. As priests unto the Gentile nations, they were to serve as mediators, leading others to know and worship Yahweh.[7] Regrettably, Israel failed to fulfill her mission as a nation of priests and, instead, strayed into idolatry, ultimately facing destruction at the hands of Assyria and Babylon. However, God's original intent of establishing Israel as a kingdom of priests would ultimately find its realization through the New Testament church, which he established to be a "royal priesthood" (1 Pet. 2:9).

3) Holy Nation

God's most eminent attribute is holiness. In Leviticus 19:2, God instructs his people to be holy because he himself is holy. To facilitate this, God appointed the tribe of Levi as priests to represent and serve on behalf of all of Israel. Leviticus primarily focuses on guiding the Israelites in living a holy life. Its purpose is for the Israelites to become holy, just as God is holy.

The concept of holiness in Leviticus extends beyond religious practices; it encompasses every aspect of life. This book addresses diverse matters including dietary laws, dress codes, architectural guidelines for houses, interpersonal relationships, personal hygiene like using the toilet or bathing, and much more. Its central message is that holiness should pervade all aspects of life. Israel was to become a sanctified people by being faithful to God's Word.

3. Message of Hope—the Central Idea of the Pentateuch

The central theme running through the Pentateuch is God's desire to save humankind. God initially created man in a vibrant world filled with life. However, when Adam disbelieved God and faced death, God provided the proto-evangelium (original gospel) as seen in Genesis 3:15. As

7 Ibid., 98.

humanity grew increasingly corrupt, God rescued the seed of mankind through Noah, preserving mankind from a worldwide flood. Following the Flood, despite mankind's continued inclination toward evil, God acknowledged humanity as bearers of his image and reaffirmed the blessing of creation to be fruitful and multiply (Gen. 8:21; 9:6-7).

Similar to the proto-evangelium pronounced after the fall of man, God blessed Shem to continue carrying the message of hope after Noah sinned (Gen. 9:26-27). Amid the spiritual darkness after the Tower of Babel, where mankind was mired in misunderstandings of God, God called upon Abraham, a descendant of Shem, to become a beacon of light, illuminating the world with the message of life.

Through Abraham, the nation of Israel emerged, envisioned as a royal kingdom of priests. However, the Pentateuch portrays Israel as a people frequently rebelling against God. Their apostasy resulted in Moses being unable to enter the land of Canaan. Deuteronomy records a speech that Moses delivered to the people on the borders of Canaan. In Deuteronomy 28, he emphasized the dire consequences of disobedience more forcefully than he proclaimed the blessings of obedience.[8] Moses' final gospel message took the form of a stern admonition to the people.

Throughout the Pentateuch, the recorded accounts reveal man's consistent tendency to fail. Adam, Noah, Abraham, Isaac, Jacob, Moses, and even the entire nation of Israel, all leave a legacy of shortcomings and mistakes. However, in response to these failures, God extends his merciful hand of forgiveness, restoration, and salvation to mankind time and again.

To Adam, in his sinful state, God promised the coming of the seed of the woman—a foreshadowing of the Messiah who would bring redemption. To Noah, despite his failings, God revealed that the Savior would descend through Shem. In moments of crisis, God actively intervened to protect Abraham and Isaac, even when they resorted to deception to save themselves. He was present with Jacob as he fled from his deceived brother, offering a vision of a ladder reaching to heaven and promising to be with him. When Moses was unable to enter Canaan due to his sins, God demonstrated his power by resurrecting him and guiding him to a better home (Jude 1:9). God's promises extended to the nation of Israel as well: Even should they face the consequences of their sins and be taken to a foreign land, God would restore them if they remembered Him and turned

8 Deuteronomy 28 lists blessings for obeying the covenant and curses for disobedience. The section of blessings spans 15 verses (vs. 1-15), whereas the portion describing curses encompasses 53 verses (vs. 16-68) containing curses. Consequently, there are approximately 3.5 times more verses dedicated to detailing the curses than blessings.

back to Him (Deut. 30:1-10).

The Pentateuch thus portrays a consistent pattern of human failures met with God's grace and unwavering commitment to forgive, restore, and provide salvation to his people despite their shortcomings.

The Kingdom of Judah faced utter destruction at the hands of Babylon, a catastrophic event akin to a national death. However, in an awe-inspiring display of divine power, God resurrected this seemingly lifeless nation. He led his people back to Jerusalem from Babylon and reestablished a nation. It was within this restored Jewish nation that Jesus, the Savior, was born. Despite man's defeat, God's ultimate plan of salvation was fulfilled entirely by his grace.

The great men in the Pentateuch placed their hope in the God who passionately fulfills his promise of salvation, even for the helpless sinner who stumbles right after thinking they have a firm hold. This God remains our hope as we journey through these last days of Earth's history.

Chapter 02 | The Theological Structure of Genesis

The Hebrew Bible names the book of Genesis *bereshit* meaning "in the beginning," after the book's opening word, following ancient Near Eastern convention.[1] The book consists of 78,064 Hebrew characters. The modern 50-chapter division was introduced by the medieval rabbi Solomon ben Ishmael around 1330 A.D. In Palestine and Egypt, where the custom dictated reading the entire Torah once every three years, Genesis was divided into 43 or 45 chapters. The Babylonian Jews, who read the entire Torah once a year, divided Genesis into 12 chapters.[2]

The theological structure of the book of Genesis is defined by its content and the unfolding narrative, as explored below.

1. Beginnings

As the opening phrase, "in the beginning," implies, the book of Genesis revolves around beginnings or origins. It covers the origins of the following:

Physical Universe. Skies, earth, plant kingdom, animal kingdom (Gen. 1)

Humans. Men and women, marriage, family, civilization, society, urban life, arts and handicrafts, human government (Gen. 2-5, 9-11)

Sin. Disobedience, failure, separation from God, death, anger, murder, God's judgment (Gen. 3-4, 6-9, 12, 19)

Redemption. Promise, sacrifice, worship, prayer, prophecy (Gen. 3-4, 9, 12)

Nations. The three major ethnic groups: Semites, Hamites, Japhetites; individual nations; languages (Gen. 9-11, 36)

1 In the Hebrew Bible, each book in the Pentateuch is named after its beginning verses. Genesis, *bereshit* ("in the beginning"); Exodus, we'elle shemot ("These are the names"); Leviticus, wayyiqra ("And he called") were all named after the first word(s) of the book. Numbers, bemidbar ("in the wilderness") and Deuteronomy, debarim ("Words") take their titles from the first line.

2 Each part is called a parashah (pl. parashot or parshiyot) or sidra (pl. sedarot). Nahum M. Sarna, Genesis (Philadelphia, PA: The Jewish Publication Society, 1989), xi.

Israel. Abrahamic mission and covenant, the chiefs of the twelve tribes (Gen. 12, 15, 17, 35, 49)
Faith. Personal relationship and companionship with God (Gen. 15:6; Heb. 11:3-22)[3]

2. *Toledot*: God at Work in history

The book of Genesis is not a mere compilation of disconnected stories; rather, it presents a series of narratives with a coherent and intentional purpose. To achieve the unity of the narrative, Genesis employs a significant device called *toledot*. This term, derived from the word *yld*[4] meaning "to conceive, to beget," is used 13 times in Genesis, and 39 times in the Old Testament.

Toledot has three functions. First, it serves as a "major structural word" that introduces and unfolds new content, similarly to a chapter in a book. *Toledot* divides the book of Genesis as follows:[5]

Creation (Gen. 1:1-2:3)
Toledot of heaven and earth (Gen. 2:4-4:26)
Toledot of Adam (Gen. 5:1-6:8)
Toledot of Noah (Gen. 6:9-9:29)
Toledot of Shem, Ham, and Japheth (Gen. 10:1-11:9)
Toledot of Shem (Gen. 11:10-26)
Toledot of Terah (Gen. 11:27-25:11)
Toledot of Ishmael (Gen. 25:12-18)
Toledot of Isaac (Gen. 25:19-35:29)
Toledot of Esau, the ancestor of Edom (Gen. 36:1-8; 36:9-37:1)
Toledot of Jacob (Gen. 37:2-50:26)

Secondly, *Toledot*, akin to a camera's zoom lens, focuses on specific individuals and their immediate descendants.[6] *Toledot* in Genesis spans from Adam to Noah, Shem, Ham, Japheth, and further follows Shem's lineage to Abraham's father, Terah. The journey continues from Abraham

3 V. Paul Flint, Strangers & Pilgrims: A Study of Genesis (Neptune, NJ: Loizeaux Brothers, 1988), 9-10.

4 A Hebrew root is a verb consisting of three consonant letters. Since it is impossible to pronounce three consecutive consonants, the basic form of the verb (called Qal, perfect, third-person masculine singular) is used as a representative. Thus, the root of toledot is yld (and the representative form is the verb *yalad*.

5 Allen P. Ross, Creation and Blessing: A Guide to the Study and Exposition of the Book of Genesis (Grand Rapids, MI: Baker, 1988), 69-70. Abraham belongs to toledot of Terah.

6 T. Desmond Alexander, From Paradise to the Promised Land: An Introduction to the Pentateuch, 2nd ed. (Grand Rapids, MI: Baker Academic, 2002), 102.

to Isaac, Jacob, and the twelve sons of Jacob, ultimately centering on the Israelites. Against the backdrop of this genealogy, Israel assumes a pivotal role in the salvation of mankind, culminating in the birth of Jesus Christ, who is the promised seed of the woman. The ultimate goal of this genealogical account is to highlight God's chosen people, Israel, and the significance of Jesus Christ in the grand scheme of salvation.

Thirdly, *toledot* serves a crucial purpose in affirming the historicity of the Genesis account. When the aforementioned prominent figures are introduced, the phrase *elleh toledot*, meaning "these are the generations of ...," is used. This phrase acts as an anchor, firmly establishing the historical lineage of Israel from the very beginning of Creation. The descendants are like a keystone in biblical history,[7] while the phrase acts as a seam connecting the preceding and subsequent material.[8] The genealogies presented through *toledot* underscore the fact that characters such as Adam, Noah, and Abraham are not mere myths or legends, but actual historical figures. The events depicted, such as the Creation, the Fall, the Flood, and the Tower of Babel, are portrayed as genuine historical occurrences rather than products of mythical imagination.

Acknowledging the historicity of the Genesis stories is of immense theological importance. God's work of salvation unfolds within human history. In this context, history becomes the story of salvation, and every significant event plays a part in God's grand plan. The human transgression is an actual historical event that took place within the fabric of time; consequently, God's redemption through the cross of Calvary must also manifest as a historical event. The establishment of God's eternal kingdom of peace is not merely a wish or aspiration within the hearts of humanity but an experiential reality that will unfold at the Second Coming of Jesus Christ, at the appointed time set by God.

Through *toledot*, the history of Israel finds a profound connection to Creation. Jewish belief holds that the purpose of Creation is intricately tied to the creation of Israel. This unique perspective carries significant implications for all of us. Israel's very existence had the evangelical mission of serving as instruments in bringing about the restoration of the lost Eden and reconciliation of humanity with God. The divine will to bring salvation remains a mystery accessible only to believers, who alone can comprehend and accept its profound nature. This divine plan was "ordained before the ages" by God and remained "hid from ages and from generations" until it was fully unveiled through the advent of Jesus Christ (1 Cor. 2:7; Col. 1:26). Throughout their history,

7 W. Gunther Plaut, Genesis: Commentary (New York: Union of American Hebrew Congregations, 1974), 19.

8 Kenneth A. Mathews, Genesis 1-4:26, ed. E. Ray Clendenen, The New American Commentary, vol. 1 (Nashville, TN: Broadman & Holman Publishers, 1996), 41.

Ancient Israel experienced and hoped for the kingdom of God, but only in the form of faint shadows prefigured in elements like the sanctuary system, the covenant, and the law.

As Christians, we transcend the faint representations of the Old Testament and, through our profound experience of the reality of Jesus Christ, already catch a foretaste of life in the eternal kingdom. Ancient Israel perceived the shadow of the gospel and found its purpose in the Creation; for the Church of God, as the spiritual Israel that continuously experiences Jesus Christ as the living reality of the Gospel, grounding our identity in Creation is even more important.

We have existed in God's heart since the beginning of time, and were born in these end times with a special mission. We are beings with immeasurable value, as we have been entrusted with the great work of restoring God's creative providence to the earth. The eternal God has raised us up in these last days of history, when all of creation yearns and groans to be restored through the everlasting gospel.

Toledot in Genesis is a list of individuals who have died. The etymology of *toledot* (*yld*, "to conceive, to beget") would suggest that it should be a list characterized by creation, life, and production. However, after the Fall, human existence is marked by a procession of generations and mortality. Even someone like Methuselah who lives for nearly a millennium ultimately meets death as the inevitable endpoint. The book of Genesis, which commences with God's magnificent creation, ultimately concludes with Joseph's death in Egypt. The first book of the Old Testament concludes with the expectation of a historical figure who will ultimately break the chains of the *toledot* of death and initiate the *toledot* of life. And the New Testament opens with God's response to the desperate yearnings of mankind: "This is the *toledot* of life of Jesus the Messiah, the son of Abraham and David" (Matt. 1:1, Zalkinson-Ginsberg Hebrew New Testament (HNT)).

3. Narrative Typology

God has woven valuable lessons for the future within the historical experiences of the past. The accounts of the patriarchs in the Bible are not merely stories of that time; they also serve as previews of Israel's later experiences. Furthermore, these narratives foreshadow the coming of Jesus Christ and offer glimpses into the experiences of the church and God's people in the last days.

The concept of typology, which is an essential aspect of biblical hermeneutics, involves understanding the past and the future in terms of shadows and realities, types and antitypes. Through typology, the past is connected with the future, with a primary focus on what lies ahead, ultimately culminating in the end of time. This approach enables us to discern deeper meanings and spiritual significance from the biblical narratives, as they hold relevance not only in their historical context but also to the unfolding of God's plan for the future. It emphasizes the continuity and divine purpose that stretches across time, leading to the ultimate fulfillment of God's plan in the end times.

The biblical characters were profoundly aware of the interconnectedness between the past and the future. Jacob, Balaam, and Moses spoke about the fate of God's people using poetic language (Gen. 49:1-27; Num. 24:14-24; Deut. 31:29-32:43). These poems all begin with *beaharit hayyamim* ("in the latter days, in the end"): "that I may tell you that what shall befall you in the last days"; "I will advise you what this people will do to your people in the latter days"; and "evil will befall you in the latter days" (Gen. 49:1; Num. 24:14; Deut. 31:29).

Jacob's blessings in Genesis 49 focuses on the future of his twelve sons "in the last days." It is not merely a portrayal of rosy visions; instead, Jacob acknowledges his sons' past deeds alongside prophesying of their future. Last words of Jacob include mention of Reuben's sin of incest and Simeon and Levi's cruel revenge on the people of Shechem, which connects with a somber picture of the times to come (Gen. 49:2-7). In contrast, Jacob praises Judah for his crucial role in saving the family and prophesies that the Messiah, the Savior of all mankind, will descend from his line (Gen. 49:8, 10).

This intertwining of the past and the future demonstrates a close connection between the two. Things that happened to God's people in the past serve as a harbinger of things that will happen to them in the "future" (*beaharit hayyamim*). In other words, past events are understood as lessons for the future.[9] It is akin to casting a stone into a calm lake, creating larger and larger waves that ripple towards the end of the lake; thus, *beaharit hayyamim* entails an eschatological perspective.

J.H. Sailhamer's method of interpreting past narrative texts as foreshadowings of future events is known as "narrative typology."[10] In Genesis, Sailhamer proposes two examples of this approach:[11]

Genesis 12:10–13:4 as a foreshadowing of Genesis 41–Exodus 12. Abraham's flight to Egypt in Genesis 12 serves as a symbolic precursor to the more significant event of the Israelites moving to Egypt and residing there. Just as Abraham left Egypt with Lot, who became the forefather of Moab and Ammon, similarly, a "mixed multitude" accompanied the Israelites during the time of their

---

9 John H. Sailhamer, 'Genesis,' Genesis-Numbers, The Expositor's Bible Commentary (Grand Rapids, MI: Zondervan, 1990), 9.

10 Ibid.

11 Ibid., 9-10; John H. Sailhamer, The Pentateuch as Narrative: A Biblical-Theological Commentary, Library of Biblical Interpretation (Grand Rapids, MI: Zondervan Publishing House, 1992), 37-44.

exodus (Gen. 13:1; Ex. 12:38. Cf. Gen. 19:36-38; Deut. 23:3-4).[12]

The spread of sin in Genesis 1-11 and the defilement of Israelites' camp in Leviticus 11-16. The creatures listed in Leviticus 11 follow the same order as those that were created in the Genesis account. In Genesis 1, God used the word "good" to describe his creation, thereby making a distinction between good (tob, "good") and evil (ra`, "bad"); similarly, Leviticus 11 distinguishes between "clean" and "unclean" animals. Genesis 3 describes the pain of childbirth that resulted from Adam and Eve's sin, while Leviticus 12 provides instructions for after childbirth. Genesis 3 tells us that immediately after man sinned, he became naked and afraid; Leviticus 13 deals with skin diseases, which is an unclean state of the body before a holy God. Just as Adam and Eve were expelled from Eden (Gen. 3:22-24), lepers were required to live in isolation outside the camp (Lev. 13:46). The Flood account in Genesis 6-9 has at least 13 parallels in the laws of Leviticus, while the Tower of Babel account in Genesis 11 has at least two parallels in the laws of Leviticus.[13]

By approaching the Bible with the perspective that the literary content of Genesis serves as a foreshadowing of later events and characters in the history of salvation, we can attain a deeper and more profound understanding of its message. The primary subjects of typology are historical figures, events, and institutions from the Old Testament. These hold significance not only for Old Testament Israel but also for Jesus Christ, the Church, and even us in the last days.[14] When we realize this, we become aware of God's intentional guidance of individuals, nations, and historical accounts to bring about eternal salvation. This realization adds a profound dimension to our appreciation of how God's divine plan unfolds throughout history.

Many types are closely related to Jesus Christ, who is at the center of redemptive history. Below are examples of types that directly represent the person and work of Jesus Christ.

Adam and Eve. Just as Adam and Eve maintained a loving conjugal relationship through a divinely instituted marriage, Christ and the Church form a community marked by boundless and selfless love, akin to the ideal found in a marital union (Gen. 2:20-25; Eph. 5:22-33; cf.

---

12 Just as Lot, the ancestor of the Moabites and Ammonites, was definitively separated from Abraham after the destruction of Sodom, Moses demanded that Moabites and Ammonites be permanently excluded from the congregation of the Lord (Gen. 19; Deut. 23:3-4). Similarly, Nehemiah, based on the command previously delivered by Moses, separated from Israel the ʿereb ("mixed multitude") when dealing with the issue of intermarriage with Gentile women (Neh. 13:1-3).

13 For a more detailed analysis, see Sailhamer, Ibid., 40, 41.

14 Richard M. Davidson, "Biblical Interpretation," Handbook of Seventh-Day Adventist Theology (Hagerstown, MD: Review And Herald Publishing Association, 2001), 83.

Gen. 2:24 and Eph. 5:31-32).

Adam. The first Adam's sinful acts brought death to all mankind, but the last Adam, Jesus, brought life to all through his righteous deeds (Gen. 3:6-12; Rom. 6:14-21; 1 Cor. 15:22, 45).

Tunics of skin. The tunics of skin that God provided to the naked Adam serves as the first sacrifice experienced by humanity. This sacrifice symbolically represents Jesus Christ, who is the "Lamb slain from the foundation of the world" (Gen. 3:21; Rev. 13:8).

Noah's ark. Just as people in the antediluvian era were saved through Noah's ark, mankind finds salvation by being baptized into the resurrected Jesus Christ (Gen. 7:23; 1 Pet. 3:21; Rom. 6:3-4).

Melchizedek, King of Salem. Melchizedek became a "priest of the Most High God" through God's direct appointment; similarly, Jesus, despite belonging to the tribe of Judah and not the priestly tribe of Levi, a family of priests, also became a priest forever (Gen. 14:18; Ps. 110:4; Heb. 5:6, 10; 6:20; 7:11, 15, 17).

Abraham and Isaac. Abraham's willingness to sacrifice Isaac on Mount Moriah symbolizes the profound love for humanity and obedience demonstrated by God the Father and God the Son, as revealed through the crucifixion (Gen. 22:9-18; Rom. 5:8).

Jacob's ladder. The ladder, which served as a sign of God's presence to sinful Jacob, represents Jesus Christ, who bridges the gap between heaven and sinful mankind (Gen. 28:10-19; John 1:47-51).

Joseph. Joseph was deeply cherished by his father, sold into slavery, delivered from the pit of death, saved the people of his day from death by famine, and forgave his brothers. His story embodies a microcosm of the story of Jesus Christ, who forgave and offered redemption to all.

The typological messages in the Bible relating to Jesus Christ enable God's people, living in the presence of the Holy Spirit and the immanence of Jesus Christ, to perceive the Old Testament not merely as stories of others but as an account of their own experiences in this age. As we read any book in the Bible, we go beyond past records and become aware of God's active presence in our lives through his living Word in the present.

The characters in Genesis come alive and become relevant to our lives. Like Enoch and Noah, we walk with God; like Abraham, we hear his voice; and like Jacob, we encounter and wrestle with Him. Through baptism, we enter the ark, identifying with Noah and his family who survived the Flood. As we pass through the waters of baptism, we pass through the waves of death and sin in Jesus Christ, moving toward God's embrace, where He is preparing a new heaven and a new earth (Gen. 7:7, 23; 1 Pet. 3:20-22). When we recognize our sinfulness and experience moments of despair like Jacob, Jesus, the antitype of the ladder that reached the heavens, comes to us with the comforting message, "I am with you" (Gen. 28:12-15; John 1:51).

Through understanding these typological messages, we come to wonder at the exquisite harmony found in the Bible and to gratefully acknowledge God's providence and impact on our lives today. We come to recognize that the events recorded in the Bible carry gospel truths of immeasurable importance for us in the present age.

4. Major Theological Themes

As the story of beginnings, Genesis serves as a treasure trove of numerous theological themes. Among these significant topics are:

God. God is the object of our faith. How we comprehend God shapes our perception of people, the world, and salvation. In Genesis, we gain valuable insights into God's character and actions, helping us understand his nature and his ways.

Mankind. Religion invites profound contemplation on the essence of humanity. In the book of Genesis, we find a portrayal of what it means to be human in the context of our relationship with God.

Sin and judgment. In the book of Genesis, we encounter narratives about the Fall and the subsequent judgment of humanity after Creation. These accounts provide us with insights into the nature of sin and God's response to it.

Salvation. God is the source of blessings for mankind, and his desire is to rescue and save us. Those who turn to God are not turned away but are embraced as part of his divine family. In Genesis, we witness a narrative that beautifully illustrates God's love and his intention to restore humanity.

Remnant. Amidst a wicked and corrupt world, God always has faithful individuals who remain devoted to Him. The Flood account particularly highlights the remnant that God safeguarded as the seed of humanity. In the book of Genesis, we gain valuable insight into the nature of the remnant of the last days.

Revelation. God did not leave mankind to wander aimlessly in pursuit of salvation. Instead, He has consistently revealed the way to live and the path to follow. In the book of Genesis, we discern how God's revelations hold significance for the destiny of the world, the church, and each individual.

Law. God bestowed the Ten Commandments and other divine decrees upon humanity through Moses. These divine laws are manifestations of principles already present in the Genesis stories (cf. Gen. 26:5). Lessons relevant to the Ten Commandments, the laws and the Sabbath that are found in Genesis affirm that God's law is a blessing.

Sacrifices. After the fall of mankind, God provided the proto-evangelium, the first gospel, and tenderly clothed the naked Adam and Eve with tunics of skin. The sacrificial system instituted in Eden foreshadows Jesus Christ, the Lamb of God who redeems the world from sin. The stories of salvation depicted in the sacrifices of the patriarchs in Genesis continue to bring comfort and hope to those living under the grace of the cross.

Creation. God, as the Creator, brought into existence the heavens, the earth, and all that dwell within them. The creation motif in Genesis is evident in the themes of judgment and re-creation, bearing witness to the fact that the Creator is also the Redeemer who will renew all things. The Flood, serving as a model of God's judgment, instills hope in humanity for a new world, reflecting the motif of creation's renewal.

Eschatology. God is the Alpha and the Omega, the First and the Last (Rev. 1:8; 21:6; 22:13). The concept of the beginning and the end being interconnected is evident in the book of Genesis, which addresses the origin of mankind and the genesis of history. Moreover, Genesis offers glimpses into the future and the unfolding of the end times. As we grasp the relationship between origins and eschatology, recognizing the interconnectedness of Genesis and Revelation, our faith in God as the ultimate ruler of history is fortified.

These theological themes represent foundational truths of the everlasting gospel. In the book of Genesis, they exist in their embryonic form and gradually unfold with the increasing revelation. Each theme is interconnected with the others, and a proper comprehension of one is vital to understanding the rest. As we examine the Genesis stories through these themes, the magnificent blueprint of salvation comes to light. In the upcoming chapter, we will embark on a journey through the book of Genesis, seeking to uncover the core truths of Christianity.

5. The Interpreter's Attitude: A Call to Return to the Five Major Principles of the Reformation

Before delving into our journey through Genesis, we must prepare our minds and attitudes, particularly concerning how we approach the Bible. It is undeniable that the history of the Christian

Church revolves around doctrinal matters. Diverse interpretations of the main themes and texts of the Bible have led to varying ideas and attitudes toward God, humanity, the church, and society. In the current age of religious uncertainty, we must recommit ourselves to these five principles advocated by the Reformers, seeking a solid foundation for our faith.

Sola Scriptura (*"Bible Only"*). The Bible alone holds the central position in the Christian life. Our beliefs, actions, and relationships should faithfully align with the teachings of the Bible.

Solus Christus (*"Only Christ"*). Christians are identified by the name of Christ Jesus. Our calling is to embody Christ's presence in the world and be living witnesses of his message. We should diligently seek to recognize Jesus Christ as the focal point of redemptive work throughout the Bible.

Sola Fide (*"Faith Alone"*). As Christians, we must wholeheartedly embrace God's Word as it is. By faith, we accept God's promises and joyfully obey his commands. Through faith and obedience, we can fully experience God's salvation, not only in the hereafter but also in this present life.

Sola Gratia (*"Grace Alone"*). Christians humbly recognize that their salvation is a result of God's abundant grace extended to the undeserving. A thorough study of the Bible will not engender spiritual pride or legalism, but rather inspire us to echo the words of the Apostle Paul: "But by the grace of God I am what I am: and his grace which was bestowed upon me was not in vain; but I labored more abundantly than they all: yet not I, but the grace of God which was with me" (1 Cor. 15:10).

Soli Deo Gloria (*"Glory to God Alone"*). Christians are called to live God-centered lives. Our utmost loyalty should be to God, seeking his glory alone as we live out our lives in our families, churches, nations, and the world.

Many believers are primarily aware of the three principles of Sola Scriptura, Sola Fide and Sola Gratia. While these are essential, we must take one step further. By embracing Solus Christus and Soli Deo Gloria as guiding principles in our study of the Bible and our faith life, we can truly live an eternal evangelical life that centers entirely on Christ and brings glory to God.

PART II

Great and Merciful God

Chapter 03 The Names of God

Chapter 04 God's Works

Chapter 05 God's Attributes

Chapter 06 God's Character

Chapter 03 | The Names of God

1. The Theological Significance of God's Names

The protagonist of Genesis is God. The book begins with, "In the beginning God created the heavens and the earth," and ends with Joseph's parting assurance, "God will surely visit you, and you shall carry up my bones from here" (Gen. 1:1; 50:25).

The Bible does not entertain any doubt about the existence of God; it takes his presence as an inherent truth. In Genesis, the focus lies in understanding God's nature and actions. The book portrays God not as an abstract concept but through the experiences of people who encountered Him, it vividly illustrates God's character and attributes. Most importantly, the various names of God found in the book of Genesis offer profound insights into his identity and reveal different facets of his being.

In the Bible, the first demonstration of man's God-given creative abilities was through the act of naming. "Out of the ground the Lord God formed every beast of the field and every bird of the air; and brought them to Adam to see what he would call them. and whatever Adam called each living creature, that was its name" (Gen. 2:19). "And Adam said: This is now bone of my bones and flesh of my flesh; she shall be called Woman, because she was taken out of Man" (Gen. 2:23). The act of naming is a distinctive intellectual action exclusive to humankind.

The Hebrew word for name, *shem* (comes from an Arabic term, ws'm, meaning "to mark or brand" [1] and signifies a sign or distinguishing mark. Similarly, the Greek word for name, *onoma* (ὄνομα), is derived from a verb meaning "to know."[2] From the perspective of the original language, a name serves to distinguish and identify a person or thing. In a sense, human beings are composed of "body, soul, and name," making an individual's name an indispensable element in distinguishing and defining them.[3]

---

1 Walter C. Kaiser, 'šēm,' *Theological Wordbook of the Old Testament*(=TWOT), (Chicago, IL: Moody, 1980), 934.

2 'God, Names Of', *Tyndale Bible Dictionary*, ed. Walter A. Elwell et al. (Wheaton, IL: Tyndale House Publishers, 2001), 539.

3 Bietenhard, 'ὄνομα, ὀνομάζω, ἐπονομάζω, ψευδώνυμος', *Theological Dictionary of the New Testament*(=TDNT), ed. Gerhard Kittel (Grand Rapids, MI: Eerdmans, 1964-1976), 5:243.

God reveals his existence to humanity through his name. A name carries more significance than just being a title. John described his purpose in recording Jesus' deeds as causing his readers to "believe that Jesus is the Christ, the Son of God, and that believing you may have life in his name" (John 20:31). In this manner, He equated Jesus' name with Jesus Himself, highlighting the profound importance and power of a name.

The Bible, through over 300 divine names, provides a vast panorama of God's nature, character, power, and relationship with us.[4] These names of God encapsulate fundamental truths about Him that we can experience and comprehend.

The primary Hebrew names of God are *Elohim*, *Yahweh*, and *Adonai*, and the Bible includes various compound divine names combining with *El* and *Yahweh*. When arranged in the order of their appearance in the book of Genesis, the names are: *Elohim*, *Yahweh*, *El Elyon*, *Adonai*, *Eloi*, *El-Shaddai*, *El Olam*, and *Yahweh Jireh*. Let's explore these names in the sequence they appear in the Bible, starting with *Elohim*.

2. Elohim

(1) Elohim is our first encounter with God in the Bible.

"In the beginning, *Elohim* created the heavens and the earth" (Gen. 1:1). *Elohim* means God and is used 2,601 times in the Old Testament, with 219 occurrences in Genesis alone. Despite the plural form of *Eloah*,[5] it does not imply polytheistic gods but rather points to one God. *Elohim* is used in conjunction with a singular verb. Its plural form is interpreted as signifying the plurality of God's attributes as the God of gods, including his majesty, intensity, excellence, absoluteness, and exclusivity. The idea of the Trinity is also seen as inherent in this divine designation.[6]

(2) Elohim is God the Creator.

In Genesis chapter 1, the term Elohim, which appears 32 times, is exclusively used to refer to

---

4 Jong Keun Lee, *Hebrew Thinking* (Seoul, Sahmyook University Press, 2007), 40.

5 There are differing views regarding the singular form of *Elohim*,which may be identified as either *El* or *Eloah*, the latter of which appears 57 times in the Old Testament. The Book of Job uses the term *Eloah* 41 times, perhaps to avoid association with Israel. T. E. Fretheim,' 'ĕlōhîm,' *New International Dictionary of Old Testament Theology & Exegesis* (=NIDOTTE), (Grand Rapids, MI: Zondervan 1997), 405; 'God, Names Of', 539.

6 R. Kent Hughes, *Genesis: Beginning and Blessing*, Preaching the Word (Wheaton, IL: Crossway Books, 2004), 18.

the Creator. *Elohim* highlights God's excellence and power over creation, portraying him as intense, vast, and abundant in creative abilities.[7] *Elohim* is a fitting term to describe God's cosmic and global relationship with all creatures, as it encompasses the full range of God's attributes and distinguishes Him from human beings (Num. 23:19) and other creatures.[8] Isaiah affirms that it is "God (*Elohim*), Who formed the earth" (Isa. 45:18), and Jonah declares "the God of heaven, who made the sea and the dry land" (Jonah 1:9).

(3) Elohim has transcendent authority and power.

The Elohim created the heavens and the earth (Gen. 1:1). Heaven and earth are comprised of various elements, including gases like oxygen, nitrogen, and carbon; liquids such as water; and minerals like earth and rock. These elements were intentionally designed to sustain life for animals, plants, and humans. God brought into existence the heavens, the earth, the seas, and all living organisms and inanimate things that are within them.

The creation account unfolds with God first creating light and then populating the space with different environmental elements together with living organisms adapted to such environments. He filled the seas with fish and aquatic creatures, and the sky with two great lights and birds, all contributing to the harmonious balance of the earth's ecosystem.

In these orderly acts of creation, *Elohim* reveals himself as a highly scientific, intelligent, and rational being. Natural science is a means to study the raw materials prepared by *Elohim*, leading us to discover the God of immense power, order, rationality, and intelligence. By exploring and understanding the wonders of the natural world, we gain insights into the greatness and wisdom of the Creator.

(4) Elohim has absolute sovereignty over all things in the universe.

All things came into existence through the creative utterances of Elohim: "God said, let there be ..."; "let them be for ..."; "let... bring forth"; and so forth. The ten instances of *wayyomer elohim* meaning "Then/And God said," brought forth the appearance of creatures in the locations designated through those words (Gen.1:3, 6, 9, 11, 14, 20, 24, 26, 28, 29).

The power of the Word brought forth something out of nothing and established the laws of nature,

---

7 'God, Names Of', *Tyndale Bible Dictionary*, edited by Walter A. Elwell and Philip Wesley Comfort (Wheaton, IL: Tyndale House Publishers, 2001), 539.

8 G. T.; Bruce Manley, F. F., 'God, Names Of', *New Bible Dictionary* (Leicester: Inter-Varsity Press, 1996), 420.

enabling creatures to be fruitful and multiply. Everything that exists in the world, be it animate or inanimate, along with the laws of nature, owes its existence to the creative force of *Elohim*.

(5) God created time.

The first three words of the Bible, "in the beginning," signify a temporal aspect. The once chaotic world, enveloped in darkness and emptiness, transformed into a realm of order deemed good in God's eyes due to his intervention. From that moment, the earth blossomed into a beautiful and abundant world teeming with life.

To signify the transition from static time to a sacred time revealing God's glory, God created light as a demarcation for each day of the Creation week. The Sabbath was instituted to commemorate and proclaim that when creation was finished, this moment connected to the sacred and eternal world of salvation, the limitless time of redemption.

"Then God blessed the seventh day, and sanctified it, because in it He rested from all His work which God had created and made" (Gen. 2:3).

The seventh-day Sabbath exemplifies *Elohim's* sovereignty over time and history. God, who commenced a new chapter in earth's history during the Creation week, "blessed and sanctified" the seventh day. Typically, blessings are bestowed upon the earth, humanity, God's obedient people or their works (Deut. 26:15; Gen. 9:1; 26:11; Deut. 2:7; 7:13; 12:7; 14:29; 15:4, 10; 16:15; 28:12).

God blessed the creatures in the ecosystem, granting them fruitfulness and prosperity. He consecrated the seventh day as a remembrance of the blessed era brought forth by creation. The Sabbath, observed every week, testifies to God, the ruler of history, time, ages, and the entire history of humankind and its redemption.

As finite beings living in time and space, we feel anxious about our survival and seek hope amidst a world filled with sadness, terror and moral turmoil. *Elohim*, the Lord of time and space, is our source of hope. He promises "new heavens and a new earth" where tears, death, mourning, and sorrow will be no more (Isa. 65:17; Rev. 21:1).

(6) The history of salvation is the history of Elohim.

Elohim, the One who governs the stars and the earth, upholds the law of life in all things. This *Elohim* visited humanity in a fallen world. The book of Genesis narrates the stories of characters who had a living relationship with *Elohim*. Below are some examples.

Enoch. Upon the passing of the first man, Adam, the entire world vividly witnessed the inevitable reality of mortality and fell into deep despair. Amidst these dark times, *Elohim* took Enoch, a faithful companion who walked closely with Him, to heaven, his divine abode (Gen. 5:24). Enoch's extraordinary experience served as a revelation to the people of his times that Elohim holds the power of life beyond death, and that those who diligently seek the Lord, the source of life, will receive the gift of eternal life (Heb. 11:6).

Noah. When the world was corrupt and facing self-destruction, *Elohim* chose Noah, a righteous man who walked with Him, to be a messenger of righteousness and work towards saving the old world (Gen. 6:9; 1 Pet. 3:19, 20; 2 Pet. 2:5). *Elohim* selected Noah to become a second Adam who would usher in a new world, and hung a rainbow in the clouds as a sign of his covenant and promise of salvation for humankind (Gen. 8:1; 9:1, 12-16).

Abraham and Lot. During the destruction of Sodom and Gomorrah, *Elohim* remembered Abraham and guided Lot out of the doomed city (Gen. 19:29).

Joseph. Joseph breathed his last with hope in his heart. This was because he had faith in *Elohim*, the redeemer, who would lead his people from Egypt into Canaan and ultimately lead them from this world into eternity. (Gen. 50:25)

Today, *Elohim* is gathering people from all races and languages who live in obedience to him with genuine love in the blessed New Covenant fulfilled through Jesus Christ. God "will be their God, and they shall be My people" (Jer. 31:33; cf. Jer. 32:40).

(7) Elohim is plural, but it is always accompanied by a singular verb or adjective.

This unique usage is specific to the Hebrews and is not observed among other Semitic peoples.[9] At times, *Elohim* is translated as "gods" when referring to the deities of various nations. For instance, the God who delivered Israel from Egypt was called "gods" by the polytheistic Philistines. In such contexts, the corresponding plural forms of adjectives and verbs were used. As an example, in 1 Samuel 4:8, they exclaimed, "Woe to us! Who will deliver us from the hand of these mighty gods? These are the gods who struck the Egyptians with all the plagues in the wilderness." They struggled to comprehend the concept of the one God, who embodies all power and excellence.

(8) Elohim is a revelation of the Trinity.

The distinctive linguistic phenomenon associated with Elohim in the Hebrew Scriptures—use of

9 Leo G. Perdue, 'Names of God in the Old Testament,' *Harper's Bible Dictionary*, ed. Paul J. Achtemeier (San Francisco: Harper & Row, 1985), 686.

a plural noun with singular verbs or adjectives—can be seen as a clear revelation of the triune God. The book of Genesis sheds light on the Trinity through the "us" passages in which God refers to himself.

The first instance of the divine "us" occurs in the Creation account: "God said, Let us make man in Our image, according to Our likeness" (Gen. 1:26). This emphasizes that not only did God establish a covenant of life—to be fruitful and multiply (Gen. 1:22)—with humans when creating them in his image, but there was also an inner covenant within the Trinity at that moment.[10] In accordance with this covenant of life, God fashioned man in the plural but singular form, reflecting God's own plural but singular nature: "So God created man [singular] in his own image; in the image of God He created him [singular]; male and female He created them [plural]" (Gen. 1:27).

The second use of "us" is found in the story of the expulsion of humans from Eden. "Then the Lord God said, 'Behold, the man has become like one of Us, to know good and evil'" (Gen. 3:22). The third instance of "us" is found in the story of the Tower of Babel. In this account, "let us" is used to portray both the collective action of rebellious human beings ("let us build ourselves a city, and a tower") and the response of the triune God ("let Us go down and there confuse their language") (Gen. 11:4, 7). Outside of Genesis, "us" is also used in Isaiah to allude to the Trinity: "Also I heard the voice of the Lord, saying, Whom shall I send, and who will go for Us?" (Isa. 6:8).

Yet another allusion to the triune God appears in Genesis 1:2, where the Spirit of God is portrayed as moving upon the face of the waters. The Holy Spirit was holding the earth in his arms at the time of the Creation.

In the book of Ecclesiastes, Solomon, approaching faith from a philosophical, cosmopolitan standpoint, deliberately uses the term *Elohim*, which means the Creator, rather than *Yahweh*, when talking about God (Eccles. 1:13; 3:10, 13; 5:18; 7:18; 8:2, 13). Solomon refers to God as "your Creators" (*boreyka*) in Ecclesiastes 12:1. Through the inspiration of the Holy Spirit, the wisest man in the history of earth understood the concept of *Elohim* the Creator from a Trinitarian perspective.

The above biblical passages that use the word "us" not only signify the unity of the will of God the Father, the Son, and the Holy Spirit in the salvation of humanity but also demonstrate how this triune God bestows his absolute creative power to the utmost upon the redemption of mankind.

Through the act of making garments of skin during our first parents' expulsion from Eden, the triune God planted the hope of atonement through Jesus' death into the hearts of mankind.

---

10 Nathan J. Stone, *God's Names in the Old Testament, translated* by Jang Sehak (Seoul: Evangelism Publishing House, 1992), 18.

In the midst of humanity's misunderstanding of God and their dispersion in the aftermath of the Tower of Babel, God called Abraham, the future father of the nation of Israel, as his co-worker to bring salvation to all humankind.

(9) Elohim is an evangelistic God.

The Hebrew people's choice of *Elohim*, the transcendent Creator with power over all creation, as their God, must be understood from an evangelistic perspective. *Elohim* is not merely the God exclusive to the Hebrew nation but the God of the entire world, as He is the one who brought the world into being.

Upon recognizing *Elohim* as her God, Israel undertakes a sacred mission to bring all of humanity, including unbelievers, atheists, and polytheistic worshippers dispersed throughout the world, to the knowledge of the Creator who made them. Though historical Israel failed in this mission and rejected Jesus, the church as the new Israel received this commission.

Jesus Himself is *Elohim*, possessing "all authority… in heaven and on earth." He instructed his followers, "Go therefore and make disciples of all the nations, baptizing them in the name of the Father and of the Son and of the Holy Spirit, teaching them to observe all things that I have commanded you; and lo, I am with you always, even to the end of the age" (Matt. 28:18-20).

The final message of mercy sent by God to the world emphasizes that the path to salvation lies in worshipping and glorifying the Creator, *Elohim*, the One "who made heaven and earth, the sea and springs of water" (Rev. 14:6-7). The first angel's message resounds with the missionary call to acknowledge the Creator's authority and embrace his divine grace for all of humanity.

3. Yahweh

A deity name closely associated with Elohim is *Yahweh*. *Yahweh* is commonly recorded as "Jehovah" in the English Bible. From its first appearance in Genesis 2:4, the term *Yahweh* is used 6,828 times in the Old Testament, 165 of which are found in Genesis, and 1,879 times in Exodus through Joshua.

The abbreviated form of Yahweh, *yah* appears around 50 times, mainly in poetic literature. [11] Yahweh can be combined with other words to form various names of God, such as *Yahweh Jireh* ("Yahweh Will

11 E.g., Ex. 15:2; 17:16; Ps. 68:4, 18 (H. 5, 19); 77:11 (H. 12); 89:8 (H. 9); 94:7, 12; 102:18 (H. 19); 104:35.

Provide"; Genesis 22:8, 14); *Yahweh Nissi* ("Yahweh Is My Banner"; Ex. 17:15); *Yahweh Shalom* ("Yahweh Is Peace"; Judg. 6:24); *Yahweh Tsidkenu* ("Yahweh Is Our Righteousness") (Jer. 23:6; 33:16); *Yahweh Shamma* ("Yahweh Is There"; Ezek. 48:35"); and *Yahweh Tsebaoth* ("Yahweh of Hosts"; 1 Sam. 1:3; 17:45; Ps. 24:10); and *Yahweh Elohe Yisrael* ("Yahweh, the God of Israel"; Ex. 5:1; Judg. 5:3; Isa. 37:21).

(1) Yahweh is the living God who has a covenant relationship with Israel.[12]

To highlight the significance of the God whom Israel worships as *Elohim*, the transcendent Creator of the entire world, the creation account in Genesis 2:4-25 consistently refers to Him as *Yahweh Elohim* (Gen. 2:4, 5, 7, 8, 9, 15, 16, 18, 19, 21, 22).[13] Genesis connects Israel's beginnings to the world's creation through use of the *toledot* genealogy and the divine name, Yahweh. Genesis weaves together the attributes of *Elohim* the One transcending all things, with those of Yahweh the One caring for humanity and shaping world history, presenting Israel's unique perception of God as *Yahweh Elohim.*[14]

The meaning of *Yahweh* is directly explained not in Genesis but in Moses' encounter with God

12 Henry O. Thompson, 'Yahweh (Deity)', *The Anchor Bible Dictionary* (=*ABD*), (New York: Doubleday, 1992), 6:1012.

13 Genesis 1-2 presents the creation account twice. Critical scholars advocating the documentary hypothesis propose that Genesis 1:1 through the first part of Genesis 2:4, where Elohim is exclusively used as God's name, represents the Elohim document (Document E), believed to have been compiled in northern Israel around 950 B.C. In the latter part of Genesis 2:4 and onward, the term Yahweh is used to refer to God; this, these scholars contend, is the Yahweh document (Document J), thought to have been compiled in southern Judah during the David-Solomon period. A weakness in this argument arises from the fact that while Elohim and Yahweh are sometimes exclusively used within a sentence, there are also numerous sentences that use a combination of the two ("Yahweh Elohim"). It is highly unlikely that a subsequent individual that compiled Documents E and J into one document combined elements from both document into a single sentence. The more reasonable explanation is that each instance of the use of these names is motivated by the specific theological point that the author wishes to emphasize. Young Jin Kim, Reading the *Old Testament* (Seoul: Yiraeseowon, 2006), 36; Stone, 23-24; Umberto Cassuto, *The Documentary Hypothesis and the Composition of the Pentateuch: Eight Lectures*, (Jerusalem: Magnes, 1961), 23-25.

14 In the Old Testament, the books of Ecclesiastes and Jonah, which address subjects that extend beyond Israel, employ the term Elohim as the name for God. Similarly, the book of Daniel, which is set in Babylon and Medo-Persia, uses the Aramaic word *elach*, which is equivalent to "Elohim." Use of the term Yahweh is reserved for chapter 9, in which Daniel prays for the captive Jews in reliance on a covenant with God Yahweh (Dan. 9:2, 8, 10, 13, 14, 20). In contrast, Joshua, Judges, 1 and 2 Samuel, and 1 and 2 Kings, historical books of the Israelites that were written from a theocratic perspective (these books are classified as "Prophets" in the Hebrew Bible), predominantly employed the term "Yahweh." These biblical examples provide evidence that the name of God was used in accordance with the theological perspective of each respective book's author.

in Exodus. Here, God for the first time identifies himself as *Yahweh*, or "I Am That I Am" (Ex. 3:14, 15; 6:3). Although He had manifested Himself as the almighty God to Abraham, Isaac, and Jacob, He did not reveal his name as *Yahweh* to them.

In Hebrew, *Yahweh* derives from *hawa* (which is an archaic form of the verb *haya* ("to be, to become, to occur") coupled with yod a third person singular masculine pronominal prefix in imperfect verbal form. The name has been variously interpreted as "One who is," "the self-existent one" "He who will continue to be (present with His people)," and "He who causes to be, who brings into existence."[15] This conveys that God is not a static being but an active being constantly engaged with his people in a covenant relationship.[16]

Israel, in this covenant relationship, recognized only *Yahweh* as their God. Yahweh was the unique name of God revealed to Israel, and no other god could be acknowledged besides Yahweh. Due to this theological significance, ancient Israelites used terms like "my God" (*elohay*) and "God of Israel" (*elohe yisrael*), but not "my *Yahweh*" or "*Yahweh* of Israel." It was understood that *Yahweh* was inherently their God, rendering any limitations on the use of the term unnecessary. While the phrase "living God" was employed, the term "living *Yahweh*" was not used, as no other being could be considered as a truly living entity besides Yahweh.[17]

(2) Yahweh is the God who is deeply involved in the human world.

If *Elohim* represents the God who transcends creation, *Yahweh*, on the other hand, is portrayed as the God deeply involved in the created world, particularly in the human realm. The name *Yahweh* came into use to emphasize God's meticulous care for humanity within the context of creation. *Yahweh* breathed life into human beings formed from clay, akin to a potter fashioning his creation, thereby granting them life (Gen. 2:7). *Yahweh* provided Eden as a dwelling place for humankind, creating an ideal environment with abundant farmland and water resources. Additionally, he placed all the animals under human authority. As a special gift, *Yahweh* provided Adam with a companion, forming the foundation of a happy family and society. Moreover, *Yahweh* directly communicated to humans the conditions for mankind to enjoy immortality.

From the very moment of creation, *Yahweh* established a close covenantal relationship with

---

15 Robert J. Wyatt, "God, Names Of", *The International Standard Bible Encyclopedia* (Grand Rapids, MI: Eerdmans, 1982), 2:507.

16 Milton, 22.

17 Nathan J. Stone, *Names of God in the Old Testament* (Chicago, IL: Moody Press, 1944), 21.

humanity. This alliance, known as the Covenant of Creation, was jeopardized due to the Fall of mankind, which put this profound relationship into crisis.

(3) Yahweh is the righteous and holy God.

He established laws for mankind that defined good and evil, and prescribed punishment for those who transgressed (Gen. 2:17). Starting from Genesis 3, whenever scenes of God's judgment are depicted, he is referred to as Yahweh.[18] Anything that deviates from *Yahweh's* prescribed law, the foundation of life's existence, leads to self-inflicted death. Mankind was originally created on earth as a living being, a creation brought into existence by *Yahweh*. However, with Adam's sin, humanity fell into a state of spiritual death and non-existence. Subsequently, the history of humanity has been marked by a progression of death.

However, the history of death is transformed into the history of life, the history of salvation, when *Yahweh*, the living God, intervenes. As the God of the covenant, who bound Himself to humanity through creation, He takes the brush of history, previously marked by death, and paints a new narrative of life—a divine reversal of history. Throughout this process, *Yahweh* remains as the God who never gives up on mankind.

(4) Yahweh is the God who prepares the way to life

Yahweh is quick to respond to mankind's crises and consistently offers remedies in the form of further developed covenants. When Adam fell, *Yahweh* swiftly provided the proto-evangelium (Gen. 3:15). Amidst extreme depravity and the global Flood, *Yahweh* instituted the Noahic covenant, marking a new beginning in redemptive history (Gen. 6:18; 9:1-17). In response to mankind's rebellion at the Tower of Babel, resulting in the scattering of peoples and language barriers, *Yahweh* established the Abrahamic covenant (Gen. 12:1-3).

Through the Mosaic Covenant (Ex. 19-24) and the Davidic Covenant (2 Sam. 7), *Yahweh* prepared the nation of Israel to play the central role in the history of salvation. These covenants paved the way for the birth of the messiah as descendant of David. Each covenant carried the promise of salvation, and Yahweh faithfully fulfills his commitment to saving humanity. Those who

---

18 The Fall of Adam and Eve, Gen. 3:8-24; Cain's murder of Abel, Gen. 4:1-15; judgment on the antediluvians, Gen. 6-9; Tower of Babel, Gen. 11:1-9; judgment of Pharaoh due to the incident involving Sarai, Abraham's wife, Gen. 12:17; Sarai and Hagar, Gen. 16:5; judgment of Sodom, Gen. 18:16-33; judgment of Abimelech due to the incident involving Abraham's wife, Sarah, Gen. 20:3-7, 17-18.

belong to *Yahweh's* community experience the reality of God's salvation in their lives.

Apart from the representative names of God like *Elohim* and *Yahweh*, other names of God that are recorded in Genesis are predominantly associated with Abraham. When God called Abraham, he embarked on a journey of faith, leaving Ur of the Chaldeans, located in the southern part of present-day Iraq, to go to the land God showed him (Gen. 12:1; Heb. 11:8). It is difficult to fully grasp the magnitude of the adventure Abraham undertook in his obedience, especially in today's cosmopolitan world. In ancient societies, one's identity was intricately tied to family and tribe, making leaving one's home, relatives, and father's house equivalent to relinquishing economic and physical security. Without extended family protection, individuals were vulnerable in situations involving personal safety.[19]

Abraham had to trust *Yahweh's* guidance and go to the land that God would show him. God walked with Abraham, directing his path and providing protection. When Abraham severed ties with the world, his identity and destiny became defined by his personal experience with God. As a nomad in the land of Canaan, he left altars to God wherever he journeyed, signifying his encounters with the divine (Gen. 12:7, 8; 13:4, 18). Throughout his life's journey, Abraham experienced God through various names, with nearly every chapter introducing a new divine name. His encounters with God teach a profound lesson about faith and obedience.

Let us examine these names in order, beginning with "El Elyon," which appears in Genesis 14.

4. *El Elyon*

El Elyon is translated as "Most High God." *El* is a broad term that can refer to "god," whether false gods or the true God, and it is even used to refer to idols (Exod. 15:11; Deut. 3:24; Eze. 28:2; Mal. 2:11). *Elohim*, the plural form of El, was used to refer to the false gods of the Canaanites made of wood and stone (Deut. 4:28). According to the Ras Shamra tablets, which are a valuable source for understanding the Canaanite religions, El was the chief god who was the father of Baal.

El is used in Genesis in several compound names for God, such as El Elyon (Gen. 14:18-22), El Roy (Gen. 16:13), El Shaddai (Gen. 17:1), El Olam (Gen. 21:33), and El-Elohe-Yisrael. These compound names serve to emphasize specific aspects of God's character or attributes.

---

19 Gordon Wenham, *The Pentateuch*, Exploring the Old Testament, Vol. 3 (Seoul: Scripture Union International, 2007), 75.

Elyon refers to a being who is higher or loftier than any other being. In the Ugaritic texts, it was used to refer to a distinct god from *El*, but in the Old Testament, it is used to indicate God.[20] The term *El Elyon* appears in every verse in Genesis 14:18-20. In verse 22, *Yahweh El Elyon* is used, meaning "Yahweh, the Most High God."[21]

(1) Genesis 14:17-24

1) The God served by Melchizedek

When Abraham defeated the combined armies of four nations led by Chedorlaomer, the king of Elam, and rescued his nephew Lot and the people of Sodom, Melchizedek, the king of Salem, who was also known as "a priest of the Most High God," came to meet him. "Salem" means "peace," and the city later became Jerusalem, where the temple was situated. Melchizedek (*malkitsedeq*) means "king of righteousness." As a high priest, he served God, the Prince of righteousness and peace. "Blessed be Abram of God Most High, Possessor of heaven and earth" (Gen. 14:19). He addressed the Most High God as "possessor of heaven and earth." Subsequently, when Abraham made a vow before the king of Sodom, he referred to God as "Yahweh, God Most High, the Possessor of heaven and earth" (Gen. 14:22).

2) Supreme God

El Elyon has the superlative meaning of "supremely high." In ancient times, gods were often associated with specific realms or regions, such as mountains, fields, seas, or skies. Against this pagan context, *El Elyon* signifies a supreme deity who is above all other gods, emphasizing the pre-eminence of God. *El Elyon* is the universal, absolute God, transcending all things, who is to be worshipped by all people.

3) Creator and owner of heaven and earth

The qualification for God's exaltation as the supreme God is evident in Melchizedek's blessing. In Genesis 14:19, *El Elyon* is referred to as the "Possessor of heaven and earth" (*qoneh shamayim*

---

20 Ludwig Köhler and others, '*'ĕl·yôn,*' *The Hebrew and Aramaic Lexicon of the Old Testament*(=HALOT) (Leiden: Brill, 1994-2000). Elyon is used in parallel with other terms for God. El: Num. 24:16; Ps. 73:11; 107:11; Yahweh: Ps. 18:14; 21:7[H 8]; 91:9; 92:2; Elohim: Ps. 46:4[H 5]; 50:14; Shaddai: Ps. 91:1.

21 The following are the cases in which Elyon is used in direct connection with other names of God, such as *El* Elyon. Elohim Elyon: Ps. 57:3; 78:56; Yahweh Elyon: Ps. 7:17 [H 18]; 47:2[H 3].

wa'arets). While the term "lord" implies someone with control over others,[22] the corresponding Hebrew term, *qoneh* is derived from *qana* which means "to create, to possess." Some versions of the Bible interpret the term as "God who made the heavens and the earth," and the King James Version renders it as "the Possessor of heaven and earth." *El Elyon* is used to refer to the God of Israel as the One who rules over all nations.[23] Because God is the Creator and Owner of the universe, He possesses the authority and sovereignty over all gods and all things.

4) God as the source of blessings

El Elyon is a source of blessings. In Genesis 14:19-20, Melchizedek blessed Abraham in the name of the Most High God. This priestly blessing is expressed in poetic form and holds significant religious importance in Abraham's journey.[24]

The term *barak* meaning "to bless," was used prior to Genesis 14 in major junctures in the history of redemption. At creation, God blessed his creatures and humans (Gen. 1:22, 28; 5:2). After the Flood, God's blessing marked the beginning of mankind's renewed history (Gen. 9:1). Following the Tower of Babel incident, God chose Abraham from among the descendants of Shem to be a source of blessing, aiming to save mankind who had misunderstood God and become scattered across the world (Gen. 12:2, 3).

God's blessings encompass spiritual and material aspects. For Abraham, these blessings included descendants, land, and becoming the ancestor of the Messiah. At the transition between the primitive history of Genesis 1-11 and the commencement of the history of the chosen people in Genesis 12, God bestowed on Abraham of being the leader of a group of nearly a thousand people.

Melchizedek's prayer for Abraham was that God's original intention to bless the entire world through him would be fulfilled. This divine purpose was later achieved through the nation of Israel and, ultimately, through the ministry of Jesus Christ, who, like Melchizedek, hold the offices of king and priest.

5) God of power

El Elyon's abilities are absolute. In Genesis 14:14, Abraham was victorious in the battle with his

22 "주재 (主宰)", 국어대사전 (*Exhaustive Korean Language Dictionary*), Lee Hee-seung, ed. (Seoul: Minjung Seorim, 2003).

23 Terence E. Fretheim, '*El*,' *NIDOTTE* 1:400-401. Cf. 2 Sam. 22:14; Psa. 47:2[*elyon*, H. 3].

24 William David; Fry Reyburn, Euan McG., *A Handbook on Genesis*, UBS Handbook Series (New York: United Bible Societies, 1997), 324.

three hundred and eighteen elite troops, but the glory and praise are rightly attributed to the Most High God. As it is stated in Genesis 14:20, "Blessed be God Most High, who has delivered your enemies into your hand."

6) God who made Abraham victorious

Just as *El Elyon* was supreme, Abraham displayed supreme faith. Despite his burning love for Lot, Abraham's intervention in the war was not driven by mere flesh-and-blood affection. He sought God's guidance through prayer before participating in the battle, and when he achieved victory, he attributed the glory to the Most High God, who had guided him throughout.

When the king of Sodom offered him spoils, Abraham's response was immediate and resolute. He declined the king's offer, saying "I have raised my hand to the Lord, God Most High" and "I will take nothing, from a thread to a sandal strap, and that I will not take anything that is yours, lest you should say, 'I have made Abram rich'"(Gen 14:22-23). Although he was wealthy and a conqueror, he was not a captive to material things. He valued peace and was content at the knowledge that peace had been restored. Material possessions were not the driving force or purpose behind Abraham's fight. He was not seeking worldly riches obtained through a covenant with the king of Sodom; instead, he found fulfillment in the spiritual grace bestowed by the Most High God. Abraham's contentment stemmed from his reliance on God's spiritual blessings.

For those of us facing life's crises, Abraham's experience serves as a source of great comfort and courage. Even when we find ourselves entangled in unavoidable conflicts, God grants victory to those who faithfully serve Him, fear Him, and obediently follow his ways. The more intense the battles of life, the more evident is the presence of the Sovereign of heaven and earth, the Most High God.

In the end, when all the battles of this world come to a close, we will give glory to God as abundant heirs, just as Abraham did. Our victory will come from God's hand, and we will acknowledge his greatness and supremacy as we celebrate our triumph. Like Abraham, we will find true satisfaction and fulfillment in God's spiritual blessings, which exceed the temporal riches this world can offer.

El Elyon is a mighty fortress for missionaries and God's people in foreign mission fields, where they often find themselves in a lonely battle against Satan and his forces. As the ruler of all the world He has created, *El Elyon* provides strength and protection to those who put their trust in Him. Where may we find the army of God, clothed in the power of *El Elyon*, ready to engage in the good fight of faith and lead the nations to kneel in reverence and adoration before the Most High God?

5. Adonai

Adonai (*adonai*) is used about 360 times in the Old Testament and nine times in Genesis.[25] *Elohim* and *Yahweh* are titles that reveal different attributes of God. *Elohim* represents his power and glory, while *Yahweh* expresses Him as the God of righteousness, holiness, love, and redemption. These titles imply or demand that humanity, made in God's image, should obey him.[26]

Adonai, on the other hand, is a relational term. It was used among the Canaanites and Israelites to signify "master," "owner," "ruler," and "lord." Interestingly, it shares the same meaning as the Canaanite word *Baal*.[27] When used to refer to God, Adonai is translated as "Lord."

The singular form of this title, "adon" refers to relationships such as a slave and master or wife and husband. In ancient times, slaves and wives were expected to obey their masters and husbands absolutely. Those who behaved appropriately were rewarded, while those who violated the rules faced severe punishment. However, it is essential to understand Adonai not simply as a coercive being who demands submission, but as a strong protector for those under his care.

(1) Genesis 15:1-11

In Genesis, Adonai as a name for God is used exclusively in connection with Abraham.

In Genesis 15:2 and 15:8, Abraham called God Adonai Yahweh. In the preceding chapter, Abraham had displayed his strength as a mighty man of the land (*adon*) by saving his nephew Lot and the people of Sodom from the allies of the king of Shinar. However, he now found himself in a vulnerable situation, at the heart of a conflict between different peoples, and facing the possibility of retaliation. In this moment of uncertainty about how God's promises concerning the land of Canaan and his descendants would be fulfilled, Yahweh appeared to Abraham. He reassured Abraham, saying, "Fear not, Abram: I am thy shield, and thy exceeding great reward" (Gen. 15:1). Realizing that his security and prosperity were not within his own control but rather in the hands of Yahweh, who was his protector and master, Abraham promptly called on God as "Adonai Yahweh."

The fate of a servant lies in the hands of their master. In acknowledging God as *Adonai*, Abraham recognized that the future of his life rested in the hands of God. Yahweh made promises

---

25 G. Van Groningen, "God, Names Of," *Baker Encyclopedia of the Bible*, vol. 1 (Grand Rapids, Mich.: Baker Book House, 1988), 885. Gen. 15:2, 8; 18:3, 27, 30, 31, 32; 19:18; 20:4.

26 Stone, 45.

27 Reyburn, 13. The singular form of Adonai is *adon*. It is used to refer to both God and man and the proper relationship of each.

to Abraham regarding his descendants and the land, and Abraham wholeheartedly believed in the promises of his Lord. A faithful servant must unconditionally trust in the promises of their master. Abraham "believed in the Lord; and He counted it to him for righteousness" (Gen. 15:6).

(2) Genesis 18:16-33

The second scene in which Adonai appears is in Genesis 18. When Adonai, the Lord of the world, was about to judge the fallen city of Sodom, Abraham pleaded with the Lord: "Indeed now, I who am but dust and ashes have taken it upon myself to speak to the Lord (*Adonai*)" (Gen. 18:27). Abraham's righteousness had already been acknowledged by God, but he humbled himself as an ordinary human being with nothing to stand before the Lord,[28] and he pleaded for sinners, relying on God's mercy. He acknowledged wholly that the Lord was righteous and that his actions were just. Abraham pleaded with God not to be angry with him for restricting the Lord's rightful exercise of his right to judge (Gen. 18:30, 32).

The account of Abraham's intercession shows that the Adonai God is not like the capricious masters of the world. The Lord judges the world with justice (Gen. 18:25). Our Lord desires to save his servants in the world instead of punishing them.

(3) Genesis 19:1-38

In Genesis 19, Lot addressed the angels who came to destroy Sodom as Adonai, but instead of immediately following their instructions and fleeing to the mountains, he initially fled to the small city of Zoar (Gen. 19:18-22). He later realized his continued peril and eventually fled to the mountains, but ended up becoming (through his own daughters) the ancestor of the Moabites and Ammonites, who were to become enemies of God's chosen people (Gen. 19:37-38).

Adonai offers a path of salvation. When our Lord comes to save his servants and provides a way for them to live, if they respond with indifference like Lot's sons-in-law or hesitation like Lot himself, it will lead to eternal regret.

(4) Genesis 20:1-18

"But Abimelech had not come near her; and he said, 'Lord, will You slay a righteous nation also?'" (Gen. 20:4). When Abimelech, the king of Gerar, took Sarah away after Abraham deceived him into

28 Ibid., 408.

believing she was his sister, the Lord warned Abimelech in a dream not to touch Sarah, under the penalty of death if disobeyed. At this time, Abimelech referred to God as *Adonai*, but did not call him Yahweh like Abraham did, which indicates his lack of the kind of faith that Abraham had.[29]

The *Adonai* God governs the moral order of the entire world and ensures the safety of his servants. He is the Lord of the earth and everything in it, the ruler and judge of nature, with immense power to bring down fire from heaven and destroy the wicked city of Sodom. his words hold the weight of life and death. We are to obey Him as servants; at the same time, as his spiritual brides, we are to joyfully and willingly submit with love and trust.

(5) Deity name used in place of Yahweh

The most glorious meaning of *Adonai* is when it is used in place of Yahweh, the sacred title of the covenantal God. In reverence and respect for the sanctity of Yahweh's name, the Jews refrained from pronouncing the four letters (*yhwh*), and instead substituted it with Adonai.

6. El Roi

(1) Genesis 16:13

"Then she called the name of the Lord who spoke to her, You-Are-the-God-Who-Sees; for she said, 'Have I also here seen Him who sees me?'" (Gen. 16:13). This is the only instance in which the term *El Roi* is used in the Bible. The term *roi* is related to *ra'a* ("see"), and *El Roi* means "The God Who Sees Me." When proud Hagar was cast out by Sarah and wandered in the wilderness, the angel of the Lord comforted her and sent her back to Abraham. In response, Hagar called God *El Roi*: *Attah elroi* ("You are El Roi"). This is the only instance in the Bible where any human being, either male or female, gave God a name.[30]

Since the Hebrew text was originally written with only consonants, the meaning of the second word, *roi*, can vary depending on the vowels added. It can be understood as "God who watches" in the sense of God seeing all things, "God that I saw," "God who watches me," and so on. The vagueness of the word's meaning and the way it encompasses all these possibilities is part of the charm of the Hebrew language.

29 Sarna, 142.

30 Victor P. Hamilton, *The Book of Genesis: Chapters 1-17*, ed. R. K. Harrison et al., The New International Commentary on the Old Testament (Grand Rapids, MI: Eerdmans, 1990), 455.

If God is the One watching, it signifies his care and protection. If it was Hagar who saw God, it means she experienced a tangible manifestation of God's presence.[31]

No one can see God and live (Ex. 20:19; 33:20), but God revealed Himself to the ungodly, demonstrating his care for them in all circumstances. In commemoration of this encounter, Hagar named the spring where she met God as *be'er lachai ro'i* meaning "The Well of the Living One Who Sees Me." Hagar was instructed to name her child Ishmael , which means "God heard," and she received the promise that his descendants would be innumerable. Following God's instruction, Abraham named Hagar's son Ishmael (Gen. 16:11, 15).

God took care of Hagar, a disloyal slave girl who despised her mistress. He ensured that her offspring would also be called by God's name and provided for her safety and welfare. Even though she was facing the consequences of her own actions, God still took care of Hagar and the child in her womb. This shows his mercy and compassion even towards those who have faltered.

When we are aware that God cares about our needs and sufferings, we gain new found strength. Hagar returned to her previous situation, but her heart was no longer filled with despair. God promised a bright future for her and her future child. When we are conscious of God's supportive presence, we can live with hope for a better tomorrow despite our current hardships.[32] The God who sent Hagar back to her mistress most likely also healed their hurt feelings and reconciled them to each other. Hagar returned with a transformative experience that could soften "her bitterest enemy." [33]

7. El Shaddai

El Shaddai is translated as "God Almighty." *Shaddai* ("almighty") appears 48 times in the Old Testament. The book of Job is the most common source and uses *shaddai* 31 times,[34] while Genesis uses it six times (Gen. 17:1; 28:3; 35:11; 43:14; 48:3; 49:25).

The word *shaddai* is believed to have originated from various root words with meanings such as "sufficient," "lord," "god of rain," and "god of mountains." During the late patriarchal period, there

31 Sarna, 121.

32 Lawrence O. Richards, *The Bible Reader's Companion* (Wheaton, IL: Victor Books, 1991), 36.

33 Robert S. Candlish, *Studies in Genesis* (Grand Rapids, MI: Kregel, 1979). See the passage on Genesis 16:13 in this book.

34 Job 5:17; 6:4, 14; 8:3, 5; 11:7; 13:3; 15:25; 21:15, 20; 22:3, 17, 23, 25, 26; 23:16; 24:1; 27:2, 10, 11, 13; 29:5; 31:2, 35; 32:8; 33:4; 34:10, 12; 35:13; 37:23; 40:2.

was a tendency to associate this deity name with *shadad* meaning "to devastate" or "to destroy." However, this is an instance of paronomasia (i.e., a pun) and should not be accorded etymological significance.[35] The term *shaddai* is also at times etymologically linked to a word meaning "female breasts," which later came to mean "mountain." As mountains symbolize power, *El Shaddai* is a name that refers to "the all-powerful and all sufficient God who can do anything and meet any need."[36]

(1) Genesis 17:1-16

"When Abram was ninety-nine years old, the Lord appeared to Abram and said to him, "I am Almighty God; walk before Me and be blameless."" (Gen. 17:1) God revealed Himself to Abraham and Jacob using the name *El Shaddai*. This divine appearance occurred when Abraham was ninety-nine years old, Sarah was ninety, and it seemed impossible for them to have direct heirs between them.

In a time when all hope seemed lost, God renamed Abram to Abraham and Sarai to Sarah,[37] and he promised them a son named Isaac as their heir. This promise was fulfilled within the foretold timeline (Gen. 17:1, 5, 15; 21:1-2). The new names given to Abraham and Sarah, "Father of the Nations" and "Queen," served as confirmation that Isaac would indeed be born, and not only would Abraham become the father of a great nation, but he would also be the father of many nations.[38]

(2) Genesis 28:3

"May God Almighty bless you, And make you fruitful and multiply you, That you may be an assembly of peoples" (Gen. 28:3). Jacob, through a deceitful act, sought to obtain the blessings of birthright and patriarchal blessing, originally destined for his brother. Despite his actions, he still encountered the power of Almighty God. Fleeing to his uncle's house in Paddan Aram to escape his brother's wrath, he relied on God's protection and received the blessing of El Shaddai from his father, Isaac.

---

35 Christopher J. H. Wright, 'God, Names Of', *ISBE* 2:506. Ruth 1:20ff; Job 5:17; 6:4; Psalm 68:14 [MT 15]; Isaiah 13:6; In Joel 1:15, the destructive aspect is contextual.

36 Warren W. Wiersbe, *Be Obedient* (Wheaton, IL: Victor Books, 1996). See the section on Genesis 17:1 in this book.

37 Abram means "Honorable Father," Abraham means "Father of the Multitude," Sarai means "My Mistress," and Sarah means "Mistress" or "Princess, Chieftainess."

38 Wenham, 80.

Though Jacob left his home with little material wealth, with God's presence, he could prosper and become the father of many tribes. Jacob's story reminds us that if we have the Almighty God in our lives, we are immeasurably rich, regardless of our material possessions.

(3) Genesis 35, 43-49

When Jacob finally returned to Canaan after enduring twenty years of hard work in Paddan Aram, God met him at Bethel, a place that held memories of his earlier promises to be with Jacob. On this occasion, God revealed Himself using the name *El Shaddai* and reaffirmed his commitment to fulfill the patriarchal blessings that had been passed down from Isaac (Gen. 35:11).

When Jacob's sons were forced to take Benjamin to Joseph in Egypt, Jacob hoped that the Almighty God, who had taken care of him throughout his wanderings, would protect his sons and bring them back safely (Gen. 43:14). Later, Jacob acknowledged that the Almighty God had indeed fulfilled his promises, as he blessed Joseph's two sons, Ephraim and Manasseh, treating them as his own (Gen. 48:3-5). In his final moments, Jacob prayed for the Almighty God's blessings upon Joseph (Gen. 49:25).

El Shaddai is the One who makes the impossible possible. He enabled Sarah to give birth to a child at a physically impossible age, delivered Jacob from the cunning and tightfisted Laban and made him prosper (Gen. 21:2; 31:41-42), and completely fulfilled his promises to Jacob. God is our everything. Regardless of life's burdens and challenges, we can find complete satisfaction in the Almighty God alone.

8. *El Olam*

El Olam means "Eternal God" and is used in Genesis 21:33 as an equivalent to *Yahweh*. Instead of merely indicating an endless continuation of time, *El Olam* places more emphasis on the abundance and vastness of God's being.[39] Later, the term *olam* was used in God's covenant with King David (2 Sam. 7:13, 16).

(1) Genesis 21:22-34

"Then Abraham planted a tamarisk tree in Beersheba, and there called on the name of the LORD,

---

39 Fretheim, '*El*,' *NIDOTTE* 1:401.

the Everlasting God" (Gen. 21:33). Abraham established a friendly treaty with Abimelech, the Philistine king. Witnessing Abraham's prosperity as God walked with him, Abimelech made an oath in God's name to be honest with Abraham and his descendants. Before sealing the treaty, Abraham requested that Abimelech's servants return the ownership of the well that had been taken from him, and his request was granted. Subsequently, both parties named the place Beersheba, meaning "Well of Oaths." After parting ways with Abimelech, Abraham planted a tamarisk tree in Beersheba and called upon the name of Yahweh, referring to Him as *El Olam*, or "The Eternal God."

Abraham's claim for ownership of the well from the Philistine king, Abimelech, was a significant act. Although Abraham had already made a covenant using sheep and cattle, he took an additional step to ensure there would be no further disputes over the well, by setting aside seven ewes and giving them to Abimelech as a symbolic gesture signifying that he had dug the well. In Hebrew, the words "seven" and "oath" are pronounced the same, adding deeper meaning to this act of assurance.

At this point, Abraham had received the promise of heirs from God, but he had not yet obtained the land that God had spoken of. He remained a wandering foreigner, as pointed out by Abimelech. The Hebrew verb used in Genesis 21:23, *gur* is translates as "to stay as a foreigner," implying that the land where Abraham resided was a temporary dwelling place. Abraham had just begun his possession of the promised land—it began with a simple well, which was a necessary means of survival in an arid region.[40]

Abraham planted a tamarisk tree as a memorial. The tamarisk tree, is an evergreen with needle-like leaves that can root up to 30 meters deep, allowing it to absorb groundwater. Its ability to thrive while other trees wither makes it a perfect symbol of resilience and eternity. The tree provides sustenance to goats throughout the year, showing its significance in supporting life. For Abraham, this tamarisk tree served as a constant reminder of the living God, the eternal source of his strength. Even during the hardships of his journey as a stranger in a foreign land, he found solace in knowing that there is an everlasting God who sustains him. This unwavering faith in the eternal God allowed Abraham to firmly anchor his life on this earth.

The trees of the earth will eventually be cut down, the wells may disappear, the young ewes will grow old, and the treaties of mankind may be abolished, but God remains eternal. Even Abraham,

---

40 In Genesis 23, when Sarah died, Abraham purchased the family's burial place from the Hittites for four hundred shekels of silver, and the burial place at Mamre (Hebron) included a cave and a field (Gen. 23:16-20). Beersheba was a city in the southern part of the Judean desert and was the southernmost point of Israel's territory, as evidenced by the phrase "from Dan even to Beersheba," which is used to refer to the entire Promised Land (Judg. 20:1; 1 Sam. 3:20).

God's friend, would eventually pass away. However, God's "eternal covenant" (*berit olam*) (Gen. 17:7, 13, 19) with Abraham and his descendants presented a profound promise to mankind. Through this covenant, Jesus Christ, a descendant of Abraham, was born and succeeded through David, establishing a throne that would endure forever and ever (2 Sam. 7:13, 16).

The eternal God enables us, as sojourners on this earth, to experience a spiritually unfading life, renewing our minds and bodies daily, akin to the enduring nature of Abraham's well and the tamarisk tree. In the not-so-distant future, *El Olam* will bestow upon us the gift of the New Jerusalem, where we can dwell by the river of life and partake in the blessings of the tree of life.

9. Yahweh Yireh

(1) Genesis 22:1-19

Yahweh Yireh is a significant word that appears only in Genesis 22:14. "And Abraham called the name of the place, The-Lord-Will-Provide (*yhwh yireh*); as it is said to this day, 'In the Mount of the Lord it shall be provided.'" In different translations, the meaning is rendered variously; for example, the New International Version (NIV) and the English Standard Version (ESV) use "The LORD Will Provide,"[41] while the American Standard Version (ASV) states in a footnote that the term means "Jehovah will see, or provide." Since the root word of *yireh* is the verb *ra'ah* which means "see," Yahweh Yireh can be understood as "Yahweh Will See." In the second half of the verse, the verb is used again, and the King James Version (KJV) translates it as "it shall be seen." The secondary meaning of the verb *ra'ah* is "to prepare," and in the context of current verse, "see" and "prepare" have a similar meaning.[42]

The righteous and holy God who foresees the need of redemption for fallen humans provides for what is needed. "With Him prevision and provision are one and the same thing."[43]

Genesis 22 emphasizes God's "seeing" the event at issue and preparation for it. God commanded Abraham to offer Isaac as a burnt offering to test him. The original text of the Bible highlights a sequence of verbs: "take," "go," "offer for a burnt offering" (verse 2). Abraham's response to this command was immediate: "rose up early in the morning," "saddled," "took," "clave," "rose up,"

41 English Bibles typically use all capitals when using the English word "LORD" for Yahweh.

42 Sailhamer, *The Pentateuch as Narrative: A Biblical-Theological Commentary*, 88.

43 Stone, 62.

"went" (verse 3). Abraham did not question the reason behind the incomprehensible command of God, who had previously promised to create a great nation through Isaac. Instead, he moved steadily and silently to carry out the command. As Abraham and Isaac walked on, leaving the servants behind, Isaac's voice broke the silence: "Behold the fire and the wood: but where is the lamb for a burnt offering?" (verse 7). Abraham promptly replied: "My son, God will provide Himself a lamb for a burnt offering" (verse 8).

Elohim yireh ("God will see/prepare")—a phrase similar to *Yahweh Yireh*, was Abraham's answer to Isaac (Gen. 22:8).

The biblical writer may have deliberately slowed down the story by adding peripheral narratives that appear to have little impact on the core of the story, in order to provide space for readers to contemplate the inner thoughts that Abraham experienced throughout the events.[44]

Abraham, though unable to fully comprehend God's commands, placed his unwavering trust in the Almighty God, whom he had experienced during the miraculous birth of Isaac. He firmly believed in the promise that Isaac would be the one to inherit his legacy. Even though Isaac was as good as dead once Abraham received God's command to offer Isaac as a burnt offering, Abraham steadfastly clung to God's promises during the three days that followed. The same Almighty God, who has the power to bring into existence what seems impossible, had already declared, "Is anything too hard for *Yahweh*?" (Gen. 18:14). Now, through this new trial, Abraham gained even deeper insight into God's boundless power and mercy, and became convinced that God could even raise the dead to ensure the continuity of his inheritance.[45] God would take care of the future.

Abraham's unwavering faith was ultimately vindicated at the moment he had bound up Isaac, placed him on the altar, and was on the verge of sacrificing him. At that critical moment, God intervened and stopped him, providing a ram with its horns tangled in the nearby bushes as an alternative sacrifice. Isaac, in this pivotal event, became a gift to Abraham of resurrection from the dead: "Accounting that God was able to raise him up, even from the dead; from whence also he received him in a figure" (Heb. 11:9).

Abraham had faith in God even before he witnessed God's action. He had already expressed this unwavering faith when he told his servants, "I and the lad will go yonder and worship, and come again to you" (Gen. 22:5). Abraham's deep trust that Yahweh in his omniscience would foresee and provide what was needed was rewarded. The world believes that which it sees, but God demands

44 Sailhamer, *The Pentateuch as Narrative: A Biblical-Theological Commentary*, 178.

45 Charles T. Fritsch, *Genesis*, The Layman's Bible Commentary, vol. 2 (Atlanta, GA: John Knox, 1959), 74-75.

the opposite.[46] We see once we believe.

The toponym *Moriah* is likewise related to *ra'ah*, meaning "to see" or "to prepare." It may be translated as "Visible of the Lord,"[47] and the Vulgate Version of the Latin Bible paraphrases it as "Land of Revelation."

The latter part of Genesis 22:14, *behar yhwh yera'e* may be translated as "In the mount of Yahweh it shall be prepared" or "In the mount of Yahweh it shall be seen (or appear)." David experienced a manifestation of God here, on the threshing floor of Araunah, a Jebusite; and Solomon later built the temple in Jerusalem at this place, under David's direction (2 Sam. 24; 1 Chron. 21; 2 Chron. 3:1). It was here that the only begotten Son, Jesus Christ, was later crucified as the Lamb of God who takes away the sin of the world; and here also was He resurrected, fulfilling the promise of the gift of resurrection, just as Abraham had received Isaac back from the dead. God fully met humanity's ultimate needs through Jesus Christ, on the very mount where Abraham had offered his only son Isaac.

---

46 Flint, 148.

47 Judson Cornwall, Smith Stelman, *The Exhaustive Dictionary of Bible Names* (North Brunswick, NJ: Bridge-Logos, 1998), 178.

Chapter 04 | God's Works

The book of Genesis portrays the actions of the living God, from Creation to the calling of Abraham and the forefathers of the nation of Israel. It provides profound insights into the works of God and his interactions with humanity throughout history, setting the foundation for the rest of the Bible. In this chapter, we will examine what God is like through his works.

1. God the Creator

The Bible opens with a powerful declaration: "In the beginning God created the heavens and the earth" (Gen. 1:1). This statement challenged the ancient Near Eastern beliefs, as it contrasted with the Babylonian creation myth Enuma Elish, in which the earth and sky were created as the result of a power struggle among the gods.[1] In Genesis, God effortlessly brought forth the heavens and the earth through his Word. Even celestial bodies like the sun, moon, and stars, worshipped as gods by the surrounding nations, were merely creations designed by God to serve as luminaries.

The book of Genesis uses various Hebrew words like *bara'* ("create"),[2] *asah* ("make"),[3] *wayomer* ("speak"),[4] *yatsar* ("form"),[5] and *banah* ("build")[6] to describe God's work of creation, each conveying unique meanings. Understanding these words sheds light on the significance of God's

---

1 The Enuma Elish records how Marduk became the supreme god of Babylon. In that account, Marduk killed Tiamat ("sea"), a goddess who had tormented the gods, and her husband, Kingu. He split the body of Tiamat to create an upper heaven consisting of water and a solid earth, and made human beings out of the blood of Kingu. Around 1750 B.C., Hammurabi made Babylon (located in southern Iraq) the capital of the kingdom and designated Marduk as a "great god" (among other great gods). Nebuchadnezzar I, a figure from about 1120 B.C., officially elevated Marduk to "king of the gods." W. G. Lambert, 'Enuma Elish', *ABD* 2:526-528.

2 The word *bara* meaning "to create," is used seven times in Genesis 1-2 and four times in the rest of the book: Gen. 1:1, 21, 27 (3 times); 2:3, 4; 5:1, 2 (2 times); 6:7.

3 The word *asa*, meaning "to make," is used 10 times in Genesis 1-2: Gen. 1:7, 16, 25, 26, 31; 2:2 (twice), 3, 4, 18.

4 The infinitive of *wayomer* is *amar*. *Wayomer* was used as a creation command: Gen. 1:3, 6, 9, 11, 14, 20, 24, 26, 28, 29.

5 Gen. 2:7, 8, 19.

6 Gen. 2:22.

creation. Let's explore these words and their meanings in the verses that pertain to God's creative work.

(1) Barah' ("create")

This word is a theological predicate reserved solely for the actions of God, and signifies the notion of "initiating something new."[7] Throughout the creation account of Genesis 1-2, this verb is exclusively employed at pivotal moments when significant new phases of the creative process unfold. In these verses, we witness the demonstration of God's extraordinary creative power, encompassing the origin of matter (verse 1), the emergence of sentient creatures (1:21), and the unique creation of humankind (1:27).[8]

1) Genesis 1:1

"In the beginning God created the heavens and the earth" (Gen. 1:1). During the first four days of Creation, God brought into existence light, the sky, the sea, the land, the plant kingdom, the two great luminaries, and the stars, providing a material environment for living beings. The term *barah'* denotes *creatio ex nihilo* ("creation from nothing"). Unlike the ancient Near Eastern belief where pre-existing matter was used for creation, God did not rely on existing matter to create the universe. Matter originated with God, as Hebrews 11:3: "Through faith we understand that the worlds were framed by the word of God, so that things which are seen were not made of things which do appear." The reference to "the worlds" encompasses the heavens, the earth, and everything within them, which were created without "things which do appear", or pre-existing materials. Revelation 4:11 reinforces this idea, stating: "Thou hast created all things, and for Thy pleasure they are and were created." In this understanding, God's will precedes the material world's existence, and He exercises absolute sovereignty over it, allowing it to exist or disappear according to his divine purpose.

The absolute sovereignty of God over the material world is emphasized in the designation of the sun and moon as "luminous bodies" (Gen. 1:14-16). These celestial bodies, which pagans worshipped as gods, were merely referred to as *ma'or* meaning "lamp."[9] The sun god Ra, who was considered the supreme deity in Egypt during the time of the Exodus, was proven powerless during the ninth plague of darkness brought by Yahweh.[10] For three days, darkness enveloped the

---

7 Thomas McComiskey, E., '*bārā'*,' *TWOT* 127.

8 Fritsch, 26.

9 Ex. 25:6; 27:20; 35:8, 14, 28; 39:37; Lev. 24:2; Num. 4:9, 16.

10 Wolf, 137.

Egyptians, making it impossible for them to see one another; however, in the dwelling place of the children of Israel, there was *or* ("light") (Ex. 10:21-23).

God's transcendent power over the laws of nature stems from his role as their creator and originator. During the time of the Exodus, Joshua witnessed God's dominion over the sun, the most prominent force in nature. Reflecting on that experience, in the midst of the Israelites' battle with the Amorites, Joshua beseeched God to halt the sun and moon, and God in response caused the sun to stand still for almost an entire day (Josh. 10:12-14). When Hezekiah fell ill and, facing death, implored God to extend his life, God as a sign of deliverance caused the shadow of the sun to go back ten steps (Isa. 38:8). The seven eschatological plagues of Revelation 16 are directed at the sea, rivers, water sources, the sun, and the air (Rev. 16:3, 4, 8, 17). These elements are under the absolute control of God, the Creator, who established both the universe and its governing laws. Ultimately, the new heavens and new earth will exist in a state where natural lamps and sunlight are unnecessary, for all things will find complete fulfillment in God alone, the Sovereign One (Rev. 22:5).

2) Genesis 1:21

"So God created great sea creatures and every living thing that moves, with which the waters abounded, according to their kind, and every winged bird according to its kind. And God saw that it was good" (Gen. 1:21). On the fifth day of Creation, the once static world transformed and a diverse array of life forms came forth. The natural world came alive with sensory creatures roaming and exploring their environments. God filled the seas with magnificent sea beasts and other aquatic creatures, while the heavens became home to the soaring birds. On the sixth day, God continued his creative work, bringing forth the inhabitants of the earth—livestock, wild beasts, and crawling creatures. Genesis 1:21 highlights the principle that each creation was made "after their kind." The Hebrew word min ("kind") is used to denote scientific classifications.[11] This reveals God as a rational and scientific Creator.

Hattanninim is translated as "great whale" in the King James Version (KJV) and "great creatures of the sea" in the New International Version (NIV). "Tanninim" derives from *tanan* meaning "stretch," and refers to whales, crocodiles, and other giant sea animals.[12] According to Canaanite

11 Gen. 1:11, 21, 24; 6:20; 7:14. The word *min* was used to distinguish between clean and unclean creatures, especially in relation to birds: Lev. 11:14-16, 19, 22, 29; Deut. 14:13-15, 18.

12 Carl Friedrich Keil and Franz Delitzsch, Biblical *Commentary on the Old Testament* (Peabody, MA: Hendrickson, 2002), 1:37.

mythology as recorded in the Ugaritic texts, this creature was a primordial dragon god that appears alongside Leviathan and who assisted the sea god *Yam* in his fight against Baal.

Genesis 1:21 can be interpreted as a refutation of the Canaanite faith.[13] It asserts that the beings they worship are nothing more than God's creations. Before God, all the powers of the world are insignificant beings whose existence depends on his Word. Later biblical authors pointed to God's creation of these mighty sea creatures on the fifth day to support their argument that the dragon, representing an evil force hostile to God, cannot but succumb to God's absolute sovereignty.[14]

When people do not believe in God, they may foolishly turn to worshiping things like beasts and even insects (Rom. 1:23). However, living things are merely God's creations, and God holds authority over all of them. In the Bible, we see instances where God used various creatures and natural phenomena to carry out his divine plans. These include his deployment of frogs, lice, flies, and locusts, and striking the Egyptians' livestock with diseases (whereas the livestock of the Israelites were left unharmed), when bringing the ten plagues upon the land of Egypt in order to deliver Israel (Ex. 8-10). These plagues affected religious objects and deities worshiped by the Egyptians. Each of these plagues was a demonstration of Yahweh's supremacy over a particular god in the Egyptian pantheon, highlighting that Yahweh is the ultimate God over all other gods.[15]

God's dominion extends over all sentient creatures. He opened the mouth of a donkey to rebuke Balaam, who had been spiritually blinded due to bribery; prepared a large fish to shelter Jonah for three days; and had Peter pay the temple tax using money that came from a fish's mouth Num. 22:28-30; Jonah 1:17; Matt. 17:27). These accounts illustrate God's power and his ability to use creatures and circumstances for his divine purposes.

3) Genesis 1:27

"So God created man in His own image; in the image of God He created him; male and female He created them" (Gen. 1:27). This verse contains a notable repetition of the verb *bara'* three times, correlating to the three uses of "us" (a reference to the Trinity) earlier in the passage. The Hebrew Scriptures further underscore the concept of the "image of God" through the use of chiasm structure,

---

13 Sarna, 10.

14 Cf. Isa. 27:1; 51:9; Ezek. 29:3; 32:2; Ps. 44:20; 74:13-14; Job 7:12. See John Skinner, *A Critical and Exegetical Commentary on Genesis*, 2nd ed., The International Critical Commentary on the Holy Scriptures of the Old and New Testaments, vol. 1 (Edinburgh, : T. & T. Clark, 1951), 28.

15 G. Michael Hagan, 'Exodus, Theology Of,' *Baker Theological Dictionary of the Bible*, ed. Walter A. Elwell (Grand Rapids, MI: Baker, 1996), 227.

as follows:

God created man.
In his own image
In the image of God
He created him

The most remarkable aspect of God's creative work is the creation of man in his image. Human beings stood apart, being entirely new and distinct from everything else that had been created. While animals and plants were created "according to their kind," humans were not. There is only one kind of human being,[16] and they were uniquely created "in the image of God." This designation sets humans apart as the representatives of God on Earth, entrusted with the responsibility to manage all things in the world.

The preservation of God's creation relies on man's awareness of his image of God and his behavior in alignment with that image. When man embraces and lives in the image of God, the blessed state of creation is upheld. Consequently, the well-being of the entire creation is contingent upon man's relationship with God. God instituted the Sabbath system as a means to foster and strengthen this spiritual relationship.

4) Genesis 2:1-3

"Thus the heavens and the earth, and all the host of them, were finished. And on the seventh day God ended His work which He had done, and He rested on the seventh day from all His work which He had done. Then God blessed the seventh day and sanctified it, because in it He rested from all His work which God had created and made" (Gen. 2:1–3). Genesis 2:2-3, which directly focuses on the seventh day, emphasizes that God ceased and rested from all of his *doing* and *making* through three repetitions.[17] The author purposefully emphasizes God's act of rest through this construct.[18]

God the Creator rested not because of fatigue, but rather to commemorate his completion of his work of creation, and to offer his companionship to humanity. Through the Sabbath, God invites mankind, made in his image, into his rest. In the act of worship, where God and mankind meet,

16 Sarna, 13.

17 In Genesis 2:2-3, the Hebrew Scriptures emphasize God's rest by placing the word *asah* ("to do," "to make") three times at the end of each phrase.

18 Sailhamer, 'Genesis', 39.

humans have the opportunity to renew the image of God, their original form, every Sabbath.

The seven-day week was not established based on natural phenomena but was solely ordained by God for the benefit of all people. The Sabbath commemorates the anniversary of creation, and its meaning can only be truly grasped by human beings. The Sabbath is the sole day of the creation week that is not marked by the phrase "So the evening and the morning were the ...th day"; thus, it symbolically remains open to all who wish to partake of its blessings. The rest provided by God during creation is still available to modern humans who have lost their spiritual rest while living in a sinful world. We may begin experiencing this creation rest in this life by accepting Jesus Christ as our personal Savior, the way of salvation provided by God. Moreover, this rest will be fully restored in the future eternal kingdom, the new creation (Ps. 95:11; Heb. 3:11; 4:4, 9, 10).

Bara' is used four more times in two places outside of the creation account: first, in Genesis 5:1-2, listing Adam's *toledot*, and second, in Genesis 6:7, the Flood account.

5) Genesis 5:1-2

"This is the book of the genealogy of Adam. In the day that God created man, He made him in the likeness of God. He created them male and female, and blessed them and called them Mankind in the day they were created" (Gen. 5:1–2). Genesis 5 lists ten patriarchs in the genealogy from Adam to Noah. Through this genealogy, we witness that God's initial blessing to "be fruitful and multiply; fill the earth" (Gen. 1:28) continues even in a sinful world.

Adam's genealogy also demonstrates the progression of redemption, leading towards the fulfillment of the promise of the "seed of the woman" mentioned in the proto-evangelium (original gospel) of Genesis 3:15. Despite the eventual fate of each patriarch being death, the genealogy's preface highlights God's creation, offering a contrast to the genealogy of Cain, which concludes with Lamech, a murderous man.

The genealogy of Adam signifies a return to the time of God's creation, urging people to look forward to the coming Messiah, who will usher in an age of re-creation. However, before the arrival of the "seed of the woman," mankind plunged into a path of self-destruction. Amidst the crisis, the only hope for humanity lay in Noah, another Adam, chosen by God to restore the lost Eden. God's unwavering will to restore the lost paradise is persistently carried out despite any crisis or adversity.

6) Genesis 6:7

"So the Lord said, 'I will destroy man whom I have created from the face of the earth, both man and beast, creeping thing and birds of the air, for I am sorry that I have made them'" (Gen. 6:7). The Creator God has the authority to judge all of his creation. As humans faced judgment because of their sinful acts, the creatures that were subordinate to man at creation came to share in the same judgment.

(2) Asah

("to make," "to do") is the third most commonly used verb in the Old Testament (2,624 times), after *amar* ("to speak") and *hayah* ("to be"). Around one-sixth of its total usage is related to theological contexts, with Yahweh as the subject. The versatility of this word necessitates understanding its nuances through contextual cues. In the creation account, *asah* specifically pertains to God's act of creation. The term *asah* stands as the most comprehensive description of God's actions throughout the entire realm and process of creation, not only in the book of Genesis but also throughout the other books of the Old Testament.[19]

In Genesis 1, we observe God's creative style expressed through the sequence of "God said" followed by "God... made" (Gen. 1:6-7, 14-15, 24-25). The verb *asah* depicts the fulfillment of God's intentions. Creation through his spoken Word and creation through his actions are harmonious and not contradictory. Psalm 33:6 affirms that there is no distinguishable difference between God's creative words and his actions, emphasizing the potency of his speech:[20] "By the word of the Lord [Yahweh] the heavens were made (*na'asu*), And all the host of them by the breath of his mouth."

(3) Wayomer ("speak")[21]

One of the most remarkable aspects of Genesis 1 is its repeated use of the phrase "God said," which appears ten times. All things in existence came into being through these ten creation

---

19 Thomas McComiskey, E., ''*śh*,' 701. "'*śh* describes Yahweh's creative activity in all its dimensions: Yahweh made the earth (Exod 20:11; 31:17; 2 Kgs 19:15; Isa 45:12, 18; Jer 10:12 = 51:15), the sea (Exod 20:11; Jonah 1:9; Psa 95:5), and the dry land (Jonah 1:9), heaven (Exod 20:11; 31:17; 2 Kgs 19:15; Psa 96:5), the "firmament" (*raqîa'*, Gen 1:6f.), the heavenly bodies (Gen 1:16; Job 9:9), sun and moon (Psa 104:19), the "windows (in heaven)" ('*ᵃrubbôt*, 2 Kgs 7:2, 19), the animals (Gen 1:25; 3:1; Job 40:15), humanity (Gen 1:26; 5:1; 6:6; 9:6; Jer 27:5; individuals, 1 Sam 12:6), and the nations (Deut 26:19; Psa 86:9). Yahweh creates *ḥayyîm* "life" (Job 10:12)." J. Vollmer, ''*śh*', *Theological Lexicon of the Old Testament* (=TLOT), ed. Ernst Jenni et al.(Peabody, MA: Hendrickson, 1997), 2:949-950.

20 Sarna, 8.

21 The Hebrew word amar ("to speak") is the most frequently used word in the Hebrew Bible, appearing 5,282 times. H. H. Schmid, '*āmăr*,' *TLOT* 1:160.

commands.[22] In the Bible, the number ten symbolizes "sufficiency" or "fullness."[23] The most prominent biblical use of this number is the Ten Commandments.

This highlights the parallel between the giving of the Ten Commandments, representing the moral law, to the Israelites, and the universal bestowal of natural law to all peoples by the same God—both the moral law and natural law originate from the goodness of the same divine source, and they play fundamental roles in upholding order and harmony in the world.

God is the all-powerful Creator who brings forth creation through his Word. Moreover, He is the Lawmaker, establishing the laws that govern all things. Every time his creative Word is spoken, designated entities come into being, and the unchanging laws of nature, which He has ordained, stand firm.[24] Through the marvels of nature, we witness the evidence of a highly intelligent Designer —the Creator—whose existence is attested to by the intricate and harmonious order present in the world.

God, the Creator and intelligent Designer, assumes the role of the evaluator of his creatures. Seven times, He deems his creation "good" in his sight.[25]

God's intention for creation is to bestow a blessing. The Hebrew word *barak* meaning "to bless" appears three times (Gen. 1:22, 28; 2:3). The repetition of this action reveals a pattern of behavior, showcasing God's delight in blessing his creation. God's propensity to bless is evident, and we naturally anticipate his blessings upon us. Additionally, the number three carries the connotations of being "final" and "complete."[26] Living creatures and human beings have been fully blessed by

---

22 Gen. 1:3, 6, 9, 11, 14, 20, 22, 24, 26, 29.

23 The number 10 carries significant importance in the Bible, symbolizing "sufficiency" or "fullness." In the genealogies of Genesis, there were ten generations before and after the flood (Gen. 5; 11:10-30). Abraham believed that if there were ten righteous people, Sodom could be spared (Gen. 18:32). Israel's redemption came through ten plagues inflicted on Egypt (Ex. 7:8-11:10). God presented the Ten Commandments as a comprehensive law for Israel, who, unfortunately, tested Him ten times during their wilderness journey (Ex. 20:2-17; Deut. 5:6-21; Num. 14:22). "Ten played a prominent role in later Jewish life and practice. The tetragrammaton was uttered by the high priest ten times on the Day of Atonement. Ten persons constitute a congregation in the synagogue and must be present at a nuptial blessings. A row of comforters of the bereaved numbered ten." B. C. Birch, 'Number', The International Standard Bible Encyclopedia, Revised (=ISBE), 3:560.

24 God is more than a Creator; He is the Lawgiver. He distinguishes between light and darkness, separates land and sea, and assigns names to them. He commands the stars, determining signs and appointed times. Living creatures receive his word to multiply and flourish. Humanity is tasked to conquer the land, and the seventh day is sanctified. God establishes limits within the natural order and designates specific functions for his creatures. By faithfully following his divine instructions, every created being achieves its rightful purpose. Gordon J. Wenham, *Genesis 1-15*, Word Biblical Commentary, vol. 1 (Waco, TX: Word Books, 2002), 38.

25 Gen. 1:4, 10, 12, 18, 21, 25, 31.

26 'Three, Third', *Dictionary of Biblical Imagery*, ed. Leland Ryken et al. (Downers Grove, IL: InterVarsity Press, 1998), 866-867.

God with abundant life. By consecrating the seventh day with a blessing, he brought the age of blessing to its fullest expression (Gen. 1:22, 28; 2:3). Just as each utterance of God's word ushers in a new creation and a day filled with blessings and life, He continues to bring forth an age of life and blessing through his spoken word.

(4) Yatsar ("form")

"And the Lord God formed [*wayyitser*] man of the dust of the ground" (Gen. 2:7). The Hebrew word *yatsar* in the text denotes the act of forming and shaping. The participle form *yotser* refers to a person who crafts artifacts, often through carving, molding, or shaping, and in the Bible, is used to refer to a "potter" (Isa. 29:16; 45:9).[27]

God, as the Divine Potter, skillfully formed both man and beast out of the dust (Gen. 2:7-8, 19). He also shaped the mountains (Amos 4:13), formed the dry land (Ps. 95:5), and created the leviathan (*liwyathan*, "sea monster") (Ps. 104:26).[28]

In the above examples, it is evident that the word *yatsar* is not a general term for creation, but is rather used specifically to refer to the actions involved in the act of creation.[29]

Just as a potter skillfully crafts various vessels according to his design from clay, God, too, formed both humans and animals from the same material, *adama* ("soil"). This underscores the need to recognize God's absolute sovereignty over all things in the universe.[30]

God specifically chose ancient Israel as his treasured people; yet, sadly, they fell from their exalted position and became as clay pots (Lam. 4:2). The true value of a person lies in surrendering oneself to God, the divine Potter, who skillfully molds and shapes each person. God's best works are manifested in those who willingly submit to his divine will. Humans are only different from animals in that they are uniquely made in the image of God. Those who reject God's authority are likened to perishing beasts. In the face of mortality, there is no distinction between man and beast; death comes to all (Ps. 49:12, 20; Eccles. 3:19; 9:4).

(5) Banah ("build")

"And the rib which the Lord God had taken from man He made (*wayyiben*) into a woman,

27 1 Chron. 4:23; Sam. 29:16; 30:14; 41:25; 45:9; 64:8 (Heb. 7); Jer. 18:2, 3, 4, 6; 19:1, 11; Lam. 4:2; Zech. 11:13.

28 The mention of leviathan as one of God's creatures in Psalm 104:26 clearly intends to refute the myths of the ancient Near East.

29 A. H. Konkel, '*yatsar*,' *NIDOTTE* 2:504.

30 Isa. 49:16; 30:14; 45:9; 64:8; Lam. 18:6; Rom. 9:21.

and He brought her to the man" (Gen. 2:22). The Hebrew word *banah* ("build") was used in this verse.[31] This term is employed in architectural engineering, referring to the construction of cities,[32] altars, towers, and houses.[33] Adam was like an unfinished building until Eve was "built."[34] God used man's ribs as building materials for constructing woman,[35] and through both men and women, He constructed humanity (Gen. 16:2; 30:3).[36]

Yahweh "builds the house" by blessing a married couple with children (Ps. 127:1). The word *tsela*, translated as "rib," denotes a component used in the construction of buildings and utensils, and was employed in the construction of the sanctuary and temple (Ex. 25:5; 26:20).[37] God values and desires to preserve the sanctity of marital relationships akin to the sacred architecture of a temple. He establishes his kingdom on earth through the families of devoted believers. Just as God provided detailed instructions for constructing tabernacles and utensils, when a home is built according to God's design and principles, it becomes a sanctuary where God dwells—a place that radiates life and reflects his divine presence (1 Cor. 3:16).[38]

God was pleased with David's desire to build a house for him, and made a promise to establish the kingship of the house of David forever through Jesus Christ, the last Adam.[39] Through our

---

31 The word *banah* is only used in relation to creation in Genesis 2:22 and Amos 9:6. However, in Akkadian and Ugaritic, this word is regularly employed when referring to creation. Wenham, 69.

32 Gen. 4:17; Mic. 3:10.

33 Altar, Gen. 8:20; tower, Gen. 11:4; house and cattle booth, Gen. 33:17.

34 "He (Adam) now saw himself, who had before been imperfect, rendered complete in his wife...Moses also designedly used the word *built*, to teach us that in the person of the woman the human race was at length complete, which had before been like a building just begun." John Calvin, *Commentaries on the First Book of Moses Called Genesis,* trans., John King, Calvin's Old Testament Commentaries, vol. 1 (Grand Rapids, MI.: Wm. B. Eerdmans, 1948), 133.

35 "Adam was not created ex nihilo (out of nothing) but out of the dust of the earth, and neither was Eve made *ex nihilo*... She was made of the same stuff as the man—the same bone, the same flesh, the same DNA." Hughes, 60.

36 Keil and Delitzsch, 56.

37 Tsela was used 9 times in Exodus 25-38 to refer to the tabernacle and its furnishings, in the following verses: Ex. 25:12 (2 times), 14; 26:20, 26, 27 (2 times), 35 (2 times); 27:7; 30:4; 36:25, 31, 32; 37:3 (2 times), 5, 27; 38:7. In the case of Solomon's Temple, it was used to refer to side chambers (1 Kings 6:5, 8), boards of ceder and planks of fir (1 Kings 6:15 (2 times), 16), doors (1 Kings 6:34), and beams (1 Kings 7:3). In Ezekiel's vision of the new temple, *tsela* denotes the side chambers (Ezek. 41:5, 6 (4 times), 7, 8, 9 (2 times), 11, 26). For an interpretation of Adam's *tsela* as "the side of the tabernacle," see Pinchas Stolper, 'The Man-Woman Dynamic of Ha-Adam: A Jewish Paradigm of Marriage,' *Tradition* 27, (1992): 35.

38 The verb "made" in Genesis 2:22 carries the meaning of "built," just as man "built" the temple. Warren W. Wiersbe, *Wiersbe's Expository Outlines on the Old Testament* (Wheaton, IL: Victor Books, 1993), Gen. 2:22.

39 2 Sam. 7:27, 29.

obedience to God's word, we can live a life with firm foundations, constructed by God.[40]

God originally intended man to be a temple in which the Spirit of God dwells. Jesus, the antitype of Adam, referred to his own flesh as a temple. "Jesus answered and said to them, "destroy this temple, and in three days I will raise it up." Then the Jews said, "It has taken forty-six years to build this temple, and will You raise it up in three days?" But He was speaking of the temple of His body. Therefore, when He had risen from the dead, His disciples remembered that He had said this to them; and they believed the Scripture and the word which Jesus had said" (John 2:19–22).

According to Jesus' teachings, man can be either a temple of the Holy Spirit or a den of evil spirits (Luke 11:24-26). The gospel serves as a means of rebuilding temples that have been severely damaged and torn down by sin, and this work is carried out through evangelists. An evangelist must be a wise builder, constructing their own life on the foundation of Jesus Christ and building God's house upon it (1 Cor. 3:10-11). Through the power of the gospel, individuals and churches are restored and transformed into holy temples, becoming God's dwelling place (1 Cor. 3:16; Eph. 2:22).

The model of God's first temple is Adam and Eve. The experience of a couple becoming fully united in God's blessing is akin to experiencing the Holy of Holies, where God and man meet. Thus, the love between the two should be holy and beautiful, just as described in Genesis 2:23-25. The Song of Songs further elaborates on this profound love between two souls.[41]

2. God the Judge

(1) God the Creator is the Judge.

Creation and judgment are intricately linked topics. As the Creator, God holds the authority to pass judgment. The same God who brought the physical world into existence through the ten creation commands of wayyomer [42] is also a spiritual and moral deity who governs the human world

40 For instances where God's salvation and judgment are metaphorically referred to using the construction-related analogies of building and demolition, see Psalm 28:5 and Jeremiah 2:10.

41 It appears that there was much controversy surrounding the inclusion of Song of Solomon within the biblical canon, as shown in the Mishnah. Rabbi Aqiba (A.D. 100) provided a powerful argument that resolved the canonical issue regarding the Song of Solomon. Aqiba stated as follows: "No Israelite man ever disputed concerning Song of Songs that it imparts uncleanness to hands. For the entire age is not so worthy as the day on which the Song of Songs was given to Israel. For all the scriptures are holy, but the Song of Songs is holiest of all." (Mishnah Yadayim 3:5). Jacob Neusner, *The Mishnah: A New Translation* (New Haven/London: Yale University Press, 1988), 1127.

42 Gen. 1:3, 6, 9, 11, 14, 20, 24, 26, 28, 29.

through the Ten Commandments, which serve as moral laws.

God carefully examines the world he created. The recurring phrase "God saw that it was good," mentioned seven times at the conclusion of each creation account, demonstrates that God's creation is a world of perfect order and beauty.[43] This also underscores that as the Creator, God is also the ultimate Judge who observes and renders judgment. He saw the grievous sins of humanity before the Flood, observed the endeavors of the builders of the Tower of Babel, and personally visited Sodom and Gomorrah to assess their dire state.[44]

(2) God judges between good and evil.

In the Garden of Eden, God said to Adam, "But of the tree of the knowledge of good and evil you shall not eat, for in the day that you eat of it you shall surely die" (Gen. 2:17). Since man is created in the image of God, he possesses the spiritual and moral capacity to distinguish between good and evil. Even the serpent, the tempter of Eden, acknowledged that God is the primary authority in discerning good and evil (Gen. 3:5).[45]

Through God's Word, man can understand what is good and what is evil. God created man to be a moral being with free will, making him accountable for his choices. "Let us hear the conclusion of the whole matter: Fear God and keep His commandments, For this is man's all. For God will bring every work into judgment, Including every secret thing, Whether good or evil" (Ecc. 12:13–14). The tree of knowledge of good and evil highlights that humans are not immortal. Man was a creature who loved God completely and could live eternally on the condition that he lived a life of trust and obedience. Human beings are blessed by God (Gen. 1:28). God gave man the gift of a good world.[46] God only spoke good things that blessed man.[47] Because God created man to be morally righteous and upright, it was perfectly natural for him to love and trust in Him and obey his Word.

The serpent took issue with God's Word to undermine the relationship of love and trust. "Yea,

---

43 Gen. 1:4, 10, 12, 18, 21, 25, 31.

44 Genesis 6:5, 12; 11:5; and 18:21 use the Hebrew verb *ra'ah*, meaning "to see" or "to behold." When used with God as the subject, *ra'ah* indicates a theological term associated with divine judgment. It portrays God as the One who sees and discerns, making evident his role as the Judge.

45 Keil and Delitzsch, 1:53. The inability to distinguish between good and evil is a sign of immaturity or a state of reduce mental acuity due to age (Deut. 1:39; 2 Sam. 19:35).

46 The repeated use of the phrase "God saw that it was good" after each act of God's creation reveals a world of goodness. The Hebrew word tov ("good") also carries a meaning of moral rightness. 1 Kings 8:36; Hos. 8:3; Mic. 6:8.

47 God is good (Ps. 143:10; Mark 10:18). God's will is good (Rom. 12:2). Everything God created is good (1 Tim. 4:4). God's words are good (1 Kings 8:56; Zech. 1:13; Heb. 6:5).

hath God said, Ye shall not eat of every tree of the garden?" (Gen 3:1).[48] When God judged Adam, his concern was Adam's obedience to his word (Gen. 3:11). Unfortunately, mankind's choice was tragic. "She took of its fruit and ate. She also gave to her husband with her, and he ate" (Gen. 3:6). Solomon reflects on this human condition, stating, "Truly, this only I have found: That God made man upright, But they have sought out many schemes" (Ecc. 7:29).[49]

After the transgression at the tree of knowledge of good and evil, sin became a daily part of life, and religious life was not exempt from its influence. Cain offered God an unacceptable offering, and his anger towards God and Abel was great. God spoke to Cain, warning him about the temptation of sin lurking at his door. He said, "If you do well, will you not be accepted? And if you do not do well, sin lies at the door. And its desire is for you, but you should rule over it" (Gen. 4:7).

God, the ultimate judge of good and evil, urged and warned Cain to choose the path of righteousness over evil. Should he fail to pursue goodness, he would be overcome by sin, compared to a lurking beast waiting to pounce on its prey.[50] God perceives sin as a force that seeks to assail humankind.

However, despite the formidable power of sin, we need not be ensnared by its grip. Through the divine grace bestowed upon us, we have the capacity to overcome the dominion of sin. "You should rule over it [sin]" in this verse is both a command and a promise. Cain had the ability to control sin, although he ultimately faltered. In contrast, the life of Enoch stands as a testimony to the veracity of God's assurances. Enoch's close communion with God was so profound that he transcended earthly

---

48 Has God indeed said (*ap ki-amar elohim*), the serpent introduced his words by an intensive particle that "sows a seed of doubt regarding what God has said." Reyburn, 81.

49 The background of Ecclesiastes 7:29 is the creation narrative in Genesis chapter 1. Therefore, the author of Ecclesiastes used the more universal divine name Elohim instead of the covenantal name "Yahweh," and the term "Adam" for humanity or mankind. The word *yasar* translated as "upright," carries a moral meaning, referring to righteousness (Ps. 32:4), upright and moral living (Job 4:7), and the state of being straight and not twisted (Eccles. 7:13). Graham S. Ogden, Lynell Zogbo, A Handbook on *Ecclesiastes*, UBS Handbook Series; Helps for Translators (New York, NY: United Bible Societies, 1998), 273. In Ecclesiastes 7:29, the Hebrew noun *hissabon* is translated as "inventions." This word appears only in this verse and in 2 Chronicles 26:15. It refers to the outcomes of complex thinking processes, and encompasses complex thoughts and ingenious inventions. This verse portrays the distorted nature of humanity, using various means to distort and twist God's clear words in order to fulfill their greedy desires. John E. Hartley, '*ḥšb*,' *NIDOTTE* 2:309.

50 The Hebrew word *rabats* means "to crouch." In the context of Genesis, it was used to refer to animals crouching or lying in wait to rest or to prey upon their food (Gen. 29:2; 49:9, 14). In Genesis 4:7, it is used metaphorically to describe sin as a lurking animal, lying in wait to pounce. HALOT (The Hebrew and Aramaic Lexicon of the Old Testament) explains the meaning of Genesis 4:7 as "to crouch, to lie in wait." The phrase "thee shall be his desire" in this verse depicts sin as a lurking beast, ready to seize its opportunity. '*rbṣ*,' *HALOT*. The "door" where sin lies in wait refers to Cain's mind, thoughts, and intention. Reyburn, 110.

existence, as God took him away from the world (Gen. 5:24).

The decisive judgment between good and evil unfolded during the time of the Flood. Genesis 6:5 holds profound significance: "And the Lord saw that the wickedness of man was great in the earth, and that every intent of the thoughts of his heart was only evil continually."

The world during the time of the Flood was full of evil, with mankind consistently promoting wickedness.[51] The account in Genesis 6:11-13 indicates that the once good and harmonious world, initially created by God, had undergone a complete corruption, reaching a critical point of self-destructive tendencies.[52] God's judgment intervened to save humanity from the path of self-destruction. This divine intervention serves as a pivotal moment in biblical history, signifying God's response to the overwhelming prevalence of evil and the restoration of justice.

In the New Testament, the Flood and the destruction of Sodom, both events recorded in Genesis, are employed as symbolic representations (types) of the universal judgment that pertains to the entire world.[53] The people of Sodom were described as "exceedingly wicked and sinful against the Lord" (Gen. 13:13). God told Abraham that He was judging Sodom and Gomorrah because "their sin is very grievous" (Gen. 18:20). The Sodomites demonstrated that they were deserving of judgment in their attempt to perpetrate evil deeds against the two angels who had come to examine them. "The men of the city, the men of Sodom, both old and young, all the people from every quarter, surrounded the house," intent on fulfilling their licentious desires (Gen. 19:4-5). Lot's endeavors to dissuade them from their wicked intent were of no avail, and they attempted to harm Lot also (Gen. 19:7, 9). The full measure of their iniquity led to divine judgment. The Lord, the Judge between good and evil, decreed the destruction of Sodom and the surrounding cities with fire (Gen. 19:24-25). This event foreshadows God's ultimate judgement of the world through fire in the last days.[54]

(3) God judges fairly.

Abraham said, "Shall not the Judge of all the earth do right?" (Gen. 18:25), making a plea for

---

51 Genesis 6:5, in using the singular form *adam* points to the collective phenomenon of human corruption during the pre-flood era.

52 The Hebrew term *shahat* is used to describe the corruption of humanity and the world, which is the main cause of the Great Flood. The term conveys different meanings based on its passive and active forms. In its passive form it means "to be corrupted" (Gen. 6:11, 12), while in its active form it carries the meanings "to corrupt" or "to destroy" (Gen. 6:12, 13). The people before the Flood self-destructed through corruption.

53 Matt. 24:38-39; Luke 17:27, 29; 2 Pet. 2:5-6.

54 Luke 17:29; 2 Pet. 2:6; Jude 1:7.

God to make a distinction between the righteous and the wicked. Abraham's earnest intercession on behalf of the inhabitants of Sodom was fully accepted by God, such that had there been but ten righteous individuals in Sodom, the city would have been spared from judgment (Gen. 18:32). Through the visit of the angels, it was revealed that the only person meriting deliverance in Sodom was Lot. God saved Lot, the sole righteous man in Sodom. He is a just and merciful Judge, who delivers the godly from tribulation (2 Pet. 2:7-9).

Amidst the catastrophic event of the Flood, God displayed his favor towards Noah, a man who was "a just man, perfect in his generations" (Gen. 6:9). Recognizing Noah's virtue, God chose to spare him and those who were with him in the ark from the sweeping destruction that engulfed all living creatures during the Flood (Gen. 7:1).

(4) God has the power to execute judgment.

Upon Adam's transgression, divine judgment was pronounced upon the earth and its inhabitants. The consequences of this judgment included increased toil and labor required for obtaining sustenance from the land. Women were to experience the pain of childbirth as part of God's decree. Moreover, mortality became the shared destiny of all mankind as a result of this judgment (Gen. 3:16-17).

In the case of Cain, God's judgment prevented the earth from yielding its produce in abundance (Gen. 4:12).

The Great Flood was not a mere natural catastrophe, but rather a result of God's direct intervention; it was He who caused rain to pour upon the earth incessantly for forty days and nights (Gen. 7:4, 12). During the Flood, the waters surged from the depths, and the windows of heaven were opened, serving as divine instruments to execute God's judgment (Gen. 7:11).

God's judgment upon the builders of Babel resulted in the confusion of their language and dispersion across the earth (Gen. 11:4-9).

In the judgment of the cities of the plains, God employed brimstone and fire to overthrow and destroy them (Gen. 19:24-25).

God, through his divine power, reversed the creative order established at the time of creation to execute his judgments. The once beautiful earth experienced divine curses and disruption of natural order, while the human language system was confounded, and supernatural sulfur fires rained down from heaven. The power of creation, hitherto used for bringing order and beauty, was wielded to execute divine judgment.

(5) God provides the way of salvation in judgment.

Amidst the weight of sin and the entrance of death into the human experience due to Adam's transgression, God extended hope to all mankind through the promise of the seed of the woman (Gen. 3:15).

In his mercy, the Lord marked Cain to protect him from harm, despite his grievous act (Gen. 4:14-15).

To Noah, God revealed the detailed plan for the ark of salvation, providing a way of escape from the impending flood judgment (Gen. 6:13-22).

Even in the judgment of Babel, God displayed his compassion by not inflicting harm upon human life; instead, He intervened to cause difficulties in communication and thereby scattered the people (Gen. 11:1-9). In his providence, God chose Abraham as a channel of blessing, entrusting him with the message of salvation to be shared with the scattered nations (Gen. 12:1-3).

When God executed judgment upon Sodom, Gomorrah, and the surrounding cities, He ensured the deliverance of Lot from their destruction (Gen. 19:29).

When all mankind apostatized, God established a pathway of salvation for all. In this redemptive narrative, we encounter key figures like Noah, regarded as the new Adam and symbolizing the seed of the woman, and Abraham, who represents a new beginning in God's history of salvation that extends to all mankind.

Through divine judgment, the brilliance of the good news of God's salvation becomes more evident. Just as the rainbow emerges in resplendent beauty after the rain, bringing hope and reassurance to our hearts, the gospel of God's salvation shines even brighter in the face of human failings and judgment.

(6) God cares for his people during judgment.

The narratives of the Flood and the destruction of Sodom and Gomorrah serve as types, representing the impending worldwide judgment. For God's people, this judgment brings hope and assurance. It is distressing and difficult to live in a world marred by evil intentions, immorality, and lawlessness. We see this in the example of Lot, "who was oppressed by the filthy conduct of the wicked" (2 Pet. 2:7).

Only through God's judgment can the world's lawlessness and sin be brought to an end, paving the way for a new world. When this judgment comes, God will, as in the cases of Noah and Lot, deliver and save his faithful people. Notably, God's attention to the individuals within his judgment is evident, as He deeply cares for each person. Those who walk with God and remain faithful will be preserved and not destroyed.

3. God the Redeemer

God's judgment is never without a message of salvation. Even amid the backdrop of mankind's profound sinfulness and God's stern judgment, the light of salvation shines brilliantly.

Upon Adam's fall, God provided hope and redemption through a promise of a Savior, a divine seed from the woman: "I will put enmity between you and the woman, and between your seed and her seed; He shall bruise your head, and you shall bruise his heel" (Gen. 3:15). Despite mankind's sin, the ultimate curse fell upon the serpent, with his head being bruised, symbolizing Satan's defeat by the Savior. Jesus, the divine seed of the woman, would thereby ensure eternal salvation for humanity.

God's plan for salvation is steadfast and sure. God holds the key of salvation. Adam cherished the hope brought by this promise. his perspective on his wife, whom he previously criticized ("The woman whom You gave to be with me, she gave me of the tree, and I ate," Gen. 3:12), changed, as he now saw her in the light of God's promise. The seed of the woman would restore life, conquer death, and lift condemnation. In recognition of this profound promise, Adam called his wife *Hawah*, signifying "life" (Gen. 3:20).

In the account of Cain's judgment in Genesis 4, God provided him with a protective sign: "And the Lord said to him, "Therefore, whoever kills Cain, vengeance shall be taken on him sevenfold." And the Lord set a mark on Cain, lest anyone finding him should kill him" (Gen. 4:15). In this manner, God arranged so that Cain would not face retaliation for his act of killing Abel.[55] God's merciful provision allowed Cain the opportunity to reflect and repent for his sin; however, despite God's gracious protection, Cain continued in his sinful ways, and his descendants followed a path of wickedness. Ultimately, their disobedience and corruption contributed to God's judgment through the Flood.

---

55 Umberto Cassuto, *A Commentary on the Book of Genesis: Part 1, from Adam to Noah, a Commentary on Genesis I-Vi8*, trans., Israel Abrahams (Jerusalem: Magnes, 1961), 225. The phrase "whosoever slayeth Cain, vengeance shall be taken on him sevenfold" need not be understood literally. The number seven in the Bible symbolizes completeness, implying that "sevenfold" signifies "to the fullest extent." Thus, the statement suggests that the one who kills Cain will receive a severe and complete punishment for their actions. *Ibid.*, 226. Cf. Lev. 26:18, 21, 24, 28; Ps. 79:12; Prov. 6:31.

Prior to the Flood, God mercifully provided people with 120 years to repent, issuing warnings of impending judgment. Throughout that period, God worked through Noah, seeking to save the people of that time. Every subsequent generation after the Flood lives under the shelter of God's will to save.

In the instance of the Tower of Babel, God did not resort to killing the builders. Instead, He dispersed them in diverse directions and selected Abraham to carry the vital mission of bringing salvation to the entire world. Abraham's intercession for Sodom and Gomorrah in Genesis 18:22-33 exemplifies his divine calling to partake in the gospel mission.

4. Absolute Sovereign

God, as the supreme ruler of the universe, holds absolute sovereignty over all creation. Being the eternal and omnipotent creator and sustainer of the universe, his authority is unassailable. "Infinite wisdom, goodness, and power, with the right of possession, which belongs to God in all his creatures, are the immutable foundation of his dominion."[56]

The entirety of the universe stands as the kingdom of God, governed by his absolute authority. The ten words of creation, expressed in Genesis 1 as *yayyomer Elohim* ("and God said"), signify the words of the King with unchallenged authority. "By the word of the Lord the heavens were made, And all the host of them by the breath of His mouth....For He spoke, and it was done; He commanded, and it stood fast" (Ps. 33:6, 9).

Because God is the unchanging Creator, his sovereignty over the world remains constant, even in the face of mankind's fallen state. This truth is evident in the depiction of Melchizedek, the king of Salem, who is described as "the priest of God the Most High" (Gen. 14:18). Abraham also acknowledges God's authority as the "Possessor of heaven and earth" and "God the Most High" when speaking to the king of Sodom (Gen. 14:22). Moreover, Abraham had his servant swear an oath to Yahweh, the God of heaven and earth, as the latter was departing to choose a bride for Isaac (Gen. 24:3) These instances show that God exercises equal control over both international and personal affairs.

God's absolute sovereignty is consistently directed towards the salvation of mankind.

---

56 Charles Hodge and Edward N. Gross, *Systematic Theology*, Abridged ed. (Phillips urg, N.J.: P&R Pub., 1997), 1:440.

Throughout history, God's covenant with individuals like Noah, Abraham, Moses, and David serves as a testament to his unwavering authority. These covenants were made to fulfill the promise of Jesus Christ, the descendant foretold in Genesis 3:15. In accordance with these covenants, Jesus was born as the son of Abraham and David, and further up the genealogy, of Adam, and ultimately of God (Matt. 1:1; Luke 3:38). The fulfillment of these covenants can only be attributed to God's absolute sovereignty, for He is the One who foresees the end from the beginning and governs all things through the providence of his eternal will and wisdom.[57]

The lives of Israel's patriarchs were under the providential guidance of God. Despite the failures and shortcomings of Abraham, Isaac, Jacob, and Joseph's brothers, God chose them and faithfully fulfilled all the promises He had made to them. This divine favor is solely due to God's grace. Joseph, in particular, bore witness to the providential nature of God's care over both nations and individuals: "So now it was not you who sent me here, but God; and He has made me a father to Pharaoh, and lord of all his house, and a ruler throughout all the land of Egypt" (Gen. 45:7–8; cf. Gen. 37:5-11).

The accounts of the Flood and the events of Sodom and Gomorrah stand as powerful testimonies to God's sovereignty over the natural world.

5. Protector

The earliest record of God as Protector can be traced back to the creation narrative in Genesis 2:4-25. In this account, God intimately fashioned man with his own hands and breathed life into his nostrils. He provided a bountiful and serene habitat, the Garden of Eden, where humanity could thrive. God prepared a suitable companion for man, and ensured mankind's well-being, offering them a beautiful environment with abundant sustenance.

After the Fall, God continued to demonstrate his protective care for his people. He acted as a just judge for Abel, preserving the honor of this righteous man who had seemingly died a meaningless death. During the judgment of the Flood, God shielded Noah and his family, safeguarding them from the devastating waters (Gen. 4:10; 7:23; 8:1).

God's protective hand was evident throughout the lives of Israel's patriarchs. God intervened to

57 Martyn Lloyd-Jones, *Joy Before God's Presence: God's Blessing In Psalms* (Seoul, Word of Life, 1995), 24. Korean edition of Martyn Lloyd-Jones, *Seeking The Face Of God: Nine Reflections On The Psalms*.

save Abraham's wife, Sarai, from harm when she was in the hands of Pharaoh, king of Egypt, and later with Abimelech, king of Gerar (Gen. 12:10-20; 20:1-18). During a conflict, God empowered Abraham to rescue the people of Sodom, including his nephew Lot, from the forces of Amraphel, king of Shinar (Gen. 14:13-16, 20). God also showed his protection and care for Hagar and Ishmael when they were cast out of their home by Sarai, because of their connection with Abraham (Gen. 16:1-16; 21:8-21). Furthermore, God's angel delivered Lot from the wicked in Sodom and saved him during the time of judgment (Gen. 19).

The hand of God's protection was clearly evident in Jacob's life during various critical moments. While Jacob was fleeing from his brother Esau, God revealed Himself to Jacob through a vision of a ladder at Bethel, assuring him of his presence and promising to bring him safely back to the land of Canaan, which promise He faithfully fulfilled (Gen. 28:10-22; 35:1-7). Despite being taken advantage of by his uncle Laban, Jacob was blessed by God with prosperity, and God warned Laban not to harm him through a dream (Gen. 31:24, 29, 40-42). Moreover, God intervened when Jacob faced the threat of revenge from Esau, bringing about a reconciliation that restored peace between the two brothers (Gen. 33:1-17). In the incident involving Simeon and Levi's actions against the Shechemites, God protected Jacob's family by instilling fear in their enemies, ensuring their safety (Gen. 34; 35:5).

Joseph's journey from being sold into Egypt to becoming the prime minister of the country is a remarkable testament to God's providence. Although Joseph faced challenging circumstances, God continued to bless him as he served faithfully in Potiphar's house and even during his time in prison (Gen. 39:3, 23). Ultimately, God's hand of providence was evident in Joseph's rise to power as the prime minister of Egypt. In this high-ranking position, Joseph played a crucial role in implementing God's plan to save Egypt and the surrounding nations, including his own family, from a severe famine that had struck the region (Gen. 41:37-45).

Chapter 05 | God's Attributes

1. Eternity

The Old Testament stands apart from the ancient Near Eastern creation myths, such as Enuma Elish or Egyptian myths, in that it does not mention aspects related to deities' origins, such as genealogies or conflicts.[1] Instead, it focuses on the creation of the world by God, who exists infinitely without a beginning or end. In Genesis 21:33, Abraham planted a tamarisk tree in Beersheba and called upon the name of "the Lord [Yahweh], the Everlasting God." The choice of a tamarisk, which is an evergreen tree, signified Abraham's faith in God's eternity.

Throughout the Bible, God is referred to as "the Everlasting Yahweh" (Gen. 21:33), "the eternal God" (Deut. 33:27), "the everlasting God, Yahweh" (Isa. 40:28), "the King eternal" (1 Tim. 1:17), and "the eternal Spirit" (Heb. 9:14).

The name Yahweh serves as a reminder of God's eternity. God Himself stated in Exodus 3:15 that Yahweh is "my name forever." The term Yahweh means "One who exists of his own accord," and "One who brings into being," and signifies that God exists from eternity to eternity, encompassing all time.

God's eternity is not merely an abstract concept of timelessness and transcendence. Instead, it involves a profound relationship with humankind, particularly focused on saving humanity, as humans are created in his image. God establishes an eternal covenant with his people,[2] 2 promises them an eternal inheritance,[3] and bestows upon them eternal blessings.[4]

2. Omnipotence

The events of Creation and Judgment, such as the Flood, the Tower of Babel, and the destruction

1 Horst Dietrich Preuss, *Old Testament Theology*, ed. James L. Mays, et. al. The Old Testament Library, vol. 1 (Louisville, KY: Westminster John Knox Press, 1995), 239.

2 Gen. 9:16; 17:7, 13, 19.

3 Gen. 13:15; 17:8; 48:4.

4 Gen. 49:26.

of Sodom and Gomorrah, attest to God's omnipotence. He has the ability to accomplish whatever He wills, from shaking the heavens and the earth to confounding languages and sending down fire from heaven.

Throughout history, God's omnipotence is directed towards the salvation of humanity. The fulfillment of the proto-evangelium (original gospel) promised in Genesis 3:15 is a testament to God's dominion over human history. He intervenes in remarkable ways, even opening the womb of the elderly Sarah so she can give birth to the promised seed (Gen. 17:1; 18:14). Nothing is impossible for the Creator of heaven and earth. When Sarah reacted with laughter to God's words of promise, God told her, "Is any thing too hard for the Lord? At the appointed time I will return to you, according to the time of life, and Sarah shall have a son" (Gen. 18:14; cf. Jer. 32:17, 27). Since God, the Creator, is mighty to achieve all that He says, we must wholeheartedly believe in his promises and strive to fulfill his commands through his power (Luke 1:37).

The stories of the patriarchs serve as a reminder of God's infallible works. Throughout these narratives, we witness how God communicates with people through dreams to offer guidance and protection. For instance, in Genesis 20:3, God saved Sarai by speaking to Abimelech in a dream and warning him about her identity. Similarly, He appeared to Jacob in a dream while he was a fugitive, providing encouragement and assurance (Gen. 28:12-13). God also sent Pharaoh a dream about the forthcoming plentiful years followed by a severe famine and gave Joseph the wisdom to interpret the dream, thereby delivering his people from starvation (Gen. 41; 45:7-8). God does not tyrannically wield his omnipotent power, but rather uses it with wisdom and grace to save humanity.

3. Omniscience

God is all-knowing. Nowhere do the sacred scriptures present God as acquiring knowledge through reasoning. Instead, the Bible consistently portrays God as the all-knowing and all-seeing deity.[5]

When we contemplate creation, we are struck by the evidence of God's boundless wisdom. As the Creator of the physical world, He established the laws of nature, ensuring the harmonious functioning of the universe. This demonstration of divine wisdom is a testament to his omniscience.

God's knowledge extends beyond the external aspects of creation; He intimately knows the

5 G. Vos, 'Omniscience', *ISBE* 3:599.

inner heart of humanity. He perceived the dark thoughts encroaching on Cain's heart and warned Cain about the dangers of sin, urging him to overcome it (Gen. 4:7). In the time of the Flood, God observed the pervasive evil in the hearts of humanity (Gen. 6:5). He saw the decency of Abimelech's heart and prevented him from falling into sin (Gen. 20:6).

God knows the future. He knew that Abraham's descendants would be strangers in Egypt for four hundred years (Gen. 15:13), and revealed the future destinies of Rebekah's twin sons, Esau and Jacob, when they were still in the womb (Gen. 25:23). This divine knowledge is a testament to God's absolute sovereignty, which is realized through his omnipotence and omniscience.

God possesses an intimate knowledge of the spiritual reality of humanity. "The imagination of man's heart is evil from his youth" (Gen. 8:21). Being the epitome of absolute goodness, God sets the standard for discerning between good and evil. As the all-knowing deity, only He truly comprehends what is good.[6] In his omniscience, God perceives the predicaments and crises that befall humanity, and He understands what is required to save us from these challenges. Consequently, He consistently provides us with a path to salvation.

In their journey of faith, unwavering belief in God's omniscience brings courage and comfort to the godly, especially in the midst of suffering and misunderstanding. This belief allows them to live truthfully before God, free from hidden evils, and encourages them to seek his wisdom daily through prayer.[7]

4. Omnipresence

God is everywhere. There is no place where God is not present.

God often meets humanity in unexpected places, in situations where humans least expected to encounter Him. Hagar, who found herself fleeing from her mistress Sarai with a baby in her womb, encountered God's presence in a situation of great distress, and exclaimed, "Have I also here seen Him who sees me?" (Gen. 16:13). Jacob, on the run from his brother Esau, met God unexpectedly in a dream, and said, "Surely the Lord [Yahweh] is in this place, and I did not know it" (Gen. 28:16). Joseph's life took an unexpected turn when he was sold into slavery in Egypt, but he experienced the presence of God even within these dire circumstances in a foreign land (Gen. 39:2, 3, 21, 23).

6 Bruce K. Waltke and Charles Yu, *An Old Testament Theology: An Exegetical, Canonical, and Thematic Approach*, 1st ed. (Grand Rapids, MI: Zondervan, 2007), 275.

7 Vos, 600.

The act of building an altar is a powerful expression of faith in God's omnipresence.[8] Without the conscious awareness of God's presence, there would be no reason or motivation to construct an altar. Throughout the Bible, we see instances where God revealed the mark of his presence by accepting sacrifices offered on altars. For instance, God acknowledged Abel's sacrifice, and "smelled a sweet savour" when Noah gave his burnt offerings (Gen. 4:4; 8:20, 21). Abraham built altars wherever he went as an expression of his faith and devotion (Gen. 12:7, 8; 13:4, 18). Similarly, when Jacob experienced a crisis in his life, he remembered the God who had been with him in the past and, as an act of faith and a revival of his trust in God, he went up to Bethel to build an altar (Gen. 35:1, 3, 7).

God's omnipresence encompasses the entirety of the world. The rainbow, which served as a sign of God's post-Flood covenant with Noah, symbolizes God's care and protection for all living things on earth (Gen. 9:10-17). It serves as "the sign of the covenant between Me [God] and the earth" (Gen. 9:13). The covenant God made with Noah extended to all living things, underscoring the omnipresence of He who exercises control over all living beings. The rainbow serves as a profound reminder and evidence of God's omnipresence throughout the whole world.

Because God is everywhere, believers can walk with Him wherever they live. Like Enoch, we can walk with God to heaven (Gen. 5:24), and like Noah, we can become perfect in our generation and walk with God in the midst of an immoral world (Gen. 6:9). Because of our belief in God's omnipresence, we have the privilege of worshipping God wherever we may be and whatever our circumstances. There is no place or situation beyond God's care and guidance, and his children can lead lives of discipleship, consecrating every aspect of their existence to Him. We can believe and understand that the distance from God is the same everywhere under heaven, for his presence is unfailing and constant.

---

8 Omnipresence refers to God's attribute of being present everywhere and transcending all limitations of space and place. It signifies that God exists in every location without any restriction. Along with omniscience and omnipotence, it is among God's unique attributes.

Chapter 06 | God's Character

1. Holy

(1) The Sabbath as a testimony to God's holiness

God is holy. Holiness means being set apart from daily common things. While the book of Genesis rarely explicitly deals with the concept of God's holiness, it contains fundamental statements about the holiness of God that gains significant emphasis later in the Bible. God's holiness was evident from the very beginning of creation. In Genesis 2:3, God sanctified the Sabbath, an act that only the Holy One can do. Blessing and sanctifying time is an action exclusive to One who is transcendent. Through the sanctification of the seventh day, God enables humans to participate in his holiness through worship. The concept of holiness may only be properly understood in relation to God.

(2) God distinguishes between cleanness and uncleanness

God instructed Noah to distinguish between clean and unclean animals as he gathered them into the ark and led the animals to the ark in accordance with this distinction. After the Flood, Noah offered burnt offerings to God out of the clean animals (Gen. 7:2, 8; 8:20). Thus, the concept of distinguishing between clean and unclean existed even before the time of Moses, in the pre-Flood era. Just as the distinction between good and evil is not determined by human decisions, the division between clean and unclean is established by a holy God.

God revealed further details of this dichotomic taxonomy to Moses in Leviticus 11 and Deuteronomy 14. The act of distinguishing between clean and unclean among the animals that could be encountered in daily life was meant to remind God's people of the importance of living with the knowledge of a holy God even within their secular lives. The practice of avoiding unclean food served as a "visual aid," emphasizing the importance of purity for God's people throughout all ages.[1]

Noah's division of animals into clean and unclean was for the purpose of determining whether

1 Waltke and Yu, 14.

or not they could be offered as sacrifices to God.[2] In the act of worship, mankind experienced the presence of the holy God. As they left Eden, they carried with them the sacred observance of the Sabbath, the institution of marriage, and the practice of worship that facilitated fellowship with the Divine. Cain and Abel were both aware of how to offer sacrifices to God.

(3) Holiness and worship

God's holiness empowers his people to live a consecrated and set-apart life. In a time when the sins of the Cainite tribe were prevalent, the righteous descendants of Seth initiated public worship and started calling on the name of Yahweh: "Then men began to call on the name of the Lord" (Gen. 4:26). This act of worship was a way for the godly lineage of Seth to remain faithful and devoted to God amidst the prevailing unrighteousness.

Kadesh was a Canaanite city, and its name means "sanctuary" or "holy place" (Gen. 14:7, 16:14, and 20:1).[3] It is likely that Kadesh served as the focal point for the Canaanites' rituals and religious practices. The worship of a deity or deities and recognition of the deity's holiness are universal qualities bestowed upon human beings. These qualities arise from the human need for a transcendent presence beyond themselves, as humans inherently seek a connection to something greater and beyond their individual existence.

However, the pursuit of human holiness apart from the holy God, Yahweh, caused things to go terribly wrong. The Canaanite religion deteriorated into depraved worship, with the prostitute playing the role of a priestess, known as kdesha ("consecrated").[4] True spiritual and moral holiness is intimately connected to righteousness and purity, concepts that can only be fully understood through the revelation of the Creator, Yahweh.

---

2 Kenneth A. Mathews, *Genesis 4:27-11*:26, ed. E. Ray Clendenen, The New Ameri can Commentary, vol. 1B (Nashville, TN: Broadman & Holman Publishers, 1996), 372, 373.

3 The longer name for Kadesh is "Kadesh Barnea." During the exodus, twelve spies of Israel explored the land of Canaan from this place, but due to lack of faith, the Israelites received forty years of wandering in the wilderness as punishment (Num. 13-14). Miriam died and was buried here (Num. 20:1), and Moses, in disobedience to God's command, struck the rock twice instead of speaking to it, resulting in the denial of his entry into the Promised Land (Num. 20:2-13). The original name, "En Mishpat", means "spring of judgment." It is located approximately 80 kilometers south of Beersheba and has the largest oasis in the northern Sinai desert, producing around 40 m^3 of water per hour. Dale W. Manor, 'Kadesh-Barnea', *ABD* 4:1. It is believed that the name "En Mishpat" was given by nomads who gathered at this oasis to resolve their disputes. Sarna, 106.

4 Judah lay with Tamar, his son's wife, mistakenly regarding her as a prostitute. When it was time for him to pay her for her services, he inquired after the local temple prostitute, but no such individual existed in that area (Gen. 38:21-22).

(4) Holy Judge

A holy God is one who administers judgment against injustice, wickedness, and corruption. The stories of judgment in Genesis demonstrate how a righteous God chastises a wicked world, upholding justice and righteousness.

(5) God who distinguishes

A holy God is a discriminating Creator. Each day of Creation involved the act of distinguishing and separating. God created light and darkness, water and firmament, sea and land, and animals and plants, each in its own kind. The seventh day, Sunday, was designated as the Sabbath, set apart as a special day of rest.

By consecrating the Sabbath as a celebration of his creation, God sanctified the entire universe as his own. Any actions that disrupt or corrupt the natural order, which God perceived as beautiful, attack the holiness of the Creator by violating his sacred creation.

God also sets apart his people. Those who belong to the "seed of the woman" are God's chosen ones. The story of redemption unfolds towards the ultimate victory of Jesus Christ, the holy One of God, in the conflict between God's holy people and the wicked followers of Satan.[5] In a world corrupted by sin, God made a special distinction for Noah. Amidst a society that had turned away from God, He called upon Abraham to leave the temple cities (Ur and Haran) of the moon god Sin, where corrupt worship prevailed.[6]

(6) Holiness is redemptive and evangelistic.

God called Abraham out of the darkness of a pagan world to bear witness to the gospel of eternal blessing that restores the world. Everywhere he went, Abraham's altar was a quiet witness to the Gentile world about the holy God he served. The purpose of Abraham's calling was to establish a nation, Israel, that would be the source of the blessings of the world. The book of Genesis shows that God's holy people, Israel, was formed amidst all manner of trials and challenges.

---

5 The angel Gabriel referred to the soon-to-be-born Jesus as "that Holy one who is to be born will be called the Son of God" (Luke 1:35). In the New Testament, "Holy One of God" is used only twice, in Mark 1:24 and Luke 4:34. Both times, the title was used by evil spirits as they came out of a person in obedience to Jesus' command.

6 Haran is a city located in modern day southern Turkey. In the second millennium BC, this place, along with Ur of the Chaldeans, worshipped the moon god. The Assyrians revered this temple, while the Babylonians later restored the worship of the moon god. The mother of the last Babylonian emperor (Nabonidus), who died at the ripe old age of 104, was the high priestess of the temple of Ur. Later, Nabonidus' daughter became the high priestess. R. J. Hughes, III, 'Haran', *ISBE* 2:614.

God's holiness is evangelistic in nature. Even as the Sabbath arrives week after week, God persistently extends an invitation to humanity for holy fellowship with Him. This divine invitation will continue into the future, encompassing a new heaven and a new earth. Just as God called Abraham to save a corrupt world through Noah and to establish his kingdom on earth, God also calls us today to be royal priests, tasked with bearing witness to his marvelous light.

2. Merciful

The merciful nature of God is evident in his act of creation. God delights in bestowing blessings upon all living beings, including humans (Gen. 1:22, 28). By blessing the seventh day, God extended his benevolence to all spatial beings existing within time (Gen. 2:3).

After the fall of mankind, God's mercy shines even more brightly, contrasting with the sinful image of humanity. The proto-evangelium found in Genesis 3:15 reveals God's merciful intentions; through this original gospel, God mitigated the threat of judgment articulated in Genesis 2:17 and replaced it with the promise of salvation.[7]

The Hebrew words that express God's mercy are hen meaning "grace";[8] hesed meaning "mercy" or "kindness";[9] and yatab[10] meaning "to do good." Yet another word used in the Bible to signify grace is ahab ("to love"). In Genesis, it is not used to describe God, but rather is used in the context of interpersonal relationships, including with respect to parents and children (Gen. 22:2; 25:28; 37:3, 4; 44:20), spouses (Gen. 24:67, 30, 32), food (Gen. 25:2, 4, 9, 14), and courtship (Gen. 29:18; 34:3). Outside of Genesis, it is used to describe God's love for humanity (Ex. 20:6; Deut. 5:10;

7 William Dyrness, *Themes in Old Testament Theology* (Downers Grove, IL; Carlisle, UK: InterVarsity Press, The Paternoster Press, 1977), 58.

8 In Genesis, the word hen meaning "grace" appears three times in relation to God, in Genesis 6:8, 18:3, and 19:19. It is also used to describe Joseph, who received favor in the sight of the keeper of the prison based on God's providential hand in Genesis 39:21. Additionally, the word appears in various contexts signifying the impartment of "grace" between individuals (Gen. 32:5 (H 6); 33:8, 10, 15; 34:11; 39:4; 47:25, 29; 50:4). Laban used this word when requesting Jacob to stay with him, saying, "if I have found favour in your eyes" in Genesis 30:27.

9 The term is translated as kindness (Gen. 20:13; 21:23; 24:12, 14, 49; 40:14; 47:29) and mercy (Gen. 19:19; 24:27; 32:10; 39:21) in NKJV.

10 In Genesis, the word *yātab* is used in relation to God twice in Genesis 32:9, 12, in the context of Jacob's prayer for protection from Esau, with the meaning of "to bestow grace." Additionally, the word appears in the Korean Revised Version of the Bible with the meanings of "to do good" in Genesis 4:7, "to be secure" in Genesis 12:13, "to prosper" in Genesis 12:16, "to be pleased" in Genesis 34:18; 41:37, "to gain favor" in Genesis 40:14, and "to delight" in Genesis 45:16.

7:9; Josh. 22:5; 23:11; Judg. 5:31; 1 Kings 3:3; Ps. 31:24; 38:12), Israel (Hos. 3:1), the founding fathers of Israel (Deut. 4:37; 10:15), and believers (Deut. 7:13; 23:6; Isa. 43:4; Jer. 31:3; Hos. 11:1; 14:15).[11] These words capture the essence of God's compassionate and gracious nature, showing his willingness to extend goodness and favor to his creation.

(1) Grace (חֵן, hen)

At the time of the Flood judgment, Noah received the grace of Yahweh (Gen. 6:8).[12] When all of humanity was facing destruction due to their extreme corruption, God extended great grace to Noah, choosing him to be saved and to become the instrument through which mankind would find a new beginning. Without God's mercy, humanity would have faced total annihilation. The Lord, who witnessed widespread corruption in the world, did not ignore the righteousness of one individual and thus decided to save him.

The call of Noah exemplifies God's mercy, not just towards Noah alone, but towards all of humankind. The fact that God provided salvation amidst judgment reveals his inherent mercy. Genesis 6:9 emphasizes that God's grace towards Noah was not because of Noah's personal virtues, but because of his close relationship with God, as he "walked with God."

Abraham unknowingly displayed great hospitability toward God. In accordance with Eastern etiquette, he respectfully invited the three heavenly guests to his tents with the words, "if I have now found favour I in Your sight" (Gen. 18:3). He unwittingly entertained angels, and among their group was Yahweh himself (Heb. 13:2).[13] God's acceptance of man's invitation to sup with him represents an exceedingly great favor toward that man. Abraham experienced God's grace through his hospitality toward Yahweh. He received the promise of Isaac's birth, and God accepted his pleas

---

11 Yet another word used in the Bible to signify grace is *ahab* ("to love"). In Genesis, it is not used to describe God, but rather is used in the context of interpersonal relationships, including with respect to parents and children (Gen. 22:2; 25:28; 37:3, 4; 44:20), spouses (Gen. 24:67, 30, 32), food (Gen. 25:2, 4, 9, 14), and courtship (Gen. 29:18; 34:3). Outside of Genesis, it is used to describe God's love for humanity (Ex. 20:6; Deut. 5:10; 7:9; Josh. 22:5; 23:11; Judg. 5:31; 1 Kings 3:3; Ps. 31:24; 38:12), Israel (Hos. 3:1), the founding fathers of Israel (Deut. 4:37; 10:15), and believers (Deut. 7:13; 23:6; Isa. 43:4; Jer. 31:3; Hos. 11:1; 14:15).

12 The original meaning of the phrase is "found grace in the eyes of the Lord". The phrase implies that the precondition for receiving grace is not based on discerning actions but on one's attitude. The bestower of grace is always the superior party. When the term *hen* is used to describe the attitude of the superior party, it conveys humility or favoritism. Cf. H. J. Stoebe, '*ḥnn*,' *TLOT* 1:440-441.

13 Justin Martyr, Ambrose, Cyril, and other church fathers considered the three visitors as the Triune God (Trinity), but as Genesis 19:1 indicates, two of them were angels. Thomas Whitelaw, *Genesis*, ed. H. D. M. Spence-Jones, The Pulpit Commentary, vol. 1 (New York, Toronto: Funk & Wagnalls Company, 1913), 240.

on behalf of Sodom and Gomorrah.

God sent two angels to Sodom to save the righteous man, Lot. Even though Lot acknowledged that his salvation was due to God's unconditional "grace" (hen) and "unfailing love" (hesed), Lot asked for permission to flee to the nearby town of Zoar, out of fear that he might encounter death during his escape (Gen. 19:19, 20). God granted his plea despite the reluctance Lot displayed in following God's command. Abraham's plea for the righteous people in Sodom contrasts with Lot's plea to save his own life. Nevertheless, even though Lot's actions were not as decisive as one might hope, God "remembered Abraham, and sent Lot out of the midst of the overthrow" (Gen. 19:29).

(2) Mercy and Favor (חֶסֶד hesed)

Hesed is a Hebrew word that represents sincere and unwavering love and is often translated as "loving-kindness" or "steadfast love." It appears 246 times in the Old Testament, and approximately one-third of these occurrences describe God's disposition towards the faithful, including his people Israel and humanity as a whole, as well as his actions of benevolence towards them.[14]

The first occurrence of hesed is in Genesis 19:19, when God saves Lot from the destruction of Sodom. The most frequent use of the word is found in the prayer of Eliezar, Abraham's servant, at the well of Nahor, when he beseeched God to help him find God's chosen bride for Isaac. God answered his prayer and showed hesed, so that Eliezar could easily find Isaac's future wife (Gen. 24:12, 14, 27).

The presence of hesed in these narratives underscores God's unwavering love and faithfulness towards his chosen ones. It demonstrates that God's hesed is not confined to the age of patriarchy or a specific period but extends to "his children as well."[15]

(3) Do good to (יָטַב yatab)

On his journey to meet his brother Esau, Jacob humbly confessed that he was unworthy to receive all the grace and blessings that God had bestowed upon him. "I am not worthy of the least of all the mercies and of all the truth which you have shown Your servant; for I crossed over this Jordan with my staff, and now I have become two companies" (Gen. 32:10 [H 11]). The Hebrew

---

14 D.A. Baer, R. P. Gordon, '*ḥsd*,' *NIDOTTE* 2:211.

15 Ibid., 214. Abraham's servant prayed to God, saying, "Blessed be the Lord God of my master Abraham, Who hath not left destitute my master of his mercy and his truth" (Gen. 24:27). This underscores the possibility of the cessation of God's *hesed.* See also God's taking away lovingkindness (hesed) and mercies from the people of Israel (Jer. 3:43), and his declaration that He will not take away mercy (Hesed) from David, unlike what He did with Saul (2 Sam. 7:15).

word used, qaton conveys the idea of being small or worthless, and Jacob expressed his sense of unworthiness with a contrite heart. God did not abandon Jacob despite his past mistakes; instead, God remained faithful and showed him love. Jacob's confession, translated as "I am not worthy of the least of...," literally means "I am smaller than all the mercies and all the truth." The word Jacob used, qaton, means "small, worthless." Jacob was tearfully confessing his wrongful act of defrauding his older brother.[16] Despite his shortcomings, God favored Jacob and caused him to prosper, then commanded him to return to his homeland. Although Jacob was deeply anxious because of his strained relationship with Esau, he continued forward, relying solely on God's promises: "I will deal well (yatab) with you" (Gen. 32:9); and "I will surely treat you well (yatab), and make your descendants as the sand of the sea, which cannot be numbered for multitude." (Gen. 32:12). Not only did God do good to Jacob by protecting him from Esau, but He also used Jacob's life to bring forth the nation of Israel, thus doing a great good for the whole world.

God showed mercy (hesed) upon Joseph, thereby allowing him to receive grace (hen) from the keeper of the prison (Gen. 39:21). Even in the midst of a dark and challenging time, where Joseph was unjustly accused and imprisoned with no apparent hope of escape, God's grace was at work in his life. God granted to Joseph wisdom and attentive consideration for others, which not only gained him favor with the keeper of the prison but eventually led to favor from Pharaoh and his servants.[17] Through God's blessings, Joseph played a crucial role in bringing Egypt and other nations out of crisis and saved countless lives, including those of the patriarchs of Israel. This narrative illustrates how God's mercy and grace extend beyond the individual to impact their surroundings, neighbors, and even entire nations.

3. Forgiveness

(1) Proto-evangelium and coat of skins

Through the proto-evangelium (original gospel) recorded in Genesis 3:15, God decreed that Jesus Christ would take on the punishment of death that God had warned humanity about in Genesis 2:17. Although God did not expressly mention forgiveness when delivering judgment upon our first

16 Kenneth A. Mathews, *Genesis* 11:27-50:26, 551.

17 The word *yatab* meaning "to do good" or "be pleased," was used in relation to Joseph. Pharaoh and the officials regarded Joseph's proposals regarding the seven years of abundance and seven years of famine favorably (Gen. 41:37), and were pleased with Joseph's reunion with his brothers (Gen. 45:16).

parents, forgiveness was implied within this judgment. God's draping our first parents with coats of skins foreshadowed Jesus Christ's death on the cross on behalf of sinners (Gen. 3:21).

(2) God took upon Himself the suffering of sin.

After the Flood, God found pleasure in Noah's sacrifice and made a promise not to destroy all living things again, even though humanity's wickedness remained unchanged (Gen. 8:20. cf. Gen. 6:5). This contrast between God's mercy towards Noah and humanity's continued sinful state points to a future event where God himself would bear the burden of humanity's sins on the cross.

The concept of forgiveness, which entails God taking upon Himself the sins of humankind, is illustrated in the account of Abraham's intercession to God for Sodom in Genesis 18:24, where he asks, "Suppose there were fifty righteous within the city: would you also destroy the place and not spare it for the fifty righteous that were in it?" and in Genesis 18:26, where the Lord replied, "If I find in Sodom fifty righteous within the city, then I will spare all the place for their sakes." The term "forgive" is used here for the first time in Genesis. Subsequently, Joseph's brothers also used this expression to request forgiveness from Joseph after they had collectively buried Jacob (Gen. 50:17).

In these instances, the Hebrew verb used for "forgive" is nasa which essentially means "to lift, carry, take." This illustrates that forgiveness involves taking away sins and bearing them upon oneself.[18] It invites us to reflect on the image of Jesus Christ, the Lamb of God, who takes away the sins of the world.

Abraham fervently pleaded with God to spare Sodom, starting with the hope of finding fifty righteous people in the city, continuing all the way down to ten righteous individuals. Each time, his heart was filled with fear and trembling, showing his deep concern for his nephew Lot.[19] In response, God repeatedly agreed to reducing the number of required righteous individuals. This reveals that God's true will is not to punish, but to forgive and restore. The destruction of Sodom was not due to the insufficient number of righteous people, but because the city had become thoroughly unfit for the righteous to dwell.

---

18 Keil and Delitzsch, 1:14. When the verb *nasa* takes *awon* ("iniquity), *hatah* ("sin"), and *pesha* ("transgression") as object, *nasa* means "to bear away, to remove sin and its ieffects …thus to forgive or pardon." John S. Kselman, 'Forgiveness (Old Testament),' ABD 2:832. The Hebrew word for the verb "to forgive" is *salah*, and is first used in Exodus 34:9.

19 Abraham's words show that he pleaded for Sodom not flippantly, but with trembling and deep reverence: "I have taken upon me to speak unto the Lord, which am but dust and ashes"; "Oh let not the Lord be angry, and I will speak"; "Behold now, I have taken upon me to speak unto the Lord"; "Oh let not the Lord be angry, and I will speak yet but this once" (Gen. 18:27, 30, 31, 32).

(3) Restoration of relationship

The book of Genesis contains instances where forgiveness is evident, even though the term "forgiveness" is not explicitly used. For example, in the stories of Jacob and Esau, and of Joseph and his brothers, forgiveness is demonstrated through actions.

Forgiveness was already achieved when Esau ran toward Jacob, who was limping toward him, and embraced and wept with his brother (Gen. 32:31; 33:4). Similarly, when Joseph revealed himself to his brothers and wept aloud before them, it was evident that he had already forgiven them for their previous mistreatment of him (Gen. 45:1, 2). The acts of kindness and reconciliation that followed reinforce that complete forgiveness had been accomplished. In these examples, forgiveness resulted in the restoration of the right relationship between the parties involved.

(4) The patriarchs were people who experienced forgiveness.

When we analyze the stories of God and the patriarchs through this lens, we discover numerous instances where the patriarchs sinned against God and were forgiven. Abraham repeatedly fell into crisis because he lied that his wife was his sister, and each time, God intervened to take care of the situation, first by rebuking Pharaoh, and then by speaking with Abimelech, the king of Gerar (Gen. 12:17; 20:3). Although the biblical accounts are silent on what further actions Abraham took in these situations, it is highly likely that Abraham repented before God for his sin and pleaded for deliverance.

Similarly, Isaac and Jacob also committed sins, following in the footsteps of their father Abraham. Isaac repeated the deception of his father, this time regarding his wife Rebekah, and Jacob deceived his father Isaac and his brother Esau to steal the blessing meant for Esau. The altars they subsequently built reflects their journey of repentance and seeking forgiveness from God.

Throughout these accounts, we can observe God's continual forgiveness and encouragement towards the patriarchs, even in their weaknesses. He raised up the weak to be the forefathers of his chosen nation, Israel, and continued to guide history to achieve the salvation of mankind. The image of God as a forgiving deity is firmly established in the sanctuary the Israelites built as they came out of Egypt, based on God's own instructions.

4. Faithfulness

(1) Cares for his people

God demonstrates his faithful care for his people throughout the Bible. He remains true to his promises and extends his protection and provision to those who trust in Him.

In the story of Noah, God faithfully preserved Noah and his family by having them enter the ark and protecting them during the Flood (Gen. 6:18; 7:1, 23; 8:1). After the Flood, God's faithful care for all living things was evident in the establishment of the rainbow as a sign of his covenant (Gen. 9:15-16).

God's faithfulness is also evident in the fulfillment of his promise to Abraham and Sarah, who, despite their old age, were blessed with the birth of their son Isaac (Gen. 17:15-19; 21:1-3). When Abraham's servant sought a wife for Isaac, he acknowledged God's constant kindness and faithfulness in guiding their path (Gen. 24:27).

God promised his constant presence and support to the fugitive Jacob, and Jacob later affirmed that God had indeed been faithful to his word (Gen. 28:15; 32:10).

(2) Fulfills his covenants

God's faithfulness is prominently seen in the covenant He established with humanity. From the very beginning, in Genesis 3:15, God foretold the redemptive work that would come to fruition, and we witness the steady unfolding of God's plan throughout the book of Genesis.

Genesis shows us the story of the birth of the nation of Israel, which would hold a pivotal role in the history of redemption. Despite numerous adversities such as sterility, fraud, betrayal, famine, and all manner of other challenges, including misconduct and mistakes and sins committed by the patriarchs who were to play key roles in the redemptive narrative, God remained steadfast in preparing Israel for its mission of evangelism and the salvation of all mankind. Even amidst the consequences of sin, the blessings of the creation covenant, to be fruitful, multiply and replenish the earth, remained valid for all nations. God's faithfulness ensures that his original intentions and promises are not lost due to sin, but continue to be relevant and applicable to all humanity.

5. Long-suffering

God is long-suffering. In Genesis 6:3, God granted a grace period of one hundred and twenty years to the people of the pre-Flood era. Despite the wickedness and evil deeds that were already prevalent, as illustrated by Lamech's introduction of polygamy and celebration of murder, God allowed sinful mankind to continue living for more than a century. God's patience persisted until the sins of the people reached the tipping point. Some interpret the period of one hundred and twenty years as a cap on the lifespan of humans, but this interpretation is flawed given the presence of people who lived beyond one hundred and twenty years after the Flood.[20]

In light of God's holiness, the continuation of a sinful world can be attributed to the long-suffering patience of a just God. From the moment of humanity's fall until the present, history can be viewed as a testament to God's enduring patience.

God's long-suffering extends not only to his chosen people but also to the Gentile world. In Genesis 15:16, it is stated, "But in the fourth generation they shall return here, for the iniquity of the Amorites is not yet complete." It took more than 400 years for the Israelites to settle in Canaan, during which God tolerated the Amorites until their iniquities had fully ripened (Lev. 18:24-28).

God's imposition of limitations on time reminds us that his mercy and long-suffering are not everlasting. While God is indeed the God of patience and love, He is also the God of wrath. his patience and mercy have a purpose and a limit, and there comes a point when the consequences of sin and disobedience must be faced. God's long-suffering provides sinners with an opportunity for salvation. It is a period of grace during which God patiently awaits the repentance and redemption of those who have gone astray. The time of the end is also a part of God's divine plan, although its exact timing remains known only to God the Father. As Jesus stated in Matthew 24:36, no one other than the Father knows when the end will come, emphasizing the need to be spiritually vigilant and live as genuine followers of God.

20 Before the Great Flood, the average lifespan was around 900 years (Gen. 5). However, after the Flood, lifespans decreased rapidly (Gen. 11). After the Flood, Shem lived 600 years, Eber 464 years, Abraham 175 years, Joseph 110 years, Jacob 147 years, and Moses 120 years.

PART III

Humanity

Chapter 07 | Image of God

1. Genesis: A book about the origin and destiny of mankind

The Bible tells us about the origin and destiny of man. While the Pentateuch primarily focuses on God's chosen people, Israel, the book of Genesis connects the Israelites' origins to the broader history of humanity. Genesis 1-11 contains a universal history, capturing the lineage from Adam to the time of the Tower of Babel. Subsequently, Genesis 12-50 delves into the early national history of Israel through the accounts of Abraham, Isaac, Jacob, and his twelve sons, who became the patriarchs of the nation of Israel. The following books, Exodus through Deuteronomy, then provide a detailed history of the nation of Israel.

Although the Bible deals with human history, its primary focus is the Israelites and their leaders, who are the objects of God's concern; other peoples and individuals are discussed in their relation to the nation of Israel or its patriarchs. The ancestors of faith, starting from Adam, possess distinct individual traits, yet they also share universal qualities that are common to all human beings. The book of Genesis narrates the origin of mankind and its history of fall, judgment, and restoration. It serves as a fundamental source for reflecting on humanity's nature and destiny. What is humankind, and what is their destiny?

2. Biblical references to the image of God

The concept of the "image of God" is explicitly mentioned only a few times in the Bible, but its significance is profound and far-reaching. In the Old Testament, it is found in Genesis 1:26, 27; 5:1; and 9:6. In the New Testament, it is referenced in 1 Corinthians 11:7, 2 Corinthians 4:4, Colossians 1:15, and James 3:9.

This idea of being created in the image of God is not to be taken lightly or ignored, as it has a crucial impact on the understanding of human beings[1] and forms a foundational basis for the

1 Sinclair Ferguson, "Image of God," *New Dictionary of Theology*, 328.

Christian worldview, including our understanding of salvation and eschatology.

3. God's creatures

In the Old Testament, the image of God is mentioned only in Genesis. Each time it is used, it is accompanied by a verb indicating God's act of creation. There was a special consultation within the triune God with respect to the creation of mankind (Gen. 1:26), and God created man and woman in his image according to that plan (Gen. 1:27). At the time of the new creation following the Flood, God explicitly forbade murder, which entails destroying a being that bears the image of God (Gen. 9:6). Human beings did not evolve from amoeba-like microorganisms, nor did they come into existence by chance. Instead, they were intentionally created as special beings by God's providence, designed with a purpose and a unique connection to their Creator.

There are distinct limitations that set humans apart from other living things. In Genesis 1, the phrase "according to its kind" was used to express the clear distinction that exists between each living creature. While all animals and plants were created according to its kind, humans were uniquely created in the image and likeness of God (Gen. 1:11, 12, 21, 24, 25).[2]

The phrase "according to its kind" serves as a crucial keyword in the act of creation. Through God's work of distinguishing, dividing, and creating according to kinds, the world transformed from disorder into one of order and harmony, with clear distinctions between living beings. Along this line of distinction, humans were set apart as the image of God, elevated as the supreme creatures among all living things.

Just as there is a clear distinction between humans and animals, there is a clear distinction between humanity and God. This contrasts with ancient Near Eastern myths that suggest humans were created with divine substance: in these accounts, Marduk killed Kingu, the husband of Tiamat (sea goddess), and created the first human by mixing Kingu's blood with dust. According to this

---

2 The Hebrew word *min* which refers to the creation of living things according to their kind, appears multiple times in the Pentateuch: in the creation accounts (Gen. 1:11, 12 (two times), 21 (two times), 24 (two times), 25 (three times)), the flood account (Gen. 6:20 (three times); 7:14 (four times)), and the classification of clean and unclean animals in Leviticus 11 and Deuteronomy 14 (Lev. 11:14, 15, 16, 19, 22 (four times), 29; Deut. 14:13, 14, 15, 18). Outside the Pentateuch, it occurs just once, in Ezekiel 47:10. *Min*" falls under the scientific classification of organisms into species, but is also more comprehensive as it includes grouping based on visual similarities. For example, in modern taxonomy, birds and insects are classified separately, but the Bible groups winged creatures together (Gen. 1:20-21). Both perspectives are valid, and there is no need to reject either as they both provide suitable viewpoints. Mark D. Futato, '*mîn*,' *NIDOTTE* 2:934.

worldview, there is no fundamental distinction between the divine and the human, as humans were created using divine substances. Compare this with the biblical account, where the name *Adam* means "dust" in Hebrew; in essence, man is fundamentally akin to *adamah* ("ground, earth, soil"). Even though human beings were created in the image of God, and are superior to the rest of creation, they originated from the earth, and are not immortal divine beings. Unlike God, they lack eternalness, omniscience, omnipotence, and omnipresence.

Humans did not come into existence on their own, but rather through God's intentional act of creation. They are sustained by following God's instructions regarding what to eat and what not to eat (Gen. 1:29; 2:15-17). They are to live in the place appointed by God and fulfill the work that He assigns (Gen. 2:8, 15).

4. Union of mind and body

(1) Creatures with physical bodies

The phrase *tselem elohim* ("image of God") is used four times in Genesis without being explicitly defined. The Hebrew word *tselem* meaning "image," is found 17 times in the Old Testament. It generally refers to the concrete physical appearance of tangible objects, except for two instances where it appears to describe shadows or dreams (Ps. 39:6 [7]; 73:20).[3]

Genesis 2:7 provides a concrete picture of God's creation of mankind, portraying humans as creatures with physical bodies that were formed from dust. Additionally, humans exercise their God-given authority over living things by naming them, aligning with the intended purpose mentioned in Genesis 1:26 (Gen. 2:19-20). The image of God, therefore, refers to a living human being in whom body and mind are united.

(2) A being with a mind and body

Considering the usage of *tselem* and the accounts of the creation of man as the image of God

3 Waltke and Yu, 215-216. The Hebrew word *tselem* ("image") is used a total of 17 times, as follows: "image of God": 4 times (Gen. 1:26, 27; 9:6); representing idols of foreign gods: six times (Num. 33:52; 1 Kings 11:18; 2 Chron. 23:17; Ezek. 7:20; 16:17; Amos 5:26); physically representing tumors and mice: three times (1 Sam. 6:5, 11); pictorial representation of fleeting shadows and dreams: two times (Ps. 39:6 [7]; 73:20); wall painting (Ezek. 23:14); Seth as the image of Adam (Gen. 5:3). See Waltke and Yu, 205. Moreover, the Aramaic equivalent of *tselem*, which is *tsulem*, is used 17 times over the course of two chapters, Daniel 2 and 3, in connection with the image Nebuchadnezzar saw in his dream and the image of gold he set up in the plain of Dura in Babylon (Dan. 2:31 (two times), 32, 34, 35; 3:1, 2, 3(two times), 5, 7, 10, 12, 14, 15, 18, 19).

in Genesis 1-2, the longstanding theological view within Christianity that seeks to limit the image of God to the mental part, while ignoring the corporeal, by sharply dividing man into the material body and the immaterial mind/soul, reflects the influence of Greek philosophy that was prevalent at the time of the New Testament. However, this interpretation does not properly reflect the holistic, biblical view of human beings.[4] The biblical view presents humans as integrated beings, with their mental, spiritual, and physical dimensions interconnected and inseparable.

(3) Spiritual beings in communion with God

It is an incomparable privilege that we humans were created in God's image, in God's likeness. If we trace our lineage back to its origins, we encounter the great Creator God, not evolving lower creatures or mollusks. Humankind's origin is not rooted in insects or beasts but in the living God, and we bear the image of God in both appearance and character. Human beings are mental-spiritual beings capable of communicating with God, as well as corporeal beings able to represent God and reveal Him before all creation.

(4) Incarnation and the dignity of the human body

Jesus is God who humbled Himself and came to this earth as a man. He is described as "the brightness of His glory and the express image of His person" (Heb. 1:3). Jesus' incarnation represents God's self-emptying and humility. Through this act, we are given a profound understanding of the dignity of the human body, and we are called to glorify God with our bodies.

---

4 In the context of the dualistic thinking influenced by Hellenistic thought, there have been extensive discussions since the early Christian era about whether *tselem* ("image") and *demut* ("form") are synonymous and the exact meaning of each, in particular with respect to the exclusion of the physical aspect of human beings and focus on the spiritual aspect. During the early Christian era, church fathers such as Tertullianus (196-212 AD; argued that the image of God is preserved even after sin but the likeness of God is restored through the Holy Spirit at baptism), Irenaeus (c. 130-200 AD), and Origenes (c. 185-254 AD; argued that at creation, humans received the honor of being in the image of God, but the attainment of God's likeness occurs at the time of final completion) regarded the image and likeness of God as distinct. Augustine (354-430 AD) found traces of the image of God, termed *Vestigia*, in the memory, intellect, and will of humans. Medieval theology maintained a dualistic view, identifying intellectual abilities and willpower as aspects of God's image. According to such dualism, it was believed that one could perform good deeds without grace, which significantly influenced Catholic theology and laid the groundwork for natural theology, which posits that one can recognize God without special revelation. The religious reformers rejected this dualism. Martin Luther (1483-1546) considered the image and likeness as synonymous terms, while John Calvin (1509-1564) viewed the ethical aspect of the holiness, righteousness, and knowledge as the image of God. Millard J. Erickson, *Christian Theology*, 2nd ed. (Grand Rapids, MI: Baker Books, 1998), 520-523; Ferguson, 1116; Alister E. McGrath, *Christian Theology: An Introduction*, 3rd ed. (Malden, MA: Blackwell Publishers Inc., 2001), 440-443.

Our physical forms are not to be considered lowly. The Son of God honored the human body by taking on this form, reminding us that serving and meeting physical needs are essential for the salvation of souls.

(5) Need for holistic service

The Lord served holistically to restore the image of God that had been marred by sin. Matthew 4:23 describes Jesus' ministry, which addressed the whole person. He revived the sick intellect by imparting spiritual knowledge, resurrected the dead spirituality by preaching the gospel, and purified the body—the vessel of intellect and spirituality—by healing the sick.

The ultimate restoration of the image of God will be achieved on the day of the Second Coming, when the "redemption of our body" (Rom. 8:23) occurs for those born again through the Holy Spirit. At the last trumpet, we will be transformed in an instant, and our mortal bodies will be clothed with incorruptibility and immortality (1 Cor. 15:51, 54). Until that day arrives, we are called to live lives that glorify God with our bodies, recognizing them as temples of the Holy Spirit (1 Cor. 6:20).

5. Ontological and functional interpretations

(1) Ontological interpretation

Interpretations of God's image can be broadly divided into ontological and functional interpretations.[5] Traditional ontological interpretations focus on the likeness of God in human nature. Man has reason and will, fellowships with God, and loves purity and wisdom. Human beings can understand God's will and live in harmony with God's will.

In Genesis 1-2, man shares a deeply intimate relationship with God. God created man from the dust of the earth and breathed life into his nostrils, establishing a profound bond of "I-Thou." Man possesses the intellect to comprehend God's instructions on the way of life (Gen. 2:16-17). He displays creativity, physical ability, and willpower as he cultivates and guards the Garden of Eden, while also giving names to all the beasts (Gen. 2:15, 19). Furthermore, man displays emotional capacity, experiencing great joy in the God-given companionship, as well as pure love and morality in his relationship with his spouse (Gen. 2:22-25). Humans enjoyed freedom to partake from any

---

5 John C. Collins, *Genesis 1-4: A Linguistic, Literary, and Theological Commentary* (Phillipsburg, NJ: P&R Publishing Company, 2006), 61-67.

tree in the Garden of Eden, with the exception of the fruit from the tree of the knowledge of good and evil (Gen. 2:16-17). In Genesis 3:8-9, we witness that the first human, the founding father of mankind, is a spiritual being who engaged in daily communion with God, the Creator.

The image of God encompasses both "moral" qualities such as purity, holiness, and communion with the Creator, as well as "natural" attributes like intellect, imagination, and moral and psychological self-direction.[6] In the beginning, man enjoyed a holy and joyful existence by understanding God's ways, sharing pure love, and wholeheartedly obeying God's will. Due to the Fall, the image of God in humanity has been heavily defaced; however, the image of God may be restored in individuals through the workings of the Holy Spirit, who brings about rebirth, justification, and sanctification, allowing them to partake in the divine nature (2 Pet. 1:4). We are graced with a special blessing, being invited to live truthfully in love and grow into the likeness of Christ, who is the image of God's person in all aspects (Eph. 4:15).[7]

(2) Functional interpretation

1) Representatives of God

Modern scholars have given significant attention to the functional aspects of God's image.[8] In Genesis 1, God is portrayed as a sovereign king, bringing all things into existence and establishing order through his creative command. Unlike in ancient Mesopotamian mythology where humans were made to serve as slaves to the gods,[9] God's purpose in creating humans in his image was to appoint them as rulers over the animals and the world, with everything subordinate to humankind

---

6 W. T. Purkiser, *Exploring Christian Holiness: The Biblical Foundations*, vol. 1 (Kansas City, MS: Beacon Hill Press of Kansas City, 1983), 1:35.

7 Goldingay posits that when the image of God is interpreted as extending to human appearance, the difficulties posed by the incarnation of Jesus Christ are significantly reduced. John Goldingay, *Old Testament Theology: Israel's Gospel*, vol. 1 (Downers Grove, IL: InterVarsity Press, 2003), 102-103.

8 The scholars who first asserted the functional aspect of God's image were H. Holzinger (1898) and J. Hehn (1915), but they did not receive much attention. Currently, there are strong advocates for this view, including D.J.A. Clines (1968), W.H. Schmidt (1964), W. Grosse (1981), E.M. Curtiss (1984), and B. Ockinga(1984). Additionally, scholars such as G.J. Wenham (1987), W. Brueggemann (1982), W.J. Dumbrell(1984), R.W. Klein (1979), W. Janzen (1982), J. Goldingay (1986), B.W. Anderson (1984), N.H. Snaith (1979-1980), and W. Zimmerli (1967) have a favorable view of this position. Cf. Ian Hart, 'Genesis 1:1-2:3 as a Prologue to the Book of Genesis', *Tyndale Bulletin* 46 (1995): 317-318.

9 Benjamin R. Foster, 'Atra-Hasis (1.130)', *The Context of Scripture: Canonical Compositions from the Biblical World,* ed. William W. Hallo et al., The Context of Scripture (Leiden, New York: Brill, 1997), 450-451; Thorkild Jacobsen, 'The Eridu Genesis (1.158),' *The Context of Scripture: Canonical Compositions from the Biblical World*, 513-514.

(Gen. 1:26). In other words, humans have been ordained to be royal beings on earth.[10]

The royal position, representative of God, extends beyond Adam, the progenitor of humankind. In the ancient Near East, the privilege of representing the gods was confined solely to kings, but the Bible extends this role to all human beings.[11] Genesis 5:1-3 establishes a connection between creation and the genealogy of Adam, emphasizing that God's image continues to apply to all earthly descendants. Because human beings are God's representatives, murder was explicitly prohibited after the Flood, to safeguard their inherent dignity (Gen. 9:6).

2) Royal priesthood

Man was originally intended to "till" (*'abad*) and "keep" (*shamar*) the Garden of Eden (Gen. 2:5, 15). In the Bible, the words *abad* ("to serve") and *shamar* ("to keep") were used together when describing the priestly temple service (Num. 3:7-8, 8:25-26, 18:5-6; 1 Chron. 23:32; Ezek. 44:14). The role of humans, created in the image of God, was to mediate between God and creation through their labor, thereby serving as a royal priesthood.

Eden itself is depicted as a sanctuary, with holy days and fellowship with God (Gen. 2:3, 8, 15, 3:8). The imagery of the trees in the Garden of Eden later reappears as the sanctuary's gold candlestick with seven branches, while Solomon's Temple contained carvings of trees, flowers, and cherubs to recreate the atmosphere of the Garden of Eden (1 Kings 6:18, 29, 32, 35).

Man was ordained to serve as priests in the sanctuary of Eden, and as they multiplied and replenished the earth, they were meant to extend the sanctuary of God's rule to the entire earth. This is the significance behind the cultural command to "replenish the earth, and subdue it" in Genesis 1:28. The book of Revelation ends by envisioning a future time when the whole earth will become God's sanctuary (Rev. 22:1-5).

6. Temple of the Holy Spirit

Man was originally created as a spiritual being, capable of enjoying fellowship with God. According to Genesis 2:7, God breathed life into man, forming him from dust, and he became a living soul. This connection between human life and the work of God's Spirit is not insignificant, as

10 Raymond C. Van Leuwen, 'Form, Image', *NIDOTTE* 4:645.

11 Ibid., 643; Waltke and Yu, 218.

emphasized in Genesis 6:3.

In Job 33:4, we learn that the Holy Spirit, referred to here as "the breath of the Almighty," is responsible for giving life. When we consider Genesis 2:7 in light of the book of Job, it becomes evident that the Holy Spirit resides in humanity, enabling them to cultivate the earth as representatives of God and to rule over the beasts (Gen. 2:15, 19).[12]

As the temple of God's Holy Spirit, human beings should live a holy life not only when worshiping on the Sabbath, but also throughout the week in all of their daily affairs, as indicated by the commandment, "Six days you shall labor and do all your work" (Ex. 20:9). The Holy Spirit, dwelling within human hearts, should govern all aspects of life.

---

12 In ancient Mesopotamia, idols of the gods were generally believed to be the dwelling places of the gods' spirits, and the locations where idols were erected were understood to be places under the rule of that particular deity. Kings, as representatives of the gods, were commonly perceived as embodying the image of the gods because they ruled on behalf of the gods. Hart, 318.

Chapter 08 | Living Soul and Body

1. Living Soul

The word "living soul" appears only in Genesis 2:7:[1] "And the Lord God formed man of the dust of the ground, and breathed into his nostrils the breath of life; and man became a living soul" (KJV).

(1) Man as a living being

Some interpret this verse as supporting the idea of the immortality of the soul. However, the Hebrew term *nepesh hayyah*" translated as "living soul" in this context, is elsewhere rendered as "living being." It is used to refer variously to aquatic animals, land animals, reptiles, all living creatures included in the Noahic covenant after the Flood, and all living creatures that flourish by the water originating from the sanctuary in Ezekiel's vision (Gen. 1:20, 24, 30; 2:19; 9:12, 15, 16; Ezek. 47:9).

In essence, "living soul" refers to a human being as a living being. Since Genesis 2:17 warns that eating from the tree of the knowledge of good and evil will result in certain death, the concept of an immortal soul is without basis.

(2) Image of God

In light of Genesis 1:26 and subsequent verses, Genesis 2:7 should be interpreted as depicting the image of God in the form of a living being. Deceased beings cannot serve as representations of God because they lack the ability to communicate with Him, praise Him, or carry out the tasks He has assigned to them. Likewise, images crafted from stone, wood, iron, and other materials are incapable of truly representing God.[2]

---

1 Note, however, that the phrase *psychēn zōsan* (ψυχὴν ζῶσαν) in 1 Corinthians 15:45, which quotes Genesis 2:7, has been translated as "living soul" in English translations of the Bible, including in the King James Version.

2 P. J. Harland, *The Value of Human Life: A Study of the Story of the Flood (Genesis 6-9)*, Supplements to Vetus Testamentum, vol. 64 (Leiden: Brill, 1996), 178-183; Claus Westermann, *Genesis 1-11: A Commentary*, trans., John J. Scullion (Minneapolis, MN: Augsburg 1984), 153.

2. Body

As the book of Genesis delves into the origins of humanity, it offers valuable insights into a proper understanding of the nature of the body. The Hebrew terms for body used in Genesis are *gewiyya* which is used once,[3] and *basar* ("flesh") occurs 33 times.[4] *Basar* originally denotes "flesh," but its Its principal significance is apparent in the accounts of Creation and the Flood.

In the creation narrative of Genesis 2:21-24, the word *basar* appears four times. When God took a rib from Adam and formed the first woman, the term *basar* took on an extended significance. Adam referred to his wife as "bone of my bones, and flesh of my flesh (*basar*)," and God blessed him, saying, "Therefore shall a man leave his father and his mother, and shall cleave unto his wife: and they shall be one flesh (*basar*)."

(1) Flesh (basar) as a component of the body

The flesh that filled the place of Adam's rib was transformed into soft human flesh when God originally made Adam from dust and put life into his nostrils (Gen. 2:7, 21). After death it will return to its original dust (Gen. 3:19).

In the creation account, the flesh that filled up the place where Adam's rib was the same soft human flesh that God had transformed from dust by breathing into Adam's nostrils (Gen. 2:7, 21). Once Adam died, this flesh would return to its original state as dust (Gen. 3:19).

(2) Component of fundamental relationship of human society

God, who is love, fashioned a companion for Adam from his very bones, an aide to partake in his boundless affection alongside Adam. Adam greeted her with elation and uttered the earliest human expression chronicled in the Bible:[5] "This is now bone of my bones and flesh of my flesh" (Gen. 2:23). Adam perceived his initial encounter with his wife as involving an intimate, bone-and-

---

3 The term *gewiyya* appears 13 times in 11 verses in the Old Testament. It is used to refer to living human beings or to celestial beings (Gen. 47:18; Ezek. 1:11, 23; Dan. 10:6; Neh. 9:37), human corpses (1 Sam. 31:10, 12 [2 times]; Ps. 110:6; Nah. 3:3), and animal carcasses (Judg. 14:8, 9). It is more appropriately interpreted as "body" rather than "corpse." This term was also used with a negative connotation to designate servants or slaves (Gen. 47:18; Neh. 9:37). T. Desmond Alexander, '*gwyh*,' *NIDOTTE* 1:834.

4 The term *basar* appears 270 times in the Old Testament, with the highest frequency of 61 occurrences found in the book of Leviticus, which describes the priestly laws and regulations. It appears 32 times in the book of Genesis: Gen. 2:21, 23 (2 times); 6:3, 12, 13, 17, 19; 7:15, 16, 21; 8:17; 9:4, 11, 15 (2 times), 16, 17; 17:11, 13, 14, 23, 24, 25; 29:14; 37:27; 40:19; 41:2, 3, 4, 18, 19.

5 Sarna, 23.

flesh type relationship, while God proclaimed the matrimonial bond as the loftiest tie within human society, surpassing even the parent-child relationship. The two become one flesh (Gen. 2:24).

Basar epitomizes kinship, the foundational bedrock of affection that shapes human society. Reflecting the trinity of God, the couple becomes inseparably intertwined. The components of human anatomy—blood, flesh, and bones—are recurrently mentioned throughout Genesis, symbolizing the connections among siblings and relatives (Laban to Jacob: "my bone and my flesh," Gen. 29:14; Joseph's brothers regarding Joseph: "our flesh," Gen. 37:27).

(3) Typology of the gospel through the incarnation of Christ

God crafted Eve from Adam's being, making "of one blood all nations of men" (Acts 17:26). Through Jesus Christ, the ultimate Adam and descendant of the woman, God reconciles the fragmented human family, plagued by discord and strife (Acts 17:27-31; cf. Gen 3:15; Gal. 4:4). The incarnation and crucifixion symbolize God's selfless offering for humanity, a concept echoed through the embodiment of love in both the Church and the bond of a married couple (Eph. 5:22-33).

(4) The body of man and animal

In Hebrew, there exists no term exclusively denoting the physical body; instead, basar is used broadly to encompass the entirety of an individual. The union of marriage seamlessly melds two distinct individuals into "one flesh" (Gen. 2:24).[6] Similarly, the phrase "all flesh" is used in the context of the Great Flood to refer to both humans and animals.[7] In this account, the entities undergoing judgment and those meeting destruction are all corporeal beings.[8]

Human beings and animals alike are physical beings that were formed from a common source, the soil (Gen. 2:7, 19). In terms of their physical composition, there exists no inherent superiority of man over animals. Just as humans consume animal flesh, animals also partake in human remains (Gen. 9:4; 40:19). The true dignity and significance of the human body are exclusively tied to our

---

6 George E. Ladd, 'Flesh', *Baker Encyclopedia of the Bible*, ed. Walter A. Elwell (Grand Rapids, MI: Baker, 1988), 793.

7 The Hebrew word used is *kol basar* meaning "all flesh." Gen. 6:12-13, 17, 19; 7:16, 21; 8:17.

8 Among the creatures that perished in the judgment of the Great Flood were those that engaged in corrupt and violent acts (Gen. 6:12, 13), as well as others in which there was the breath of life (Gen. 6:17; 7:21). The creatures that were saved are those whose lives were preserved within the ark (Gen. 6:19; 7:15, 16; 8:17).

connection with God.[9]

(5) Finite human beings characterized by vulnerability

In Genesis 6:3, Yahweh declared, "My spirit shall not strive with man forever, for he is indeed flesh." This verse, situated within the narrative of God's judgment through the Flood, employs the *basar* motif to link human mortality and ethical deterioration. The core essence of the *basar* concept encapsulates the innate vulnerability of physical existence (Gen. 7:21), the intrinsic moral shortcomings of humanity (Gen. 6:12), and the inherent feebleness and fragility within mankind.[10]

Human beings are inherently limited in their existence. Life resides in the flesh solely through the divine breath of God, and upon his withdrawal, life ceases (Gen. 2:7; 7:22). This finitude of flesh finds manifestation in the genealogies of Genesis 5, which cyclically state "so all the days ... were ... years: and he died" (Gen. 5:5, 8, 11, 14, 17, 20, 27, 31). Genesis concludes with the death of Joseph and his embalmment in Egypt (Gen. 50:26).

The pathway to eternal life lies in devotion to God and obedience to his commands. However, the unfortunate choice made in Genesis 3 transformed the flesh into a tool of Satan, giving rise to a malevolent society that breeds fratricide and murder (Gen. 4:8, 28). During the era of the Great Flood, humanity had become evil to the point where "the wickedness of man was great in the earth, and...every intent of the thoughts of his heart was only evil continually"; this led to the withdraw of the life-giving Spirit of God from the land (Gen. 6:1-4).[11]

Though the flesh is weak and bound by limitations, nowhere does the Bible claim that the flesh is inherently sinful.[12] Within the genealogical lineage of Adam, a lineage marked by mortality, there were notable figures like Enoch, who ascended to heaven in the presence of God, and Noah, who ushered in a new era for humanity post-Flood (Gen. 5:21-24; 6:8-9). Humanity retains the agency to decide whether to yield their faculties to sin, using them as instruments of unrighteousness unto sin, or to dedicate them to God, wielding them as instruments of righteousness unto God (Rom. 6:13).

---

9 The Bible symbolically employs the imagery of cannibalism to describe the following actions: exploiting the weak (Mic. 3:3), devouring oneself in foolishness (Eccles. 4:5), and causing harm to others (Job 19:22). Actual cannibalistic actions are also recorded in the Bible, as in Leviticus 26:29, which describes a dire situation that arose as a consequence of God's judgment within a besieged city. F. B. Knutson, 'Flesh', *ISBE* 2:313.

10 Mathews, *Genesis* 4:27-11:26, 334.

11 The motif of erroneous choices in Genesis 3 is reiterated in Genesis 6:1-4. Ibid.

12 Ladd, 793.

(6) Object of God's covenant

God bestowed the rainbow as a symbol of his enduring covenant that He would never again destroy all life through another catastrophic flood (Gen. 9:11-17). The term *basar* is employed here, encompassing all living entities (Gen. 9:11, 15, 16, 17). This multicolored arc stands as an eternal covenant "between me [God] and you and every living creature of all flesh" (Gen. 9:15). God said he would "see" and "remember." He is one who remembers all of his creation. This proclamation shows that God's affection extends not only to humanity but to all living beings under their dominion, manifesting his deep love for life. Furthermore, this promise paves the way for a future when, through the redemptive work of Jesus Christ, all living beings will partake fully in God's blessings. All of creation awaits the glorious day when they shall be "delivered from the bondage of corruption" (Rom. 8:21).

(7) Circumcision, a sign of the covenant in the human body

Circumcision bestows upon *basar* a distinctive significance. Basar in this context corresponds to the foreskin (Gen. 17:11, 13, 14, 23, 24, 25). This ancient practice was embraced by the Western Semites of antiquity, including Ammonites, Moabites, Edomites, and Hebrews, with the latter observing it in a deeply religious context. Through circumcision, the Hebrews etched upon their flesh an indelible mark of belonging to the community of God's covenant people. God's declaration to Abraham resounded with the promise, "I will...be God to you and your descendants after you...and I will be their God" (Gen. 17:7, 8). "And the uncircumcised man child whose flesh of his foreskin is not circumcised, that soul shall be cut off from his people; he hath broken my covenant" (Gen. 17:14).

Even more important than carrying the sign of the covenant on the body is the circumcision of the heart (Deut. 10:16). This inner transformation calls for a life dedicated to spiritual abundance, devotion to the Lord, and adherence to his divine purpose. When Peter visited Cornelius' household, the circumcised believers who accompanied him witnessed an outpouring of the Holy Spirit on uncircumcised Gentiles, which culminated in their inclusion among God's people through baptism (Acts 10:44-48). This event marked the realization of God's promise recorded in the book of Ezekiel—that God would give a new heart and a new spirit, exchanging the stony heart for a heart of flesh (*leb basar*) (Ezek. 36:26). It also fulfilled the prophecy in the book of Joel regarding the outpouring of God's spirit on all individuals (Joel 2:28 [3:1]; cf. Acts 2:17).[13] The emblem

13 R. K. Harrison, 'Circumcision', *Baker Theological Dictionary of the Bible* ed. Walter A. Elwell (Grand Rapids, MI: Baker, 1996), 99.

distinguishing God's people today is the circumcision of the heart, signifying the infusion of the Holy Spirit's fullness within.

Chapter 09 | God's Steward

1. Person in charge of the family's affairs

A steward is an individual entrusted with overseeing the affairs of a substantial household. Their responsibilities encompass tending to the master's table, supervising household staff, and effectively managing financial matters. Stewardship embodies "the careful and responsible management of something entrusted to one's care."[1] From the perspective of creation, the concept of stewardship entails the perception that humanity and all other created beings and things belonging to God's family and under his ownership.

In this context, a steward is a member of God's household, acting as custodian for every being and everything in the world. Each person has been granted a specific sphere of influence in accordance with their divine allotment. Moses, a prime biblical example of a faithful steward, "was faithful in all His house as a servant, for a testimony of those things which would be spoken after," and "Christ as a Son over His own house" likewise fulfilled his duties as a faithful steward (Heb. 3:5, 6).

Stewards featured in Genesis include Eliezer of Damascus (Gen. 15:2; 24:2), who was a steward for Abraham, and Joseph, who initially served as Potiphar's steward, later oversaw various affairs at the prison, and ultimately ascended to the position of prime minister of Egypt (Gen. 39:6, 22; 41:40-41).[2]

The Genesis accounts of human stewardship appear against the backdrop of the Creation, the Flood, and the lives of the patriarchs Abraham, Jacob, and Joseph.

---

1 *Webster's Collegiate Dictionary, Eleventh Edition*, s.v. 'Stewardship.'

2 The Old Testament does not include a specific word for "steward," but the word appears from time to time in translations based on the context. It occurs four times in the story of Joseph (Gen. 43:16, 19; 44:1, 4). The Hebrew original is *asher al-bet* meaning "the one over the house". The role of a steward in the Old Testament varies depending on the word used and the context. As an example, Shebna was a steward responsible for finances (Isa. 22:15). T.M. Dorman, 'Steward', ISBE 4:617.

2. General Principles of Stewardship in Creation

Genesis 1-2 provides insight into the origins and fundamental principles of stewardship.

(1) Human stewardship has its origins in creation.

Stewardship corresponds to the functional meaning of the image of God. God created man to rule over creation. "Then God said, 'Let Us make man in Our image, according to Our likeness; let them have dominion over the fish of the sea, over the birds of the air, and over the cattle, over all the earth and over every creeping thing that creeps on the earth'" (Gen. 1:26).

God created one man, Adam, but God's intention was not for Adam alone to manage God's world. 'Let them have dominion' indicates, humanity, every human being is called to stewardship. Mankind's exalted status as the image of God is occupied by mankind in all things because God originally created man as a steward representing God.

Stewardship aligns with the functional meaning of "image of God." God's design encompassed mankind's role as rulers over creation (Gen. 1:26). While God initially formed a single human, Adam, his intention was not to have Adam mange the world alone. The phrase "let them have dominion" signifies that all of humanity is summoned to partake in stewardship. Humanity's elevated position, bearing the divine image, is based on God's designed role for humanity, to represent God on earth as his stewards.

(2) Human stewardship is given by the grace of God.

Human beings have reason to thank God for his grace in designating them to serve as stewards. Despite being the final creation, mankind occupies the loftiest position among all creatures. Emerging from dust, humans were created into intelligent and authoritative entities, bearing the divine image and empowered to oversee the world on God's behalf. Indeed, in the grand tapestry of creation, it is evident that God crafted all things with humankind in mind.

(3) Man is accountable to God the Creator.

In their role as rulers over creation, human beings could be tempted to perceive themselves as absolute beings. Within the confines of the Garden of Eden, two trees were placed as safeguards against this potential arrogance—the Tree of Life and the Tree of the Knowledge of Good and Evil (Gen. 2:9, 17).

The Tree of Life offered a poignant reminder of humanity's finite nature, a creation formed from dust. Human beings' continued existence required the breath of life imparted by the infinite God as well as physical nourishment (Gen. 2:7, 9, 16). Because human beings depend on "the breath of the Almighty" to give them life, comprehension, and sustenance (Job 32:8; 33:4), they are fundamentally spiritual and moral beings who must worship God, their Creator and source of being.

Humanity's fundamental duty was to adhere to God's sovereignty. The Tree of Life and the Tree of the Knowledge of Good and Evil stood as perpetual symbols of this imperative (Gen. 2:9, 16, 17). These trees encapsulated God's directive for mankind.

In Genesis 2:16, the Hebrew term for "commanded" is *wayetsav*. Its verbal form *tsiwah* is Piel that has intensive meaning. Its noun form is *mitzwah* and means "commandment." Even before the Fall, humanity was not autonomous but rather existed under God's rule. Within what might appear to be a simple commandment, a profound truth resounds—humans are not the ultimate master of this world. Instead, human existence finds its purpose solely within a rightful relationship with God, the Creator.

Mankind was bound by the compelling force of this commandment. As we can see from Genesis 2:17, obedience amounted to a matter of life and death.

It is important to keep in mind that the focus of the *mitzwah* is not the specifics of the relevant commandment, but rather recognition and acknowledgment of God's supreme authority to command. God is a moral being who deeply cares about the happiness and welfare of his people.[3] If our first parents had unwaveringly accepted this fundamental truth, they would have avoided the Fall.

(4) Through stewardship, human beings are to realize God's will within God's created world.

As human beings shoulder the responsibility of upholding and tending to creation on behalf of God, they must labor in alignment with the Creator's intent. God, the true owner of the universe, granted his creatures the blessing to be fruitful and to multiply (Gen. 1:22, 28). Through stewardship, humanity takes on the task of ensuring that the full extent of God's blessings permeates every realm under their care. In doing so, the created world may retain its original beauty and remain good in God's sight (Gen. 1:4, 10, 12, 18, 21, 25, 31). The ultimate aspiration of human stewardship lies in the management of all things to be good in God's sight.

3 F. Raymond Collins, 'Commandment', ABD 1:1098.

(5) Humans are responsible for the ecosystem.

The realm of stewardship entrusted to us, as outlined in Genesis 1:28-30, encompasses all living creatures (fish, birds, land animals, etc.) as well as the environment they live in (land, seas, sky). Our duty involves managing ecosystems to ensure the provision of sufficient sustenance and conditions for the flourishing of all living beings. Genesis 2 describes the Garden of Eden as an ideal ecological setting, and it introduces the four principal water sources—Pison, Gihon, Hiddekel, and Euphrates—alongside the mineral riches of Havila—pure gold, bedelium, and onyx—through which the Pison River flows (Gen. 2:10-14). Adam, the custodian of the earth, endowed with the authority to cultivate the land and tend to the Garden of Eden, is first seen fulfilling this role by bestowing names upon the animal world, exemplifying his status as their caretaker (Gen. 2:19, 20).

In exploring our responsibility towards the ecosystem, it is imperative to properly understand the meaning of "dominion" and "subdue" as used in Genesis 1:26 and 28. As beings subject to the authority of a moral God, who places utmost importance on the happiness and well-being of his creations, humanity bears the ethical obligation of preserving and responsibly using ecosystems. The Hebrew terms *rada* and *kabash* translated as "have dominion over" and "subdue" respectively, are in some instances used with negative connotations of oppression and exploitation through coercive force; however, in the context of Genesis 1, they carry a positive significance.[4]

Genesis 2 serves as a lens through which we comprehend the true meaning of exercising dominion over all living things and subduing the earth. Adam's dominion over all living things was manifested through the act of naming (Gen. 2:19). Because the intrinsic essence of each being is encapsulated in a name, the act of naming is not just an exercise in taxonomy. Rather, this act underscores the necessity of understanding the attributes of God's creatures and fostering an ecologically vibrant environment for them, in alignment with God's blessing to be fruitful and multiple (Gen. 1:22, 28). God looked to see what name Adam would call the animals, and whatever he called them became their name; this is a testament to the value God places on human personal discernment. Human beings are to employ their intellect and ingenuity to govern the created world and fulfill their responsibility entrusted by God.

The phrase "subdue the earth" in Genesis 1:28 does not imply a callous devastation of the ecosystem. In relation to the earth, as mentioned in the related verse of Genesis 2:5, humanity was tasked with cultivating the land. The Hebrew term for "till the land" is *abad* meaning "to work, to

4 Philip J. Nel, *NIDOTTE* 3:1055.

serve." This term is also employed elsewhere in the Pentateuch to denote the Levites' service to God in the temple.[5] Eden, the place where God situated humankind, was structured akin to God's sanctuary.[6]

Essentially, human labor is a sacred service, akin to that of a priest. Following the Fall of humanity, work became a divine instrument for the redemption of mankind.

A steward is an individual entrusted with executing the master's intentions, serving the master's purpose. God's underlying concept of creation was for his creation to be fruitful and multiply and fill the ecological realms, both on land and in the sea (Gen. 1:20, 22, 28). Humanity, bearing the divine image, must, in fulfilling the role of God's steward, reveal to the created realm the transcendent Creator who exists beyond humanity.

The concept of ecosystem stewardship finds its roots in the Creation, thus extending beyond the boundaries of specific religions like Judaism or Christianity. All of humanity, irrespective of ethnicity, race, or faith, is entrusted as stewards by God. In today's critical juncture, where pressing issues like pollution, energy, air quality, and climate change imperil mankind's future, human stewardship assumes a crucial guiding role in seeking solutions. A Christian perspective, aligned with its worldview, has the potential to offer a particularly impactful contribution towards the preservation of our planet.

(6) Human beings are accountable to the human community.

God did not create man and woman simultaneously. After forming Adam, God bestowed upon him the profound gift of human companionship, by crafting a woman from Adam's rib to serve as

---

5 Num. 3:7-8; 4:23, 30, 47; 8:11, 19, 22; 16:9; 18:6, 7, 21, 23. In the Hebrew Bible, when the verbs *abad* ("to serve") and *shamar* ("to keep") are used together, they refer to the priestly service in the sanctuary (Num. 3:7-8; 8:25-26; 18:5-6; Lev. 23:32; Ezek. 44:14). Through labor, humans, created in the image of God, have been appointed to a royal priesthood, mediating between God and the created world.

6 Gordon J. Wenham, 'Sanctuary Symbolism in the Garden of Eden Story', *Proceedings, 9th World Congress of Jewish Studies*, Proceedings of the World Congress of Jewish Studies (Jerusalem: World Union of Jewish Studies, 1986), 19-25. Eden, where humanity was placed in the beginning, is a sanctuary. There, humans worshipped God on the Sabbath (Gen. 2:3), and God walked in its midst (Gen. 2:8, 15; 3:8). Sin tainted this sacred place, leading to the human beings' expulsion (Gen. 3:22-23). Cherubim with flaming swords were placed at the entrance on the east side of Eden, reminiscent of the angels that covered the mercy seat in the Most Holy Place (the Hebrew word *šakan* meaning "placed," has the same root word as the Hebrew word "shekinah," which signifies the glory light of God's presence), to guard (*šamar* "to keep") the sacred garden (note also that the entrance to the sanctuary was on the east side). The trees in the Garden of Eden were symbolically represented by the seven-branched golden menorah in the sanctuary. Similarly, King Solomon's temple was adorned with carved wood, flowers, and cherubim on its walls and doors, evoking the atmosphere of the Garden of Eden (1 Kings 6:18, 29, 32, 35).

his partner and helper (Gen. 2:18, 20-22). The family, as the cornerstone of human society, stands as the fundamental unit for realizing the divine blessings of procreation and expansion (Gen. 1:28). This act of creating a woman as a companion to aid Adam's stewardship role highlights the significance of the family unit in fostering stewardship values, emphasizing the essential role of both men and women in this shared responsibility without discrimination.

The provision of a helpmeet was a deliberate action that was also meant to encompass the forming of broader communities. The human community was to be a community of love characterized by mutual aid, while also having a shared destiny, evident in the enduring repercussions of Adam's transgression on all of humanity. As such, the human community functions as an educational community, fostering a culture of mutual care, guidance, and support, whose aim is to encourage love of God and adherence to his laws.

Humanity was created within the relational context of kinship (Gen. 2:23). Our world constitutes a single family, united under the presence of one divine Father, God. It is imperative for Christians to engage earnestly in not only advancing the church's evangelistic endeavors but also in confronting pressing global challenges, including by tackling issues like racial and socioeconomic divisions, regional economic imbalances, pursuing disarmament and nuclear non-proliferation, and combating the threat of global warming.[7]

The divine proclamation of marriage found in Genesis 2:24—"Therefore shall a man leave his father and his mother, and shall cleave unto his wife: and they shall be one flesh"—highlights the importance of financial and spiritual independence within the context of a new family. Achieving this independence necessitates the ability to engage in suitable professional endeavors prior to marriage. For Christians, it is crucial to view their means of sustenance as a platform through which they can fulfill their divine calling. This is achieved by Christians pursuing meaningful and ethical vocations that align with their God-given purpose and contribute positively to their lives and the community.

(7) Human beings should develop appropriate knowledge, abilities, and influence to be good stewards.

To be able to contribute to the restoration and flourishing of ecosystems and human communities, human beings must acquire a comprehensive understanding across a spectrum of disciplines

7 P. N. Hillyer, 'Stewardship', *New Dictionary of Theology* (Downers Grove Inter Varsity Press, 2000), 661.

encompassing the humanities, social sciences, and natural sciences. Adam's role in tending to and protecting the Garden of Eden, as well as naming the animals, underscores his grasp of the natural sciences as well as his managerial skills (Gen. 2:15, 19). He beautifully articulated his profound sentiments upon the creation of his companion, the woman, showcasing his literary and artistic prowess (Gen. 2:23). Humanity, similarly, must develop profound expertise in the domains entrusted to them by God and exercise astute stewardship to foster wise management and preservation.

Human stewardship must be redemptive. The symbolism of the Tree of Knowledge of Good and Evil underscores humanity's shared destiny. As Romans 5 highlights, the introduction of sin and death into the world originated from a solitary individual, whose act caused all of humankind to fall into the grip of sin and condemnation (Rom. 5:12, 16-19). Nevertheless, Jesus Christ emerged as the catalyst for transforming a community of death into a community of life. Communities rooted in faith should diligently safeguard families, congregations, societies, and nations from corruption, while also working earnestly to guide individuals towards God. This is accomplished by proclaiming the splendid virtues of God and exemplifying stewardship within the unique contexts they find themselves in.

3. The Eschatological Meaning of Stewardship in the Flood

As humanity's iniquity spread, hearts and intentions turned increasingly wicked, culminating in widespread violence and corruption. In response, God enacted judgment upon the world through a massive flood. The phrase "all flesh had corrupted his way on the earth" encompasses even the animal kingdom (Gen. 6:5-7, 12).[8] Not only did humanity neglect its stewardship duties towards itself, but also towards other creatures in the ecosystem. This collective failure led to the devastating flood.

Noah, however, was a steadfast individual who faithfully carried out the stewardship bestowed upon humanity during creation's inception. The ark, fashioned according to the Creator's instructions (Gen. 6:14-16), serves as a symbolic representation of the hierarchical structure established by God at the world's genesis, akin to a "microcosm of the universe."[9] Within divinely designed vessel (Gen.

8 The phrase "all flesh" in Genesis 6:12 may be understood as encompassing both humans and the animal kingdom. Harland, 31; Gerhard F. Hasel, 'Some Issues Regarding the Nature and Universality of the Genesis Flood Narrative', *Origins* 5 (1978): 83-91.

9 Waltke and Yu, 302.

6:18; cf. Gen. 1:1-19) was mankind, charged with caring for all other creatures (Gen. 6:18; cf. Gen. 1:26-28); animals (Gen. 6:20; cf. Gen. 1:20-25); and food that would sustain them (Gen. 6:21; cf. Gen. 1:29-30).

Noah epitomized the quintessential steward, unwaveringly adhering to his Master's command. Genesis draws a stark contrast between Adam's disobedience and Noah's obedience through the Hebrew word *tsiwah* meaning "to command." Adam, initially entrusted as God's steward, deviated from God's explicit instructions, causing a global calamity (Gen. 3:11, 17); in contrast, Noah's unwavering faithfulness resulted in salvation for the world (Gen. 6:22; 7:5).[10] Following the Flood, God renewed the blessing previously bestowed upon Adam, extending it to Noah and his offspring (Gen. 9:1-2). Through Noah, humanity embraced a renewed stewardship, entrusted with dominion over all things, bestowed anew by God.

Noah's stewardship mirrors God's divine work. In Genesis 6:22, the phrase *ken asa* meaning "so did he," signifies the resemblance between Noah's actions and God's activities, through use of a verbal allusion with *wayehi ken* ("and it was so"), used in Genesis 1 (Gen. 1:7, 9, 11, 15, 24, 30).[11] Noah's deeds outwardly manifest the intentions of God. Through his person and ministry, Noah effectively represented God in his era. He is portrayed as one who "found grace in the eyes of the Lord" and as "a just man and perfect in his generations" who "walked with God" (Gen. 6:8-9).

After the Flood, God reaffirmed mankind's dominion over the animals (Gen. 9:2) and through repeated reference to these creatures in the context of the Noahic covenant, emphasized his desire for their preservation (Gen. 9:10, 11, 12, 15, 16, 17). This covenant underscores God's profound concern for the well-being and preservation of ecosystems (Gen. 9:2).[12]

---

10 The Hebrew text of Genesis 6:22 ("Thus did Noah; according to all that God commanded him, so did he") emphasizes Noah's complete obedience by repeating the Hebrew word for "did" or "acted" ('*asa*') at the beginning and end of the sentence, and by using the comprehensive term *kol*, which means "all" or "everything." A similar construction is found in Genesis 7:5 ("And Noah did according unto all that the Lord commanded him."), reinforcing the same effect. Similar idiomatic expressions were used to describe the construction of the tabernacle (Ex. 39:32, 42; 40:16) and significant moments during the Israelites' wanderings in the wilderness (Num. 1:54; 2:34; 9:5). See Wenham, *Genesis 1-15*, 176.

11 Ibid.

12 According to Waltke, the imagery from Genesis 8:9 of Noah tenderly receiving the dove that had flown back to the ark to preserve its life reveals a restored connection among God, humanity, and the rest of creation. Waltke and Yu, 303.

4. Stewardship in the tithes of the patriarchs

The word for tithing in Hebrew is *ma'aser* which originates from the verb *asar*. References to tithing are found in various passages throughout the Pentateuch, specifically in Leviticus, Numbers, and Deuteronomy. From the time of Moses, the Israelites presenting a tenth of their agricultural produce—such as grains, wine, oil and fruits—as well as their livestock including sheep and cattle as an offering to God, which would be used to sustain the Levites and priests who served in the sanctuary (Lev. 27:30-33; Num. 18:20-32; Deut. 14:22-29). Tithing began before the Mosaic era, however, as the Bible contains records of both Abraham and Jacob offering tithes to the Lord.

(1) Abraham's tithe to Melchizedek (Gen. 14:20)

Abram had fought against the allied army of King Chedorlaomer of Elam, who had assailed Sodom and Gomorrah, and emerging victorious, brought back those who had been held captive as well as war spoils. On his way he passed through the valley of Shaveh,[13] where he encountered Melchizedek, the king-priest of Salem. Melchizedek blessed him in the name of *El Elyon* ("Most High God"), and Abram presented Melchizedek with a tithe of the acquired spoils.

1) Tithing is an acknowledgment of elevated authority.

The practice of tithing is not unique to the Hebrews. In ancient civilizations, it was not an uncommon practice to pay a tithe to the temple and the king.[14] Abram, the patriarch of faith, showed deference to Melchizedek, recognizing his superior authority, by offering a tithe. Melchizedek's elevated status was due to the divine authority of the Most High God that stood behind him.

2) Tithing is a response of praise to God's blessings.

The phrases "Blessed be Abram" and "blessed be the Most High God" within Melchizedek's blessing both use the Hebrew word *barak*. This term, *barak*, pairs God's blessing together with the human expression of praise through the act of tithing. God, the sovereign ruler of heaven and earth (Gen. 14:19), is not only the Creator and Owner of all, but also the ultimate source of blessings.

---

13 The Valley of Shaveh mentioned in Genesis 14:17 refers to the King's Valley, which is where Absalom erected a pillar for himself (2 Sam. 18:18). Josephus (*Ant* 7.10.3 §243) points out that this pillar is located at a distance of two stadia (350 to 400 meters) from Jerusalem, which indicates that the King's Valley is the Kidron Valley. Michael C. Astour, 'Shaveh, Valley Of', *ABD* 5:1168.

14 The custom of tithing was present in Egypt, Syria, Lydia, Babylon, and Assyria, and it is also found in Ugarit around the 14th century BC. See E. E. Carpenter, 'Tithe', *ISBE* 4:861.

The duty of a faithful believer is to remain aware of God's blessing in all aspects of life, including the Earth's produce and personal achievements. This awareness leads to the offering of tithes and offerings, a form of praise.

The narrative of Abraham exemplifies this interconnectedness. his victory in battle prompted him to offer a tenth of the war spoils, an action that acknowledged the divine blessing behind his triumph. Tithing is a testament that life's blessings are not taken for granted; rather, they are attributed to God's providence. By tithing, we openly declare that the wellspring of strength and authority rests solely in God, reinforcing our profound recognition of his sovereignty.

3) Tithing consecrates our battles as God's battles.

Melchizedek blessed Abraham in the name of the "Most High God, which hath delivered thine enemies unto thy hand" (Gen. 14:20). By paying a tithe to the priest of this Most High God, Abram consecrated the battle he had fought and his victory therein to God. After Israel emerged as a nation, the principle of allocating a portion of the spoils of war as gifts to the priestly tribe was enacted as law (Num. 31:28; 2 Sam. 8:11; 1 Chron. 26:27).[15] Through the act of tithing, believers express gratitude for God's role in helping them to prevail in the relentless struggle between good and evil, and entrust their household and heritage to God's faithful care.

4) Through tithing, Abram confessed that it was by God's grace alone that he and his descendents would come to possess the land of Canaan.

In this narrative, Abram was referred to as "Abram the Hebrew" signifying his status as an outsider (Gen. 14:13).[16]

After parting ways with Lot, Abram received God's promise that He would grant him the land of Canaan as well as many descendants. In response, Abram relocated his tent to the plain of Mamre in Hebron and erected an altar to honor Yahweh (Gen. 13:14-18). Here it was that Abram

---

15 Johann Peter Lange, Tayler Lewis, and Abraham Gosman, *Genesis, or, the First Book of Moses, Together with a General Theological and Homiletical Introduction to the Old Testament* (New York: C. Scribner & co., 1868), 405.

16 At first glance, there is no apparent need for Genesis 14:13 to describe Abram as "Abram the Hebrew" given that the book was originally written for Hebrew readers. It is likely that "the Hebrew" here was included deliberately; the Hebrew verb *shakan* used in "dwelt," can also imply the act of temporarily dwelling within a tent. Hence, "Abram the Hebrew" connotes Abram's status as a foreigner or an outsider, emphasizing his identity as someone residing temporarily as a foreigner or expatriate. In Jonah 1:9, Jonah identified himself to the Gentile sailors using this term. Reyburn, 317.

became involved resolving the armed conflict between the forces of the king of Elam and those of Sodom (Gen. 14:12). Despite emerging victorious from the conflict, Abram remained a foreigner and stranger in the land.[17] By offering tithes to God and refusing the king's offer of wealth, Abram showed his firm belief that the fulfillment of the promise of land and descendants rested solely on the power and grace of God.[18]

5) Tithing is man's response to God the Giver.

The Hebrew term for "to deliver (into one's hands)" is *miggen* and has a correlative meaning with *natan*,[19] and it is paired with humans, who make offerings to God. Mankind's offerings are in response to the blessings given by God. God is the ultimate source of all blessings, and human beings demonstrate their gratitude by presenting a portion of the abundant blessings they have received from God.

6) Tithing is the dedication of one's life to He who gave life.

A battle with a formidable enemy entails a fight for one's life. By offering a tithe following his victory in battle, Abraham expressed his thanks to God for the new life he had gained and consecrated his life to God.

7) Tithing is an expression of humility.

Through his tithing to Melchizedek, Abraham demonstrated reverence for Melchizedek, who as a priest of the Most High God surpassed even his own spiritual standing. Melchizedek also became a type for Jesus Christ, superior even to Abraham (Heb. 7:3, 9-10). The act of tithing, therefore, becomes a confession of the believer's allegiance to the divine sovereignty and a commitment to lead a life marked by unwavering faith and loyalty.

---

17 Even after the Hebrews came to possess the land of Canaan, they were to fundamentally regard themselves as sojourners and strangers in the land, as the ultimate possessor of the land is God. See Lev. 25:23.

18 Gordon J. McConville, 'Abraham and Melchizedek: Horizons in Genesis 14', He Swore an Oath, second edition (Grand Rapids, MI: Baker Book House, 1994), 115.

19 The term *miggen* meaning "to deliver," appears three times in the Hebrew Bible, consistently in conjunction with *natan* meaning "to give." See Gen. 14:20; Hos. 11:8; Prov. 4:9. In Genesis 15:1, the term *magen* meaning "shield," evokes Genesis 14:20, which depicts God as the One who bestows victory and protection. Wenham, *Genesis 1-15*, 317.

8) Abraham set the model for the institution of tithing.

In ancient times, the practice of offering tenths was directed towards both the sacred temple and the monarch.[20] Abraham's act of tithing to Melchizedek set a crucial precedent for future Israelites, illustrating the importance of tithing to uphold the sanctuary system and support the priesthood. Notably, Abraham's tithing to Melchizedek occurred in Jerusalem, the designated location for Israel's only legitimate sanctuary. This is significant, as Jerusalem was to serve as a hub for spreading the gospel to the global community. The Levitical model of tithing, a firmly rooted scriptural institution established by God, was designed to facilitate the dissemination of the gospel worldwide. By adhering to this framework, believers actively participate as collaborators in God's divine mission.

(2) Jacob's vow to God at Bethel to give a tithe (Gen. 28 :22)

As Jacob was fleeing from his brother Esau, he had a dream where he witnessed God on a ladder. God promised to be with Jacob and make him a source of blessings. After waking up from the dream, he vowed that he would give a tenth of his possessions as an offering to God should he be able to return to his father Isaac's house in peace.

1) Tithing is a sign of gratitude for God's grace.

Jacob was deeply discouraged and burdened with guilt for having deceived his brother. It was through a divine revelation that he found renewed hope for his life. God, in his wisdom, did not delve into Jacob's transgressions but instead extended a promise of his presence and guidance as Jacob embarked on his journey, ensuring his every need would be met. Despite his lack of any earthly possessions, Jacob was embraced by God's grace, which promised him a future brimming with abundance.

Overflowing with gratitude, Jacob entrusted his future, still veiled in uncertainty, into God's care through his commitment to give a tithe. Whereas he had previously relied on his own endeavors, he now recognized that his forthcoming path would be sculpted by the grace of God.

2) Tithing is a sign of faith in God's promise to provide for all of life's needs.

The conditions of Jacob's vow to tithe—God's personal presence, watching, care, and return

20 The example of surrendering a tenth of one's possessions to the king is found in Ugarit. Samuel presented this possibility as one of the burdens that the people would bear should they accept a monarchy (1 Sam. 8:15, 17). See Sarna, 110.

to his homeland (Gen. 28:20-21)—reflected promises that God had already made to Jacob in his dream (Gen. 28:13-15). He embraced the promises in faith. his steadfast faith is emphasized in his unequivocal declaration, “I will surely give the tenth to Thee” (Gen. 28:22)[21]

3) Jacob's tithing served as a model for Israel's tithing system.

The recipient of Jacob's tithe isn't explicitly mentioned, but his story carries profound implications. After his encounter with God, Jacob set up a stone pillar, naming it Bethel which signifies “house of God” (Gen. 28:19). He pledged to sustain this pillar with tithes, envisioning it as the Beth Elohim a sanctified abode for God. Upon his return to Canaan, he constructed an altar at Bethel, designating it as El Bethel signifying “God of Bethel” (Gen. 35:3, 6-7). Subsequently, God bestowed the name Israel upon Jacob, along with promises for both the nation of Israel and the land. In commemoration of this, Jacob erected another stone pillar, naming the place Bethel. Jacob's actions foreshadow a forthcoming practice among the Israelites, wherein they would offer tithes primarily to support and maintain the dwelling place of God.[22]

21 The original Hebrew text of “Of all that Thou shalt give me I will surely give the tenth unto Thee” (Gen. 28:22) emphasizes that tithing will take place in a certain and thorough manner by using the Piel participle absolute form *asser* of the verb *asar*, meaning “to set apart,” right before the first person singular imperfect verb form. The English Standard Version renders it as “I will give a full tenth to you.” Sarna understands Jacob's tithing as a one-time offering after his return to Canaan. Ibid., 201. However, the Hebrew participle expresses an action performed “thoroughly, repetitively,” potentially suggesting that Jacob not only faithfully carried out the promised complete tithe after returning to Canaan but also continued to tithe consistently thereafter. See GKC §113n.

22 Carpenter, 862.

PART IV

Sin and Judgment

Chapter 10 | Words for Sin and the Fall of Adam

Right after the creation narrative concludes, Genesis delves into the account of humanity's transgressions. In the book of Genesis, specialized terms connected to sin emerge early on. This book does not romanticize Adam, Noah, and the forefathers of the nation of Israel; instead, it candidly exposes their wrongdoings and errors, demonstrating how God passed judgment and extended salvation to both individuals and the world. Within the Genesis narratives, we unearth the foundational principles of sin and divine judgment that reverberate throughout the entirety of the Bible. A grasp of these principles lays the groundwork for a comprehensive comprehension of pivotal theological themes like redemption, the covenant and law, the remnant, eschatology, and the Messiah.

1. Technical terminology for sin

There are various Old Testament terms for sin and transgression, but the main ones are *hattat* ("sin"), *awon* ("iniquity, guilt") and *pesha* ("sin, treason").[1]

1 The terms that represent sin can be translated in various ways depending on the context, sometimes even interchangeably, making it challenging to fix a single term to use in translations. In the well-known Davidic penitential psalm, Psalm 51, David uses *hattat awon* and *pesha* to refer to sin. Other terms representing sin include *asam* ("sin, sinful act"), which refers to specific results arising from sinful actions (Gen. 26:10; Lev. 5:19; 7:5; 2 Kings 12:16 [H 17]); Prov. 14:9; Jer. 51:5), *ma'al* ("sin"), which signifies disloyalty towards God that entails severe consequences, such as idolatry (Num. 22:16, 22, 31; Deut. 9:1; 10:13; Judg. 9:2, 4); *ra* ("evil"), which depicts the wretched state of sin in the eyes of God (Gen. 6:5; 13:13; Num. 14:35; Jer. 13:10); and *resha* ("wickedness" or "injustice"), referring to sinning before God by acting selfishly for personal gain at the expense of the community (Prov. 10:2; Eccles. 3:16; Mic.6:10), in contrast to *sedek* ("righteousness"), meaning to do good to the community. See Waltke and Yu, 275. In the New Testament, terms denoting sin include: (1) *hamartia* (ἁμαρτία "miss the mark"), meaning deliberately missing the mark of God's standard (Matt. 1:21; Rom. 5:12, 13; 1 John 1:9); (2) *parakoe* (παρακοή "do not try to listen, listen incompletely"), implying blocking one's ears against God's Word which leads to disobedience or disloyalty to God, and which term is used three times in the New Testament (Rom. 5:19; 2 Cor. 10:6; Heb. 2:2); (3) *parabasis* (παράβασις "pass by, violate, slip"), which implies entering forbidden territory and refers to deliberate violations of God's law, and which term is used seven times in the New Testament (Rom. 2:23; 4:15; 5:14; Gal. 3:19; 1 Tim. 2:14; Heb. 2:2; 9:15); (4) *paraptoma* (παράπτωμα "fall beside, trip and fall"), which refers to making a mistake, is used frequently in Romans (especially with respect to Adam's Fall and the prevalence of sin: see Rom. 5:15, 16, 17, 18, 20), and is used 19 times in the

(1) Hattat (חַטָּאת "sin")

The first technical term for sin in the Bible, and the most common word for sin, is *hattat*. It has its origins in the verb *hata* ("to miss the target, not to reach, to get lost"), which is used 595 times in the Old Testament.[2] Etymologically, sin is "deviation."[3] *Hattat* emphasizes behaviors, attitudes, and lifestyles that deviate from what God has ordained. Therefore, sin is failing to meet God's standards (Lev. 5:5, 16; Ps. 51:4).[4] Only an all-knowing God knows what true good is. Man must conform his heart and actions to the law of life established by God.

In Genesis, *hattat* appears in the accounts of Cain and Abel, the destruction of Sodom, Jacob and Laban, and the words spoken to Joseph by Joseph's brothers after Jacob's death (Gen. 4:7; 18:20; 31:36; 50:17). It also appears in the form of the verb *hata* and other derivatives in the narratives concerning Lot's migration to Sodom, Abraham and Abimelech, Joseph and Potiphar's wife, the Egyptian officials, Reuben's words to his brothers, and Judah's words to Jacob and Joseph (Gen. 13:13; 20:6, 9; 31:36; 39:9; 40:1; 41:9; 42:22, 32).

(2) Awon ("sin, guilt")

The term first appears in the story of Cain and Abel to refer to "punishment" (Gen. 4:13).[5] It appears 231 times in the Hebrew Scriptures, and is derived from the verb *awah*, which means "to bend, twist, distort." Literally, God "overturns" the earth (Isa. 24:1), life's paths are symbolically "made

---

Old Testament (Matt. 6:14, 15; Mark 11:25; Rom. 4:25; 5:15 (two times), 16, 17, 18, 20; 11:11, 12; 2 Cor. 5:19; Gal. 6:1; Eph. 1:7; 2:1, 5; Col. 2:13 (two times)); (5) *anomia* (ἀνομία "lawlessness, law breaking"), which is used in passages such as "Whosoever committeth sin transgresseth also the law: for sin is the transgression of the law" (1 John 3:4) and occurs 15 times in the New Testament (Matt. 7:23; 13:41; 23:28; 24:12; Rom. 4:7; 6:19 (two times); 2 Cor. 6:14; 2 Thess. 2:3, 7; Titus 2:14; Heb. 1:9; 10:17; 1 John 3:4); and (6) *adikia* (ἀδικία "unrighteous act"), which is the first evil listed in Romans 1:29. See John M. Fowler, 'Sin', *Handbook of Seventh-Day Adventist Theology*, ed. Raoul Dederen (Hagerstown, MD: Review and Herald Publishing Association, 2000), 238-239; G. F. Kittel, *Theological Dictionary of the New Testament (Abridged)* (Grand Rapids, MI: William B. Eerdmans Publishing Company, 1985), 49-51, 772-773, 848, 654, 23.

2 The root is used 237 times as a Hebrew verb, 356 times as a noun, and 2 times in Aramaic. The term hattat in meaning and origin is closely related to the New Testament terms *hamartano* (ἁμαρτάνω "to sin") and *hamartia* (ἁμαρτία "sin") Simon J. De Vries, 'Sin, Sinners', *The Interpreter's Dictionary of the Bible*, ed. G. A. Buttrick (New York/ Nashville: Abingdon Press, 1962), 4:361; '*hattat,*' *HALOT*.

3 *Ht'* is used in Judges 20:16 to describe missing a target with sling stones, and in Job 5:24 to refer to the loss of livestock; hence, the term indicates a sense of deviation or departure.

4 Fowler, 237.

5 This is translated into various terms such as "sin" (Gen. 15:16; 19:15; 44:16; Num. 5:15; Job 20:27; Ps. 78:38), "guilt" (Ex. 28:38), "sin" (Ex. 20:5; 28:43; Lev. 19:8), "iniquity" (Lev. 16:21), "evil" (Ex. 34:7, 9), "iniquity" (Lev. 5:1), and "punishment" (Lev. 5:17).

crooked" (Lam. 3:9), what is right is "distorted" (Job 33:27), and the heart is "crooked" (Prov. 12:8).

Awon refers to sin in the collective sense. The term refers collectively to the sins of the Sodomites that led to destruction (Gen. 19:15). In the sanctuary service, *awon* is the general term that refers to all sins. On the Day of Atonement, which represented the culmination of the priestly service, the goat for Azazel was cast out into the wildreness bearing "all the iniquities" of the children of Israel (Lev. 16:21-22).[6] *Awon* includes not only sin, but also guilt, which is the result of sin. "Even if the penalty is deferred or even cancelled, the offender remains a guilty person, for guilt concerns the unalterable past."[7] People today distinguish between sin, punishment, and guilt, but in the Old Testament "the action of man and what happens to him are presupposed to be directly related as one process within the basic divine order."[8] Sin is always punished.[9]

In Genesis, *awon* appears in the context of Cain's appeal to God, the condition of the Amorites prior to the Exodus, the angels' urging of Lot, and Judas' words to Joseph (Gen. 4:13; 15:16; 19:15; 44:16).

(3) Pesha (עֶשַׁפ "sin, treason")

Pesha (2 Kings 3:7; 2 Chron. 21:8; Isa. 59:13) derives from the verb *pasha*, which appears 134 times in the Old Testament, 41 times in verb form and 93 times in the noun form. The term refers to a deliberate transgression by a subordinate against a superior. Theologically, *pesha* refers to an "apostasy" or "rebellion" in which a person openly and blatantly defies God,[10] and is a very

6 Leviticus 16:21-22 (KJV) states the following: "And Aaron shall lay both his hands upon the head of the live goat, and confess over him all the iniquities (*awonot*) of the children of Israel, and all their transgressions (*pishhem*), in all their sins, putting them (*hattotam*) upon the head of the goat, and shall send him away by the hand of a fit man into the wilderness: And the goat shall bear upon him all their iniquities (*awonotam*), unto a land not inhabited: and he shall let go the goat in the wilderness." While the "sin" in verse 21 appears to encompass both "iniquities" and "transgressions", verse 22 focuses solely on "iniquity", incorporating both "sin" and "transgressions" within the scope of 'iniquity'. For the treatment of sin, see: Alex Luc, ' *'wn*,' *NIDOTTE* 3:351; Jacob Milgrom, *Leviticus 1-16: A New Translation with Introduction and Commentary*, 1st ed. (New York: Doubleday, 1991), 25, 1043.

7 L. L. Morris, 'Guilt and Forgiveness,' *New Dictionary of Theology*, 285.

8 Carl Schultz, ' *'wh*,' *TWOT* 651.

9 When Judah discovered Joseph's silver cup in Benjamin's sack, he indirectly witnessed the divine hand of God, who ensures that sin is ultimately punished. He declared, "God has found out the iniquity of your servants " (Gen. 44:16). Judah believed that their dire situation was a result of God having found out "the means to punish" their iniquity (*awon*). See A. Cohen, *The Soncino Chumash: The Five Books of Moses, with Haphtaroth, Soncino Books of the Bible* (London/ Jerusalem/ New York: The Soncino Press, 1983), 274; Sarna, 305.

10 Alex Luc, '*psh*',' *NIDOTTE* 3:706.

serious act that breaks one's relationship with God.[11] As the biblical narrative progresses, *pesha* is increasingly used to refer to the "total" transgression of an age, people, or individual, and their total break with Yahweh.[12] Whereas *hattat* ("sin") and *awon* ("iniquity") mean deviation, *pesha* refers to the breakdown of an alliance due to apostasy and rebellion, violation of norms and standards, and breach of covenants.[13]

In Genesis, the term *pesha* is used three times, in Jacob's words to Laban and Joseph's brothers' words to Joseph (Gen. 31:36; Gen. 50:17 (two times). As these two stories show, *pesha* is a "crime, a criminal act" that breaks relationships within the community, such as thievery (Gen. 31:36; Ex. 22:9[8]) or kidnapping (Gen. 50:17).[14]

2. The Fall of Adam

While some might regard humanity's fall as an instance of God overreacting to a relatively trivial transgression, Adam's apostasy is in fact an event that has considerable implications for mankind, the universe, and God Himself.

(1) historical event

To think of the fall of mankind in Genesis 3 as a myth or a metaphor without historical truth is to shake the very foundations of the Christian faith. Dismissing the account in Genesis 3 of mankind's fall as a mere myth or metaphor devoid of historical truth has the potential to destabilize the very bedrock of the Christian faith. The crucifixion of Jesus Christ cannot be separated from Adam's transgression. Notions of the resurrection, ascension, Second Coming, and the promise of a renewed paradise stand on shaky ground unless firmly rooted in the historical reality of Adam's sin.

---

11 R. Knierim, 'Crime', TLOT 2:1036. Pesha is used alongside other terms that denote sin and is translated variously in the New King James Version, as in the following examples: "forgiving iniquity and transgression and sin" (Ex. 34:7); "you have made your iniquity to be remembered, in that your transgressions are uncovered" (Ezek. 21:24[29]); "forgive the trespass of your brothers and their sin" (Gen. 50:17); "there is neither evil nor rebellion in my hand" (1 Sam. 24:11[12].

12 Ibid., 1036-37.

13 Eugene Carpenter, Michael A. Grisanti, *'psh'*', *NIDOTTE* 3:707.

14 Knierim, 'Crime', *TLOT* 2:1033. In Genesis 50:17, when Joseph's brothers confess their *pesha* to him, the usage of this term aligns with its typical meaning, revealing the hierarchical relationship between superiors and inferiors. The term highlights the social distinction between Joseph and his brothers. Luc, *'psh','* *NIDOTTE* 3:706.

1) Toledot

The historical authenticity of Adam and Eve's sin, as depicted in the book of Genesis, finds substantiation within the framework of the text itself. The *toledot* ("history, origin") structure[15] alongside the chronogenealogies of Chapters 5 and 11 reinforce the historical underpinning of this event.[16] The phrase "This is the book of the genealogy of ..." can be translated as "This is the book of the family history of..." [17]

2) Chronogeneology

The narrative of Adam's Fall, as recounted in Genesis 3, unfolds within the broader span of Genesis 2:4-4:26, highlighting it as a unique occurrence on Earth. The historical authenticity of these events gains credence through the meticulous chronogenealogy present in both Genesis 5 and Genesis 11:10-26. These genealogies meticulously connect successive generations, anchoring them in time and history. Each father-son link is established with specific ages and life spans—A begetting B at the age of x, followed by the passing of y years after B's birth, ultimately culminating in the father's demise at the age of z.

What sets the two genealogies apart from other genealogies in the Bible is their distinct temporal framework.[18] These genealogies interweave a chronological tapestry that extends from Adam to Noah and later, from Noah's son Shem to Terah, who is the father of Abraham. This serves as a foundational anchor for Israel's historical narrative, stretching back to the time of the Flood and the very act of creation.[19]

Genesis 5 and 11's genealogical accounts manifest a profound interest in the progression of time and the course of history. They stand as assertive declarations that the Creation and the Fall are veritable historical realities, etching themselves into the annals of time.[20] This is further mirrored

---

15 See the discussion in the "Toledot" section of Part 1, Chapter 3, The Theological Structure of Genesis.

16 Hasel referred to the genealogies in Genesis 5 and 11 as "chronogenealogies." Gerhard F. Hasel, 'Genesis 5 and 11: Chronogenealogies in the Biblical history of Beginnings', *Origins* 7, no. 1 (1980), 23-37; Gerhard F. Hasel, 'The Meaning of the Chronogenealogies of Genesis 5 and 11', *Origins* 7, no. 2 (1980), 53-70.

17 Wenham, Gordon J. *Genesis 1-15, vol. 1*, WBC, 49.

18 Prominent genealogies that stand out notably in the Old and New Testaments include the following: Gen. 22:20-24; 25:1-4, 12-18; 29:31-30:24; 35:16-20; 35:22-26; 39:9-14, 40-43; 46:8-27; 1 Sam. 14:50-51; 1 Chron. 1-9; Ruth 4:18-22; Matt. 1:1-17; Luke 3:23-38. These do not contain the chronogenealogical elements observed in Genesis chapter 5 and chapter 11.

19 Hasel, 'Genesis 5 and 11: Chronogenealogies in the Biblical history of Beginnings', 25.

20 Hasel, 'The Meaning of the Chronogenealogies of Genesis 5 and 11', 69.

in the Chronicles and the Gospel of Luke, where Adam is positioned as respectively the inaugural and culminating figure within the genealogical lineage (1 Chron. 1:1; Luke 3:38). Through this meticulous lineage, Jesus Christ—the pivotal figure in history—is historically linked to Adam, which solidifies their interconnectedness through the ages.

3) historical crime and historical redemption.

Outside of Genesis, Adam is referenced nine times in the Bible. The historical reality of Adam's sin is universally accepted in these references, including in the three genealogies recorded in 1 Chronicles 1:1, Luke 3:38, and Jude 14. The Israelites' rebellion against God is compared to Adam's transgression (Hos. 6:7).

Jesus is the final Adam, conclusively ending the reign of sin and death that was inaugurated by the first man, Adam. Romans 5:14-21 draws a parallel between Adam, the catalyst of sin, and Jesus Christ, the remedy for sin; Adam is presented as a foreshadowing of "Him Who was to come" (Rom. 5:14).

The New Testament underscores the historical and theological significance of Adam and Eve's transgression. The legacy of sin and death originated with the first man, Adam, while grace, righteousness, and life abound as gifts from God through Jesus Christ, who is the antitype to Adam's type.

The early church, whose members had been present as the historical events of Jesus' death, resurrection and ascension were unfolding, perceived Jesus' resurrection as a manifestation of the restoration of life that had been lost in Adam (1 Cor. 15:22, 45). Addressing matters of order between men and women in the church, they looked to the accounts of the creation and sin of Adam and Eve as their theological foundation (1 Tim. 2:13-14). The New Testament regards Adam and Eve's fall as a historical and theological event.

At the point of Adam and Eve's spiritual downfall, a significant divergence occurs: man treads the path of pride and selfishness, while God embarks on a redemptive journey driven by love—a pivotal moment captured in history.[21]

(2) The Great Controversy between Good and Evil

Genesis 1–3 presents a striking juxtaposition of active agents. The initial chapters of the Bible depict God as the speaker and doer. However, in the opening of chapter 3, a significant shift occurs as the serpent challenges and distorts God's Word, directly opposing its essence. This serpent is one

21 Robert H. Mounce, *Romans*, The New American Commentary (Nashville, TN: Broadman & Holman, 1995), 141.

that challenges God's divine authority.[22]

"But the serpent was more cunning than any beast of the field which the Lord God [Yahweh] had made" (Gen. 3:1). The conjunction "but" (waw) holds significance beyond its surface function. From a world where God's creation was deemed "very good" in God's sight (Gen. 1:31), and where Adam joyfully greeted his bride by exclaiming, "This is now bone of my bones and flesh of my flesh; she shall be called Woman" (Gen. 2:23), the word "but" takes us to a pivotal moment of crisis. The serpent,[23] God's adversary, was lurking in the grove, intent on destroying this peaceful world.

What kind of creature is this serpent?

Serpents, like all animals, were placed under mankind's authority (Gen. 3:1; cf. Gen. 1:26, 28; 2:19-20). Meanwhile, God had revealed to mankind through the Tree of Life and the Tree of the Knowledge of Good and Evil that whereas human beings are moral and spiritual beings, they do not hold supreme authority over creation—this belongs only to God, who is the source of all life. "And the Lord [Yahweh] God commanded the man, saying, 'Of every tree of the garden you may freely eat; but of the tree of the knowledge of good and evil you shall not eat, for in the day that you eat of it you shall surely die'" (Gen. 2:16, 17). This was a revelation from God to mankind. The act of revelation emanates solely from God to man, and among all earthly creatures, only humans, created in God's image, are recipients of this divine unveiling. The serpent may have been cunning,[24] but it was incapable of imparting or receiving divine revelation. Animals do not have the gift of articulate speech, which fosters rational exchanges.[25]

And yet, in Genesis 3, the serpent takes on a speaking role. Eve receives information from the serpent that appears to transcend the earlier revelation she had received: "Then the serpent said to

---

22 From the perspective of Hebrew grammar, there is a clear distinction in content between Genesis chapters 1-2 and chapter 3. Unlike the continuous use of the *wayyiqtol* verb form in the previous chapters, chapter 3 begins with a new subject introduced by a noun and starts with a perfect verb form, revealing a distinct shift in narrative structure. Furthermore, the basic Hebrew construction of verb + subject is altered to subject + verb—*we-hannachash hayah*—that serves to emphasize "the serpent." Barry L. Bandstra, *Genesis 1-11: A Handbook on the Hebrew Text* (Waco, Tex.: Baylor University Press, 2007), 166; Bruce K. Waltke and M. O'Connor, *An Introduction to Biblical Hebrew Syntax* (Winona Lake, IN: Eisen brauns, 1990), 129.

23 The Hebrew text attached the definite article (*ha*) to "serpent" (*nachash*), resulting in "the serpent" (*hannachash*).

24 "Now the serpent was more cunning than..." is rendered in the Septuagint as "the most wise" (φρονιμώτατος *phronimōtatos*). The Greek word *phronimōtatos* which comes from the word *phronimos* (φρόνιμος), meaning "wise." Jesus used this word to refer to wise people (Matt. 7:24; 10:16; 24:45; Luke 16:8).

25 The Bible records a highly exceptional instance of an animal—a donkey—speaking. This event occurs when the donkey rebukes Balaam. It is a unique occurrence that took place due to God's providential intervention to prevent Balaam from participating in cursing God's people, Israel. See Num. 22:27-30; 2 Pet. 2:15-16.

the woman, "'You will not surely die. For God knows that in the day you eat of it your eyes will be opened, and you will be like God, knowing good and evil'" (Gen. 3:4-5). Behind this serpent, assuming the role of an intelligent entity that presumed to understand the depths of God's intentions and tempted mankind with godlike aspirations, lurked the influence of spiritual darkness. The serpent was a conduit, manipulated by a malevolent authority.

This great Evil is depicted in the Bible as the serpent of old, the Devil, Satan, a murder from the beginning, a liar, and the father of lies (Rev. 12:9; 20:2; John 8:44). This entity was subject to condemnation because of his selfishness and pride, which caused him to aspire to "be like the Most High" and to deviate from the divinely appointed order (Isa. 14:12-14; 1 Tim. 3:6; Jude 6). Comprehending the enormity of sin necessitates an awareness of this grand struggle, the great controversy between Christ and Satan, Good and Evil. Central to this cosmic clash is the essence of God's unassailable sovereignty and his intrinsic character.[26]

In Luke 10:18, Jesus declared, "I saw Satan fall like lightning from heaven." Humanity does not stand on neutral terrain within the overarching conflict. Instead, two distinct courses unfold before us: one involves acknowledging our reliance on God and his Word, embracing faith and obedience, while the other succumbs to the allure of Satan's enticement to aspire to divinity and treads the perilous route of self-sufficiency and destruction.

In the proto-evangelium, Satan is depicted as vanquished, his head destined for bruising. Satan can never defeat God. By standing on the side of Jesus, human beings partake in a victory that has already been won by Jesus Christ, the seed of the woman.

(3) Separation from God

Since sin is a matter between God and Satan, Good and Evil, to violate God's Word is to abandon God and join the ranks of Satan. The act of sinning reveals that the heart has already departed from God.

Persistent sinning hardens the human heart and eventually separates the believer from God. God said that He would "surely hide [his] face" when his beloved Israel would follow other gods (Deut. 31:18). God is mighty to save, but obstinate sin creates barriers that even God cannot breach. "But your iniquities have separated you from your God; and your sins have hidden his face from you, so that He will not hear" (Isa. 59:2). But your iniquities have separated you from your God;

---

26 Fowler, 241.

and your sins have hidden his face from you, so that He will not hear. A perilous delusion unfolds when one indulges in lawlessness yet falsely believes to be aligned with God. One may maintain this self-delusion on this earth, but the truth will come to light when Jesus returns, at which time the individual will face eternal rejection, an everlasting detachment from God. "And then I will declare to them, 'I never knew you; depart from Me, you who practice lawlessness!'" (Matt. 7:23).

(4) Spiritual death

The judgment in Genesis 2:17— "for in the day that you eat of it you shall surely die"—was not literally carried out on the very day Adam and Eve first sinned. However, although their physical existence was preserved due to God's gracious intervention, in God's eyes, sin signifies spiritual death. Separation from God, the source of life, equates to spiritual death. A being estranged from God resides in darkness; a lightbulb that is cut off from the source of electricity cannot be lighted.

Remarkably, Jesus radiated the light of life upon those ensconced in the shadows of death. Those who believe and follow Him experience spiritual resurrection and eternal life (Isa. 9:2; Matt. 4:16; 8:22; John 5:24).

(5) Accountability

1) Adam and Eve were held accountable for their sin.

God's judgment upon Adam stemmed from his overt act of disobedience, rather than mere listening to the words of the serpent, looking upon the forbidden fruit, or desire for it. This judgment is rooted in a definitive act:[27] "Because you have heeded the voice of your wife, and have eaten from the tree of which I commanded you, saying, 'You shall not eat of it': Cursed is the ground for your sake; in toil you shall eat of it all the days of your life." (Gen. 3:17). The ultimate choice of the sinful act encompasses the entire spectrum of moral failings, including lack of decisiveness in rejecting the sin, selfishness, and imprudence. It stands as a reminder that each transgression, regardless of its nature, ultimately constitutes a breach of all commandments.

---

27 In Genesis 3 and James 1:13-15, we can identify four stages of sinning. First, one listens to the words of the tempter (Satan) and inclines their ear (Gen. 3:1, 4-5). Second, they are drawn and enticed by their own desires, falling into the snare (Gen. 3:6, "So when the woman saw that the tree was good for food, that it was [a]pleasant to the eyes, and a tree desirable to make one wise"; James 1:14, "But each one is tempted when he is drawn away by his own desires and enticed."). Third, they commit sin as an outcome of their desires (Gen. 3:6, "she took of its fruit and ate. She also gave to her husband with her, and he ate"; James 1:15, "Then, when desire has conceived, it gives birth to sin"). Fourth, the consequence of sin is death (Gen. 3:19, "For dust you are, And to dust you shall return"; James 1:15, "and sin, when it is full-grown, brings forth death"). See Flint, 40-41.

2) Adam received an explicit command from God.

God gave an explicit command to Adam, and when judgment befell humanity following their transgression, the ensuing questioning and verdict were anchored in the foundation of God's explicit command (Gen. 2:16; 3:11, 17). In these verses, the Hebrew verb *tsiwa*, meaning "to command," is employed. This linguistic choice underscores the authoritative and unequivocal nature of God's instruction, which amounts to a *mitzwah*.[28] In a world untainted by guilt, it was not necessary for God to give a more comprehensive articulation of his laws, in the manner of the Ten Commandments or the 613 detailed commandments of the Pentateuch.[29] A single command, "you shall not eat" of the Tree of the Knowledge of Good and Evil (Gen. 2:17), sufficed. The words *lo to'akhal mimennu* ("you shall not eat [of it]") constitute a categoridal prohibition,[30] and such command served as the cornerstone upon which the pronouncement of judgment is grounded.

3) Adam and his wife already knew of the forthcoming deception through their intimate fellowship with God.

The serpent's assertion in Genesis 3:5 sought to introduce uncertainty about God's love and divine authority. However, Adam and Eve's experiential knowledge of God left no room for doubt regarding his intentions and character. Genesis 2 unveils a profoundly intimate deity who breathes life into man, crafts a companion, and tends to mankind's needs. "Adam and Eve were surrounded with God's love."[31] The mention of Jehovah God walking in the garden following mankind's

---

28 *Mitzwah*, commandments, are generally understood as specific instructions given by God that must be obeyed, rather than merely general laws to be observed. Thus, it emphasizes concrete directives rather than abstract principles. R. K. Harris, 'Law in the OT,' ISBE 3:77. See Gen. 26:5; Ex. 15:26; 16:28; 20:6; 24:12.

29 The number 613 derives from an analysis of all the commandments found in the Torah. Shimon Kayyara (ca. 9th century, Halochot Gedolot) analyzed them for his own purposes, but his legal analysis was incomplete. Later, Eliezer ben Samuel of Metz (1115-1204, Sefer Yeraim) conducted further analysis. The most well-known analysis was conducted by Moses ben Maimonides (1135-1204), and later Moses Ibn Jacob Hagiz (1672-1751, Eleh Ha-Mitzvot) provided a commentary on Maimonides' 613 commandments. See Jacob Neusner and others, *The Encyclopedia of Judaism.* (New York: Continuum, 1999), 3:1211, 1222, 4:1660. Among the 613 commandments, there are 248 positive commandments that are expressed as "do," and 365 negative commandments that are expressed as "do not." The number 248 corresponds to the total number of parts in the human body, and 365 corresponds to the days in a year. These numbers are understood as signifying that God's commandments are meant to be practiced with one's entire body throughout the year.

30 In Hebrew, prohibitive commands use the structure of *al* + jussive form of a verb, or *lo* + imperfect form of a verb. The former is used for a specific occasion, while the latter is declarative command that is binding for both the present and the future, and has a stronger meaning than the former. Victor P. Hamilton, *Handbook on the Pentateuch*, 2nd ed. (Grand Rapids, MI: Baker Academic, 2005), 188.

31 Bill T. Arnold and Bryan Beyer, *Encountering the Old Testament: A Christian Survey*, 2nd ed., Encountering

transgression alludes to an exceptionally clos rapport between God and the inaugural couple, underscoring an intimate fellowship (Gen. 3:8).[32] God, either personally or through his celestial messengers, forewarned humanity's progenitors of Satan's downfall and the impending temptation he would wield against them. =

4) Human beings have free will; hence, Adam's sin stemmed from a deliberate choice.

Regardless of Satan's smooth speaking and the allure of the forbidden fruit, Adam and Eve had free will and possessed the ability to resist the temptation. Armed with intellectual comprehension and tangible experience of God's commands and true nature, our first parents engaged in a conscious act of defiance in yielding to Satan's enticements. Their transgression was a deliberate act of rebellion. Consequently, they faced the sobering consequences of their choices: the burden of arduous toil, the pangs of childbirth, and the inevitability of mortality (Gen. 3:16-19).

(6) The apostasy of all mankind

The sin of Adam and Eve was not just a mere individual indiscretion, but amounted to the fall of all mankind. At that time, there were only two human beings: Adam and Eve. In Hebrew, *adam* signifies "human, mankind" or the individual Adam, the progenitor of the human race. Notably, Genesis 3 employs *ha-Adam*, meaning "that person" (Gen. 3:8, 9, 12, 20, 22, 24). The recurring use of this term underscores a profound truth: Adam's transgression is the transgression of all humanity.[33] As the forefather of the human lineage, Adam's misstep resounds through generations. "Through one man sin entered the world, and death through sin, and thus death spread to all men, because all sinned... By the one man's offense death reigned through the one" (Rom. 5:12, 17). Psalm 51:5, penned by David, eloquently conveys the weighty repercussions of sin: "Behold, I was

---

Biblical Studies (Grand Rapids, MI: Baker Academic, 2008), 81.

32 Genesis 3:8, "Yahweh walking (*mithallek*) in the garden," employs the intensive reflexive verb form (Hithpael) to indicate a repeated and habitual interaction between God and humans. It suggests the possibility that the omnipotent God and the human race's forebears engaged in daily communion. Enoch (Gen. 5:22, 24), Noah (Gen. 6:9), Abraham (Gen. 17:1, 24:40), and others were known to habitually journey with God. Robert Jamieson, A. R. Fausset, and David Brown, 'Gen 3:8,' *A Commentary, Critical, Experimental and Explanatory, on the Old and New Testaments* (Oak Harbor, WA: Logos Research System, Inc, 1997); Mathews, *Genesis 1-4:26*, 239; Wenham, Genesis 1-15, 76.

33 Adam as personal name occurs first in Genesis 4:25, "And Adam knew his wife again." Before this verse the word *adam* indicate a human being Johnson Lim Teng Kok, *Grace in the Midst of Judgment: Grappling with Genesis 1-11* (Berlin: W. de Gruyter, 2002), 137 n. 223.

brought forth in iniquity, and in sin my mother conceived me."

The universal nature of Adam's transgression finds resonance throughout the book of Genesis. This truth is illuminated through various incidents, such as the heinous acts of Cain and Lamech, as well as the pervasive moral decay prior to the Great Flood (Gen. 4:8, 23-24; 6:5). Despite the deluge, humanity's sinful disposition endured (Gen. 8:21); even Noah, the renewed Adam, succumbs to inappropriate behavior (Gen. 9:21). The Tower of Babel emerges as another testament to mankind's audacious defiance against God (Gen. 11:1-9). Even the esteemed patriarchs—Abraham, Isaac, and Jacob—were not immune to sin (Gen. 12:10; 20:2; 26:7; 27). Genesis does not idealize these ancestral figures but candidly portrays their vulnerabilities and transgressions, underscoring the universal human propensity for sin. The narrative underscores that sole redemption and salvation lie within God. As a testament to mankind's fallibility and mortality, the genealogies of Genesis uniformly end in death, and Genesis concludes with the account of Joseph's death and interment (Gen. 5; 11:28, 32; 50:26).

Chapter 11 | Words for Judgment

Adam and Eve (Gen. 3), Cain and Abel (Gen. 4), Noah's Flood (Gen. 6-9), the Tower of Babel (Gen. 11), and Sodom and Gomorrah (Gen. 18-19) are some of the representative judgment accounts in Genesis. Judgment encompasses not only God's condemnation and punishment for humanity's sins but also God's profound love, aimed at achieving mankind's salvation.

Except for the account of Sodom and Gomorrah's judgment, the rest of these instances deal with the concept of judgment without using judgment-specific terminology; this is in fact a feature that is found in other parts of the Bible.[1] Nevertheless, delving into the lexicon of judging can offer insights into the multifaceted aspects of judgment. In the Old Testament, common terms associated with judgment include the Hebrew root[2] "*shapat*", meaning "to judge"; "*din*," meaning "to judge"; and "*rib*," meaning "quarrel, lawsuit," and their related forms.[3]

1. The Hebrew root *shapat* and its derivatives

(1) Hebrew root shapat

The Hebrew root *shapat* appears 642 times in the Old Testament (including in both noun and verb form) and eight times in Genesis.[4] This term denotes the process of restoring a proper order between

1 When Abraham interceded for Sodom, he called the Lord "the Judge of the Earth" (Gen. 18:25).

2 Originally, Hebrew was written only with consonants, and the Hebrew root consisted of three consonants. The vowels were invented by Masoretes (meaning "tradition") scholars and added to the Hebrew Bible.

3 The Hebrew words *šapat, din*, and *rib* are all technical terms for judgment. However, if the concept of judgment is expanded to include terms related to retribution, the vocabulary of judgment becomes very diverse. Zerafa has surveyed over fifty Hebrew and Greek words in the Old and New Testaments that express the concept of retribution. P. Zerafa, 'La Retribuzione Nella Bibbia', *Angelicum* 74(1997), 145-170.

4 The Hebrew root šapat (špṭ) has several derivatives in Genesis. The verb *šapat* ("to judge") occurs in Gen. 16:5, 19:9 (two times), and 31:53. The noun *šopet* ("judge") occurs in Gen. 18:25. The noun *mišpat* ("justice") occurs in Gen. 18:19, 25, and 40:13 *kammishpat harishon* ("in the previous manner," "as before"). The last is the ancient name of Kadesh, *en mishpat* ("the well of judgment," or "the eye of judgment"), Gen. 14:7. Cornwall, 69, B. Johnson, '*mišpāṭ*,' *TDOT* 9:96.

two individuals or groups through intervention of a third party's "shapat," ultimately restoring a state of "shalom," meaning "peace." The concept of "shapat" extends beyond judicial rulings and encompasses acts of governance. Through "shapat," those who have suffered unjustly find deliverance and justice, while wrongdoers face definitive and ultimate retribution.[5] Due to these considerations, the terms encompass a range of significances. For this reason, "shapat" has a wide variety of meanings, depending on the context. The actor administering "shapat" is either God or humans. The meanings of "shapat" within the context of the original Hebrew text are explored below.

1) Human administration of shapat

***1.** Establish or maintain justice*. The primary responsibility of a king or leader was to maintain justice in the land, especially for the vulnerable (Lev. 19:15; Ps. 72:4; Prov. 29:14; 31:8-9; Isa. 1:17; Zech. 7:9-10). This is also a defining trait of the anticipated messianic king (Isa. 11:3-4; 16:5).

2. Judge or punish as God's representative (especially in the book of Ezekiel). For example, Babylon inflicts punishment on the unrighteous Jerusalem (Ezek. 23:24; cf. 24:14).

3. Adjudicate and resolve judicial disputes among the people. This is the most common usage of shapat (Moses, Ex. 18:13, 16; appointed judges, Ex. 18:22, 26; Deut. 1:16; 16:18; 25:1; 2 Chron. 19:6). Because judges are acting as adjudicators on behalf of God, they are to judge fairly, avoiding injustice and bribery (2 Chron. 19:6-7).

4. Rule, govern. Examples include the regency of Jotham due to Uzziah's leprosy (1 Kings 15:5 [correct reference?]; 2 Chron. 26:21), and the rulers of the people in Daniel's penitential prayer (Dan. 9:12).

2) God's activities of shapat

1. Rule the earth. Yahweh is the universal Sovereign who righteously governs the earth and the world (1 Chron. 16:33; Ps. 96:13).

2. Judge. Defending one party to a dispute and condemning the other party (Gen. 16:5; Judg. 11:27; 1 Sam. 24:12, 15[13, 16]). In the temple, God judges between the two parties according to their works (1 Kings 8:32; 2 Chron. 6:23).

3. Establish justice through rescue or advocacy. David pleads for God to deliver him from Saul's hands (See 1 Sam. 24:15[16]; 2 Sam. 18:19, 31).

---

5 'špṭ *HALOT.*

4. Establish judgment through punishment. House of Eli (1 Sam. 3:13); the Israelites (Ezek. 33:20; 35:11; 36:19); the eschatological judgment of God in the valley of Jehoshaphat (Joel 3:12 [4:12]).

3) shapat in Genesis

In Genesis, the word shapat is used four times.

Sarai confronted her husband, accusing him of permitting their slave girl, Hagar—whom she had given to Abram—to behave disrespectfully after conceiving. Sarai expressed her desire for Yahweh to "judge" ("shapat") between Abram and herself (Gen. 16:5). Subsequently, a divine messenger addressed Hagar as "Hagar, slave of Sarai," instructing her to return to her mistress and submit, thereby reestablishing their relationship and settling the conflict (Gen. 16:8, 9).[6]

Upon their parting, Laban and Jacob invoked God's judgment, constructing a heap of stones as a boundary marker and vowing not to encroach upon each other's territory (Gen. 31:53).[7]

When Lot attempted to dissuade the Sodomites from their wicked acts, they scorned him, remarking that he was attempting to assume the role of a judge (Gen. 19:9).

(2) Judge or ruler— "shopet"

A judge ("shopet") is a person who has the office of judging or governing.

1. A public office in Israel. Judges were appointed at the time of the Exodus (Ex. 18:24-26). Judges and officials were to be appointed in every town to administer justice (Deut. 16:18-20).

2. Judges of the book of Judges. These judges received recognition for their authority through their military exploits that rescued God's people from foreign oppression (Judg. 2:16, 18; 3:10).

3. Rulers. Absalom's desire for the throne (2 Sam. 15:4); rulers of the earth (Ps. 2:10)

There are a total of nine instances in which God is referred to as the judge or ruler ("shopet"). Abraham prayed that the "Judge of all the earth" would "do right" (mishpat) (Gen. 18:25). Jephthah asked God to judge Ammon for itsunjust territorial claims (Judg. 11:27). The psalmist presented

---

6 The phrase in Genesis 16:6 is an allusion to the story of the Garden of Eden. "Good" (hattob) alludes to the Tree of the Knowledge of Good and Evil (Gen. 2:17), and the phrase "as your eyes see" is an allusion to the phrase "to be pleasing to the eye" (Gen. 3:6, the BHS Hebrew text includes the word "eye"). Mathews, *Genesis 11:27-50:26*, 186.

7 The stone heap that Jacob and Laban built was called "Yegar Sahadutha" and "Galĕd"), to denote "a pile of evidence." It was also called "Mispa" which means "tower", in the hope that Yahweh would watch over them (Gen 31:47, 49). Their faithfulness would be based on their faith in God, the Judge who sees everything.

God as a righteous judge who maintains justice in the world (Ps. 7:11[12]; 50:6; 75:7[8]; 94:2). God is the Savior because He is the Judge, the Lawgiver, and the King (Isa. 33:22). Job placed his hope in a divine Judge (Job 9:15; 23:7).

(3) Trial or justice—"mispat"

"Mispat" appears 425 times in the Old Testament.

1. The laws that God gave to the Israelites through Moses (Ex. 21:1)

2. Trial. Judges, representing God, must be truthful and impartial (Deut. 1:17; Zech. 7:9; 8:16)

3. God's judgment. The wicked cannot stand in the eschatological judgment (Ps. 1:5; 9:16[17]). The righteous put their hope in God's judgment to escape the oppression of the wicked (Ps. 7:6[7]; 9:4[5]). The nations will be judged by God (Zeph. 3:8).

4. Justice, fairness (Isa. 1:17, 21; 5:7; 10:2; Jer. 5:1; 7:5; Hab. 1:4). God chose Abraham to walk in the path of justice (Gen. 18:19) and judges his people who have fallen and strayed from the path of justice (Isa. 4:4; Jer. 5:1; 7:5; Ezek. 5:6-7; 20:11, 13, 16, 19, 21, 24; Hos. 5:1, 11; Mal. 3:5). Like Job, the prophets desired God to judge them in justice (Jer. 10:24; Mic. 7:9). Because trials ("mispat") are the means through which the righteous are acquitted and the wicked are condemned (Deut. 25:1), the righteous plead with God to "judge me" and "defend me" (šoptenî) (Ps. 7:8; 35:24; 43:1).

The various usages of the Hebrew root shapat make it clear that the dual aspects of condemnation/punishment and defense/deliverance play an important role in both divine and human acts of judgment. Various forms of the term can be used in a positive or negative sense. Judgment does not inherently have a negative connotation.[8]

(4) Names reflecting "shapat"

Because judgment also has a positive connotation, we can see examples in the Old Testament where "judgment" was used in the name of an individual or location. Examples include "En Mispat," meaning "Well of Judgment, Eye of Judgment" (Gen. 14:7); "Elishaphat," meaning "God Judges, God the Judge, One Whom God Judges" (2 Chron. 23:1); "Jehoshaphat," meaning "Yahweh Judges, One Whom Yahweh Judges, Yahweh is the Judge";[9] "Shapat," meaning "Judge, He Has

8 Gerhard F. Hasel, 'Divine Judgment', *Handbook of Seventh-Day Adventist Theology*, ed. Raoul Dederen et al., Commentary Reference Series (Hagerstown, MD: Review and Herald Publishing Association, 2000), 816-817.

9 Jehoshaphat is the name of the following individuals: (i) a secretary during the time of David and Solomon (2

Judged";[10] "Shiphtan," meaning "Their Judgment, Most Just Judge" (Num. 34:24); and "Shaphatiah," meaning "Yahweh's Judge, Yahweh is the Judge, Yahweh is the Defender."[11]

2. The Hebrew root *din* and its derivatives

(1) Hebrew root "din"

"Din" has the basic meaning of "to judge" and is used synonymously with shapat (Ps. 9:8[9]; Prov. 31:9). "din" is used 24 times in the Old Testament as a verb (23 times in Hebrew, 1 time in Aramaic),[12] and 24 times as a real noun. While "shapat" refers predominantly to acts of mediation and judicial decisionmaking, "din" is more narrowly associated with formal legal processes wherein authoritative and binding decisions are rendered during litigation.

1) Human acts of judgment

Eleven of the occurrences of "din" in verb form relate to human judgment. The most common

---

Sam. 8:16; 20:24; 1 Kings 4:3; 2 Chron. 18:15); (ii) one of the twelve deputies appointed by Solomon (1 Kings 4:17; cf. verse 7); (iii) the fourth king of Judah (c. 873-849 BC) (2 Chron. 17:2; 18:1; 20:32; 1 Kings 22:42), whose name in Greek is rendered as "Josaphat" (Ιωσαφατ, Matthew 1:8); and (iv) the father of King Jehu of Israel (2 Kings 9:2; 14:20).

10 Shaphat is the name of the following individuals: (i) one of the twelve spies sent by Moses to explore the land of Canaan (Num. 13:5); (ii) the father of Elisha the prophet (1 Kings 19:16, 19; 2 Kings 3:11; 6:31); (iii) among the descendants of Judah, the youngest son of Shemaiah, belonging to a line of David (1 Chron. 3:22); (iv) the chief of the Gadite clan residing in Bashan (1 Chron. 5:12); and (v) the son of Adlai who was responsible for overseeing David's herds (1 Chron. 27:29).

11 Shaphatiah is the name of the following individuals: (i) a son of David through Abital (2 Sam. 3:4; 1 Chron. 3:3); (ii) one of the warriors from Benjamin who joined David at Ziklag (1 Chron. 12:5); (iii) an officer appointed by David over the Simeonites (1 Chron. 27:16); (iv) a son of Jehoshaphat, king of Judah; (2 Chron. 21:2); (v) the son of Mattan, who was involved in throwing the prophet Jeremiah into a cistern during the time of King Zedekiah (Jer. 38:1); (vi) an ancestor of 372 people who returned from Babylon with Zerubbabel and were among the returned exiles (Ezra 2:4; Nehemiah 7:9), as well as of 81 people who returned with Ezra (Ezra 8:8); (vii) an official of Solomon whose descendants returned from Babylon with Zerubbabel and served King Solomon (Ezra 2:57; Neh. 7:59); (viii) an ancestor of the dwellers in Jerusalem from the tribe of Benjamin after the exile (1 Chron. 9:8); and (ix) an ancestor of the people from the tribe of Judah who settled in Jerusalem after the exile (Neh. 11:4). See T.M. Mauch, 'Shephatiah', *The Interpreter's Dictionary of the Bible*, ed. G. A. Buttrick (New York/ Nashville: Abingdon Press, 1962), 323-324.

12 The Aramaic verb "to judge" (!yDI, Dîn) appears once in the decree issued by King Artaxerxes of Persia (Ezra 7:25). The Aramaic noun form is used a total of six times, with five instances in singular form (Dînâ, "judgment," Ezra 7:26; Dîn, "justice", Dan. 4:34; dînä', "judicial gathering," Dan. 7:10, 22, 26), and the plural form (dayyänîn, "judges") used once in Ezra 7:25.

usages are in relation to the following acts occurring in the context of defending the rights of the socially disadvantaged or oppressed: prayer (Ps. 72:2; cf. verse 4); warning and caution (Jer. 21:12; Prov. 31:9); praise (Jer. 22:16); and condemnation (Jer. 5:28). To truly know God is to defend the poor and the needy (Jer. 22:16).[13]

2) Divine acts of judgment

Thirteen of the occurrences of "din" in verb form are used in connection with God's judgment and reign (creation, Job 36:31; all the world, Ps. 9:8[9], 50:4, 96:10, 110:6; Egypt, Gen. 15:14). God is a righteous judge (Ps. \7:9, 11 [10, 12]; 9:8[9]; 50:6; 96:13). The psalmist prays that God will save him according to his righteousness and integrity (Ps. 7:8[9]).

Since God's judgment entails punishment for foreign nations and the wicked, and protection and help for his faithful people, "It is noteworthy that God appears only as One who has the function of a merciful judge over individuals. Yahweh judges in the sense of helping and defending (Deut. 32:36; Ps. 135:14), and also in the sense of punishing (Isa. 3:13ff, Ps. 50:4)."[14]

(2) Judgement—"din"

1) Human judicial activity

Rulers were to take care of the vulnerable members of society including disabled persons (Jer. 22:16; Prov. 31:5, 8). At times, the wicked neglected to fulfill this mandate (Isa. 10:2; Jer. 5:28; Prov. 29:7). The king is to sit on the throne of judgment and preside over sweeping away all wickedness (Prov. 20:8).

2) God's judicial activity

God's "judgment" ("din") is paired with "justice" ("mishpat") (Ps. 9:4[5]; 140:12[13]). Therefore, all the saints are to praise God for their salvation, which will be effected through the proclamation of God's judgment (Ps. 76:8-9[9-10]).

(3) Judge—"dayan"

"Dayan" appears twice in Hebrew, to refer to God as the Judge. David prayed that God would be the Judge and deliver him from Saul's hands (1 Sam. 24:15), and confessed that God is the Judge

---

13 Richard Schultz, '*din*', *NIDOTTE* 1:939.

14 Hamp and Botterweck, 191.

who protects the rights of orphans and widows (Ps. 68:5).

(4) "din" in Genesis

God proclaimed that He would deliver Abram's descendants out of Egypt by "punishing" ("dan") Egypt (Gen. 15:14). The birth of the nation that would act as a conduit for bringing salvation to the world was effected through the judgment of God.

During the patriarchal era, God's judgment was perceived as a means to vindicate the wrongs suffered by an individual and bring solace to the victim. An illustration of this is found in the story of Rachel, who, upon giving birth to a son through her handmaid Bilhah, perceived this event as an instance of God righting her wrong, and named the child "dan", meaning "vindication" (Gen. 30:6; see Gen. 30:25 and 46:23).

Later, the patriarch Jacob utilized wordplay in his blessing for Dan: "dan shall judge his people" (Gen. 49:16). This prophecy saw partial fulfillment through Samson, a judge who ruled over the Israelites, who liberated the Israelites from Philistine oppression (Judg. 15).[15]

Notably, although Aholiab from the tribe of Dan played a crucial role (alongside Bezalel) in crafting the tabernacle and its furniture during the Exodus (Ex. 31:6; 36:1), the tribe had fallen to apostasy by the age of the Judges (Judg. 18:30-31). This decline continued under the rule of Jeroboam, founder of the Northern Kingdom of Israel, who installed golden calves in Bethel and Dan (1 Kings 12:28-29). The tribe of Dan was omitted from the roster of the twelve tribes comprising the 144,000 in the Book of Revelation (Rev. 7:5-8).[16]

Dinah, meaning "Justice," was the daughter of Jacob and Leah, and is the one of Jacob's daughters whose name is recorded in the Bible (Gen. 30:21). While the Bible does not include any explanation of her name, but her brothers Simeon and Levi punished the Shechemites by the sword, as judgment for the shame these people had brought on Dinah (Gen. 34).

(5) Names reflecting "din"

The Hebrew names that reflect the word "*din*" ("judgment") are as follows: Daniel ([add

15 Sarna, 340.

16 Revelation chapter 7 excludes the tribe of Dan from the twelve tribes of Israel, while including Joseph and his two sons, Manasseh. However, Ephraim is excluded. In Ezekiel's vision of the restored kingdom, Dan is included (Ezek. 48:2).

Hebrew, Däniyyë́l], "God is My Judge," "My Judge is God");[17] Dan Jaan, "Judge of the Forest," used as the name of a geographical location, Sam. 24:6); Dan, "Judgment," "One Who Judges," Gen. 30:1-6); Danite, "To Judge," "Judge," Judg. 13:2; 18:1, 11; 1 Chron. 12:35); Dannah, "You Have Judged," "Judgment," used as the name of a geographical location, Josh. 15:49); Dinah ("Judged," "defended," "Justice," Gen. 30:21; 34:1, 3); Middin, "From Judgment," "To Judge," used as the name of a geographical location, Josh. 15:61); Midian, "Quarrel," "One Who Quarrels," Gen. 25:2; 1 Chron. 1:32); Abidan, "Father Judges," "My Father Judges," Num. 1:11; 2:22; 7:60-65); Abdon, Arduous Slavery," "Judge," "Service of Judgment" or "Faithful Servant," "service");[18] Jadon, "He Whom God Will Judge," "He Who Governs," "He Who Stays," "He Will Fight (Judge)", Neh. 3:7); and Hashbadana, "Reason," "Thought During Judgment," "Wise Judge," "Thought," Neh. 8:4).

3. Hebrew root *rib* and its derivatives

(1) Basic meaning of "rib"

The basic meaning of "rib" is "to quarrel, to dispute" (Gen. 26:20-22; Num. 20:3; Deut. 33:7, 8) or "be involved in judicial proceedings" (Isa. 3:13; Jer. 2:9; Hos. 4:4; Ps. 74:22). Derivatives include "rib" ("quarrel, controversy, litigation," Gen. 13:7; Ex. 17:7; 23:3, 6; Deut. 1:12); "yarib" ("one who quarrels," Ps. 35:1; Isa. 49:25; Jer. 18:19); and Meribah (müríbâ, "quarrel," Gen. 13:8; Num. 20:13, 24; Ps. 81:8).

Although the term is mainly used in association with quarrels and litigation among human beings, the term is deployed in the Prophets to depict God reasoning with his people in a trial setting and pronouncing judgment on them (Jer. 2:5-9; Hos. 2:4-25; 4:1-3; Mic. 6:1-8).[19] God judges Israel,

---

17 Daniel is the name of the following individuals: (i) the second son of David and the firstborn of Abigail (1 Chron. 3:1; cf. 2 Sam. 3:3, where he is referred to as "Chileab"); (ii) a priest and a descendant of Ithamar (Ezra 8:2; Neh. 10:6); and (iii) the author of the Book of Daniel, which records events during the Babylonian exile. This last Daniel was a Jewish political figure in the Babylonian palace, a prophet, and a wise man (Dan. 1:6, 21).

18 The name "Abdon" has various references: (i) the son of Hillel who served as a judge of Israel for eight years (Judg. 12:13-15); (ii) a chief of the Benjaminite tribe who resided in Jerusalem (1 Chron. 8:23, 28); (iii) the eldest son of Jeiel, a Benjamite from Gibeon (1 Chron. 8:30; 9:36); and (iv) the son of Micah (2 Chron. 34:20). Additionally, Abdon is the name of one of the four cities given to the Levites from the tribe of Asher after the conquest of Canaan (Josh. 21:30).

19 The term "prophetic lawsuit" was in the past used as a technical term to describe the disputes between God and

but He is also the One who forgives, heals, and offers mercy (Ps. 103:9; Isa. 57:16). Because He is the one who defends his people in judgment, the Israelites likewise have the duty to defend the vulnerable in trial (Ex. 23:6; Isa. 1:17, 23; Prov. 23:1), and Israel may place its hope in God and plead for salvation (Isa. 49:25; Mic. 7:9; Ps. 35:1; 43:1; 119:154). "Yahweh is the judge and the defendant's counsel, and he is both the prosecutor and the attorney."[20]

(2) "Rib" in Genesis

"Rib" is used in Genesis mostly in connection with disputes that relate to a nomadic setting.

For instance, there was a quarrel between Abram's and Lot's shepherds over the pasture ("rib", Gen. 13:7; "meribah", Gen. 13:8), which dispute was resolved when Abram gave Lot priority to decide where to go. Isaac named the wells he had dug Esek, Sitnah, and Rehoboth respectively, based on his quarrel with the surrounding Canaanites (Gen. 26:20, 21, 22). Jacob was angry with Laban for pursuing him and "rebuked" him (wayyäreb Gen. 31:36). He defended the intervention of God, the righteous Judge, by pointing to his faithful service to Laban during the past twenty years and to Laban's unjust act of changing Jacob's wages ten times (Gen. 31:38-42).

(3) Names reflecting "rib"

The names that reflect "rib" are as follows: Riblah ("The Battle is Over", "Multitude of People" , Num. 34:11; 2 Kings 23:29-35; 25:6, 20, 21; Jer. 39:5); Meribah ("Waters of Contention," Ex. 17:7; Num. 20:13, 24); and Meribah Kadesh ("Kadesh = Consecrated, Sanctified," Num. 27:14; Deut. 32:51; Ezek. 47:19; 48:28).

Israel depicted in the prophetic writings, but is now widely contested and challenged. John M. Bracke, 'rib', *NIDOTTE* 3:1107.

20 Hasel, 'Divine Judgment', 817.

Chapter 12 | Events and Procedures of Judgment in Genesis

The book of Genesis contains well-known judgment accounts such as the Fall of Man (Gen. 3), the story of Cain and Abel (Gen. 4), the Flood (Gen. 6-9), the Tower of Babel (Gen. 11), and the destruction of Sodom and Gomorrah (Gen. 18-19). Why did these judgments occur? Is it possible to reconcile judgment with a loving God? Can we find God's grace in the context of judgment?

The judgment accounts in Genesis reveal a common pattern of judicial procedure, the understanding of which helps us to better understand the truth of the investigative judgment that will precede Christ's Second Coming. It is through these procedures of judgment that we discover the exquisite harmony between God's love and justice.

1. Common pattern of judicial procedure

	Period of Grace	Crime	Investigation	Sentencing	Enforcement	Mitigation
Adam	Gen. 2:7-25	Gen. 3:1-7	Gen. 3:8-13	Gen. 3:14-19	Gen. 3:22-24	Gen. 3:20-24
Cain	Gen. 4:1-7	Gen. 4:8	Gen. 4:9-10	Gen. 4:11-12	Gen. 4:16	Gen. 4:13-15,17
Flood	Gen. 6:1, 3	Gen. 6:2, 4	Gen. 6:5-12	Gen. 6:13-22	Gen. 7:1-24	Gen. 8:1-9:19
Tower of Babel	Gen. 11:1-2	Gen. 11:3-4	Gen. 11:5-6	Gen. 11:7	Gen. 11:8-9	Gen. 12:1-3
Sodom and Gomor-rah	Gen. 18:22-33; 19:1-3	Gen. 19:4-11	Gen. 18:20-21; 19:1-11	Gen. 19:12-22	Gen. 19:23-28	Gen. 19:29

The common pattern of judicial procedure found in Genesis consists of (i) a period of grace, (ii) commission of the crime, (iii) investigation, (iv) the sentence, (v) enforcement, and (vi) mitigation measures.[1] This can be diagrammed as follows.

1 Ever since Skinner identified the common pattern of "sin-investigation-judgment" in the judgment scenes of Genesis chapters 3 and 4, theologians have recognized a common pattern of judgment within the stories of Genesis 1-11. From a traditional-historical perspective, Von Rad proposed the sequence "sin-divine judgment-

2. The Fall of humanity

(1) Period of grace

Genesis 2 portrays humanity's special favor from God. He provided an idyllic environment for humans to lead joyful lives, alongside a companion (Gen. 2:8-15, 18-25). Two significant trees stood in the heart of the garden—the Tree of Life and the Tree of the Knowledge of Good and Evil—each signifying vital aspects of human existence (Gen. 2:9). The Tree of Life underscored that human immortality is not innate, but rather a gift bestowed by God in his grace. The Tree of the Knowledge of Good and Evil taught that authentic wisdom and the essence of human life, grounded in reason and spirituality, stem from the reverence of Yahweh.

"The Lord [Yahweh] God commanded the man" (Gen. 2:16). As the lawgiver who brought forth order in the material realm during creation,[2] God likewise ordained a spiritual and moral framework within the human sphere through the Tree of the Knowledge of Good and Evil. God's directive in Eden signifies the establishment of a structured society, where his command governs and guides the inhabitants of this harmonious setting.[3]

Adam and Eve once enjoyed unbroken communion with God. Through the seventh-day Sabbath, which God blessed and sanctified, humanity worshiped and communed with Him (Gen. 2:1-3). Eden, depicted in Genesis 2, holds the imagery of a sacred sanctuary. In Genesis 3:8, the verb "mithallek" ("walking"), which is a participle of hitpael of the Hebrew word "halak" ("to walk"), is used to portray God's presence moving through the garden; this is resonant of later depictions of God's presence in the tabernacle, where the verb is used (Lev. 26:12; Deut. 23:15[14]; 2 Sam. 7:6-7).[4]

Mankind, situated in Eden, held a priestly role, serving God as his consecrated priests. In Genesis 2:15, they "worked" ("work, serve") and "took care of" ("keep, observe"] the garden, and the terms

---

divine forgiveness or mitigation," while Clines, from a literary-critical standpoint, suggested "sin-Word-mitigation-punishment," and Mauldin argued for "sin-judgment-forgiveness." Clines, 61-63; Frank L. Mauldin, 'Singularity and a Pattern of Sin, Punishment, and Forgiveness: [Tower of Babel; Gen 3-11],' *Perspectives in Religious Studies 10* (1983): 42; G. von Rad, *Genesis: A Commentary*, ed. Peter Ackroyd et al., The Old Testament Library (Philadelphia, PA: Westminster Press, 1972), 152-155; John Skinner, *A Critical and Exegetical Commentary on Genesis*, 2nd ed., The International Critical Commentary on the Holy Scriptures of the Old and New Testaments, vol. 1 (Edinburgh: T. & T. Clark, 1930), 100.

2 Wenham, *Genesis* 1-15, 38.

3 John E. Hartley, 'hwc', *TWOT 757.*

4 Wenham, 'Sanctuary Symbolism in the Garden of Eden Story', 19-25; Wenham, Genesis 1-15, 76; Edward J. Young, *Genesis 3: A Devotional & Expository Study* (London: Banner of Truth Trust, 1966), 74.

used are often used elsewhere in the Bible to describe priestly duties.[5] It was for the restoration of the lost Eden that God raised Israel to be a nation of priests and a holy people in the Old Testament (Ex. 19:6), and established the church to serve as a royal priesthood and a holy nation in the New Testament (1 Peter 2:9; Revelation 1:6; 5:10). When our Edenic home is ultimately restored, God and his Lamb will establish their throne among humanity, with the redeemed serving as priests (Rev. 22:3).[6]

(2) Crime

The transgression detailed in Genesis 3:1-7 constituted a rebellion against God's divine authority, marking a rupture in their relationship and a challenge to God's merciful nature. This act was not born of ignorance but rather stemmed from ingratitude. Our first parents rejected their close communion with a compassionate God and renounced their very origin by breaking the covenant of creation. Because their action amounted to a repudiation of the creation, which was the foundation of their existence, humanity was thrust into the realm of uncreation upon the moment of sin.

Adam and Eve, in their newfound awareness of their nakedness, recognized this profound shift in the fundamental fabric of human existence (Gen. 3:7). Indeed, the exposure of nakedness stood in contrast to the role of a priest, where modesty was paramount (Ex. 20:26; Lev. 6:10).

(3) Investigation

In Genesis 3:8-13, we witness the presence of God within the context of an investigative judgment—a probing inquiry into the transgression of God's law. The once-welcomed and cherished encounters in the divine garden turned into moments of dread for those tainted by sin, compelling them to hide amidst the garden's foliage. God conducted an examination, sequentially investigating Adam, then the woman, and finally the serpent. While the serpent, unaware of its wrongdoing, was exempt, both Adam and the woman were questioned by God.

"Where are you?" (Gen. 3:9). Through this question, God summoned Adam before the Judge. Two individuals had sinned, but God called Adam individually. Each person must stand alone before God's judgment.

"I heard you in the garden, and I was afraid because I was naked; so I hid" (Gen. 3:10). The personal nature of Adam's response is reflected in his use of "I...". The Hebrew text emphasizes

---

5 In relation to the service of the Levites and priests at the tabernacle, the term `ābad is used in instances including Num. 3:7-8; 4:23, 30, 47; 8:11, 19, while šāmar is used in instances including Num. 1:53; 3:7, 8, 32; 8:26; 18:3.

6 The term latreuō in Revelation 22:3 refers to the religious service carried out by priests as servants of God.

God's voice by using the word "kolka," meaning "Your voice." This highlights the intimate "I-you" relationship between humankind and God.

Human beings bear responsibility with respect to their relationship with God. This foundational connection serves as the wellspring of all relationships. When this vital relationship becomes weakened, it triggers a spiritual crisis. Adam heard the voice of God (*šäma'Tî*, "I heard"). Awareness of God's presence triggered recognition of his state of disobedience,[7] and instead of approaching God with reverent worship, he fled, gripped by fear. The Hebrew verb "yareh" for "to be afraid," signifies both fear and reverence, and is sometimes used to describe the profound respect and love a righteous individual holds for God (Gen. 22:12, 42:18, Ex. 1:17, Deut. 5:29). This same sentiment is invoked in the context of the judgment preceding the Second Coming, where humanity is called upon to fear and give glory to God the Creator (Rev. 14:7).

"And He said, 'Who told you that you were naked? Have you eaten from the tree that I commanded you not to eat from?'" (Gen. 3:11). Adam had of his own accord become conscious of his nakedness. Personal recognition of sin is important, and Adam, having experienced God's love, should have responded by confessing his sin, not by hiding. Although he tried to evade the core issue, God went straight to the point and raised the issue of "the tree". God sees the heart of all things. "The tree" was a touchstone for determining obedience and disobedience. The investigation was aimed at elucidating whether or not Adam had obeyed, but instead of confessing his sin, Adam responded defensively, deflecting blame onto both the woman and God. "The woman you put here with me— she gave me some fruit from the tree, and I ate it" (Gen. 3:12). Adam once rejoiced in God's gift of the woman, but after the transgression, he held her accountable and even implicated God, who had blessed their union. Adam should have heeded God's command regarding the tree instead of his wife's persuasion. He sidestepped his clear responsibility and assumed the role of a victim of circumstance. Similarly, Eve shifted blame onto the serpent; although she (unlike Adam) did not invoke God in her response, the Bible is clear that the serpent was among God's creation (Gen. 3:1).

"Then the Lord [Yahweh] God said to the woman, 'What is this you have done?'" (Gen. 3:13). The Hebrew term for "What is this..." is "mah," meaning "what, how, why." In this context, it signifies an inquiry aimed at comprehending the precise nature of the event. By seeking clarity regarding the essence of the matter, God unveiled the underlying historical truth that serves as the

7 The Hebrew term 'šäma' means not only "to hear" (Gen. 3:10; 27:6; Isa. 1:6) but also "to obey" (Gen. 22:18; Ex. 24:7). Humans are meant to obey God's word as they hear it.

origin of sin.[8]

"The serpent deceived me, and I ate" (Gen. 3:13). "hissi," the hiphil form of the verb, means "to deceive." Jesus spoke of the devil who deceived humanity and led them to death, declaring, "He was a murderer from the beginning...a liar and the father of it" (John 8:44). Behind the serpent stands Satan, the cunning deceiver, who was judged through the serpent's condemnation. Drawing on the paradigm of Adam's fall, Paul confessed, "For sin, taking occasion by the commandment, deceived me and by it killed me" (Rom. 7:8).[9]

The Hebrew term "zot," rendered as "this" in God's query in Genesis 3:13, is the pivotal word in Genesis 2:23. A profound contrast emerges when these two verses are juxtaposed. The woman, who had been God's gift to Adam and the object of Adam's admiration and gratitude, had now become responsible for the introduction of unhappiness and death into the world.[10] Whereas Genesis 2:23 brims with Adam's delight in the precious gift of a companion, Genesis 3:13 reveals God's agonizing awareness of the grievous implications of their transgressions.[11]

(4) Sentencing

Genesis 3:14-19 contains God's judgment sentence. Examining the progression from investigation to judgment, the investigation unfolds in the sequence of "Adam-woman-serpent," while the sentence is pronounced in the order of "serpent-woman-Adam." This literary structure underscores the proto-evangelium (original gospel) embedded within the serpent's sentence. Even amid the pronouncement of judgment, God's salvific intent radiates.

"Because you have done this" (Gen. 3:14) indicates that the reason for judgment is works. The term "cursed" may be regarded as a word play on the term "cunning" (*arûm*).[12] This play of language highlights a fundamental damage to God's exceedingly good creation. While mankind sinned, it was the serpent and the earth that were cursed, not mankind. Humanity has never been

---

8 Lange, 232.

9 Romans 7:11 combines the themes of the deception of Satan in Genesis 3:13 and the death resulting from disobeying the command regarding the Tree of the Knowledge of Good and Evil in Genesis 2:17, to present a message regarding Paul's own experience. Paul uses the compound verb *exapataö*, "to deceive") in 2 Corinthians 11:3 and 1 Timothy 2:14, applying the ancestral failing to the circumstances of his time. See Collins, *Genesis 1-4: A Linguistic, Literary, and Theological Commentary*, 152, n.12.

10 Mathews, *Genesis* 1-4:26, 242.

11 Goldingay, 138.

12 Mathews, *Genesis* 1-4:26, 244.

subject to a curse; rather, it is the object of salvation. The Hebrew word "arar ", meaning "to curse," refers to the act by one with authority of incapacitating one of a lower rank by surrounding the latter with barriers. In Genesis 3:14 and 17, the curse signifies being banished or excommunicated from other animals, as well as the earth being cursed because of the serpent, resulting in reduced yield for humans.[13] The serpent, who arrogantly defamed God and corrupted man, became the lowliest beast, crawling on the ground.[14] Mankind was assigned the pain of childbirth, arduous labor, and the fate of returning to dust through death.

To the Jewish people, Genesis 3:15 serves as the promise of the Messiah; to Christians, it encapsulates the first promulgation of the gospel, also known as the "proto-evangelium." This passage indirectly foreshadows the incarnation and virgin birth of Jesus Christ. In the very moment when the serpent deceived Eve, instigating the fall of humanity, a curse was placed upon Satan that would ultimately bring about his defeat. The seed of the woman would bruise the serpent's head (Gen. 3:15). The divine revelation from God would shine ever more brightly throughout the ages, guiding all of humanity towards the radiant era of Jesus Christ, often referred to as the "sun of righteousness" (Mal. 4:2); in the meantime, pending a more comprehensive revelation, Satan came to perceive every child born of a woman as a potential threat.[15]

Genesis 3:15 presents human history within the framework of the great controversy between good and evil. The Bible vividly illustrates the monumental conflict between God and Satan; in this context, humanity is embroiled in a supernatural spiritual warfare in which there is a sharp delineation between God's camp and Satan's realm. This great controversy between good and evil stands distinct from the eternal dualism of good and evil as presented in Zoroastrianism, where neither force prevails unequivocally. Moreover, there is no need for us to be pessimistic regarding the ultimate outcome, in contrast to what was believed in Norse theology in the past. We can have confidence in God's triumph, assured by the promise in Genesis 3:15. With this understanding, we find encouragement knowing that those who opt for the truly human path—the path aligned with God's will for man—will ultimately emerge victorious over Satan.[16]

---

13 'arr', *TWOT*.

14 "You shall eat dust" (Gen. 3:14) does not mean that the serpent actually eats dust for sustenance. Rather, it refers to falling into a state of lowly humiliation and disgrace before one's enemies (see Ps. 72:9; Isa. 49:23; Mic. 7:17). Wenham, *Genesis 1-15*, 79. In the myth of the goddess Ishtar (deity of fertility, love, and war in Assyrian and Babylonian mythology) descending into the underworld, the cursed people are described as having dust as their portion and mud as their food. SDABC 1:232.

15 Flint, 43.

16 Waltke and Yu, *An Old Testament Theology: An Exegetical, Canonical, and Thematic Approach*, 265.

(5) Enforcement and mitigation

Genesis 3:22-24 portrays the execution of God's judgment, with God Himself as the agent of judgment. Notably, the expulsion of Adam and Eve is specified using the term "him" (*hû*) in Genesis 3:23. This masculine pronoun refers to Adam. As a result of this judgment, Adam was banished from the Garden of Eden, where he had once dwelt, to labor and cultivate the land (*ha adama*), from which he had been formed (Gen. 3:23; cf. Gen. 3:19; 2:7). As the result of their actions, humanity was condemned to live a life separated from the Tree of Life, in which they would toil all of their days and ultimately die and turn back to dust.

Yet, in Genesis 3:19-24, the profound grace of God continues to shine amid his stern judgment. Adam clung to the hope of regaining eternal life through the prophesied seed of the woman, as foretold in Genesis 3:15, and named his wife "Hawah", signifying "life." God's graciousness is further evident through the provision of garments made from animal skins, which resulted from the initial animal sacrifice. This act not only covered the physical nakedness of Adam and Eve but also symbolically concealed their spiritual shame and sins, by pointing to the redemptive work of Jesus Christ, the Lamb of God, who would take upon Himself the sin of the world (Gen. 3:21; cf. John 1:29; Isa. 61:10).

The forefathers of humanity were cast out of Eden with the precious promise of the coming Redeemer—the seed of the woman—in their hearts. Even in the bitter aftermath of their expulsion from Eden, enduring in their hearts was a radiant hope. In describing God's command to have humankind "till" (*abad*, Gen.3:23) the ground from which they were taken, his "placing" (*sakan*) of cherubim at the east of the Garden of Eden to "guard" (*samar*]) it, Genesis uses language that is reminiscent of the sanctuary system. Labor and worship served as a path for human restoration, paving the way for humankind to find its way back to God.

3. Cain and Abel

(1) Period of grace

Outside of Eden, Adam and his wife were blessed with sons, Cain and Abel (Gen. 4:1-2). Eve, who had played a part in their expulsion from paradise, emerged as the mother of all the living through God's unique grace. When she welcomed her firstborn, she recalled God's promise regarding the seed of the woman, and exclaimed, "I have acquired a man from the Lord" (Gen. 4:1). Despite humanity's loss of access to the tree of life and their ejection from Eden, God did not withdrawl the foundational blessing to be fruitful and multiply (Gen. 1:28).

The name "Cain" (*qayin*) signifies "to obtain." Eve's choice of words—using the name "man" (*îš*) rather than "son" (*ben*)—is deliberate. The term "ish" (*ʾîš*) conveys her joy at giving birth to a being that is of the same kind as Adam (Gen. 2:23-24), who was the sole man before the fall—in effect, a new Adam. However, when she gave birth to her second child, her sentiment was different. Living in a world tainted by sin had left her with a sense of emptiness, and rather than choosing a name that reflected the expectation of God's promise regarding the seed of the woman, she named this son Abel, which translates to "breath, vanity, vaporous gas" (Gen. 4:2).

"In the process of time" (Gen. 4:3) denotes "at the end of the days" and refers to a substantial span of time.[17] Time had advanced, giving rise to ample opportunities for mankind to acquire how to serve God through labor and worship. Adam and Eve's children had learned from their parents, who had had direct communion with God, about the Creation and the Fall, the plan of salvation and worship, and had opportunity to establish their own, personal faith. Now, the day had arrived when their spiritual condition would be tested through their participation in the sacrificial system.

The expression found in Genesis 4:4-5, depicting God's acceptance or rejection of the sacrifice, emphasizes that God's paramount focus is on the worshiper rather than the offered gift (*minhâ*, "gift, offering"). his true desire is for worshippers who approach Him in spirit and truth (John 4:23-24). The offerings themselves serve as visible reflections of the worshiper's inner disposition.

Cain's presentation of produce as a sacrifice reflects his arrogant dismissal of God's provision for forgiveness and salvation through the shedding of atoning blood. In contrast, Abel's offering of an animal signifies his humble embrace of the eternal truth of atonement (see Leviticus 17:11, Hebrews 9:22, and Romans 5:9).

Cain, as the progenitor of a works-based religious perspective relying on personal merits for acceptance, eventually stumbled over the divine instruction to choose righteousness and rule over sin. Tragically, he succumbed to active opposition against God and submitted to the dominion of sin (Gen. 4:7).

(2) Crime

According to the account recorded in Genesis, the conversation between God and Cain remains unresolved. Cain apparently does not respond to God's inquiry, and his words directed at Abel are

17 For the usage of "yamim" (plural of "yom", "days") to denote the passage of time, see Gen. 40:4; Num. 9:19, 20, 22.

not recorded. The account depicts a fractured and severed web of relationships, and the pace of the narrative intensifies, hastening toward the tragic culmination: the fratricidal act of murder.[18]

Genesis 4:8 succinctly depicts Cain's murder of his brother Abel as follows: "Now Cain talked with Able his brother." Cain may have employed deceitful words to lure Abel into a false sense of security, or resorted to malicious accusations and falsehoods. "[W]hen they were in the field." Cain found a secluded location wherein to perpetrate his crime without having to worry about interference. "Cain rose up against Abel his brother and killed him." This was the first martyrdom of God's faithful in the hands of the wicked (cf. Mark 23:35). This heart wrenching event etched an indelible lesson in our first parents' heart—that the wages of sin are undeniably death.

(3) Investigation

God visited Cain. To his question, "Where is Abel your brother?", Cain retorted, "I do not know. Am I my brother's keeper?" (Gen. 4:9). Evidencing his fractured relationship with God, Cain resorted to falsehoods and adopted an attitude that utterly rejected the ethical obligations that God had ordained within human society.

This had been the perfect crime, with no witnesses. The perpetrator did not have any glimmer of remorse and refused to accept responsibility. In this situation, God Himself came forward as the witness. "What have you done?" God was the unseen observer of this heartrending tableau. "The voice of your brother cries out to Me from the ground" (Gen. 4:10).[19] The Hebrew phrasing does not depict a mere mechanical inquiry or factual pronouncement; rather, it resonates as a poignant exclamation, resounding with God's anguish and emotion.[20]

God endures profound anguish whenever his creation sins. In the face of innocent suffering and untimely demise, He assumed the role of the "blood avenger" (*Goel hadam*) (Num. 35:19-21)—a champion of righteousness, a vindicator of justice. To the lonely martyr, God takes on the mantle of the nearest kinsman, the "go'el."[21]

---

18 Kok, 156.

19 In Genesis 4:10, Able's blood is written using the plural form, "the bloods of your brother". In Hebrew, the blood of animals is always in the singular *dam*, while for humans, the singular form is used to refer to blood in the natural state while the plural form is used for bleeding. Waltke and O'Connor, *An Introduction to Biblical Hebrew Syntax*, 120. See 2 Kings 9:26; Isa. 26:21.

20 The interrogative particle "ma" ("what? how? why") and the "kol" ("sound") at the beginning of the sentence are used to convey surprise. See GKC §146.1.b., §148.b.

21 The responsibility for avenging blood lay with the next of kin (often the victim's son), but when the next of kin lacked the ability or willingness to fulfill this duty towards the victim, God intervened. In cases of unintentional

(4) Sentencing

"So now you are cursed from the earth, which has opened its mouth to receive your brother's blood from your hand" (Gen. 4:11). Cain's act of murder is unequivocally pronounced. The earth is anthropomorphically portrayed, its mouth imagined as opening to receive the spilled blood of the slayer. Just as Adam's transgression ushered in a curse upon the land, so too did Cain's heinous deed defile the very earth.

Cain's sentence is two-fold: he is not only barred from the land that once sustained him but is also thrust away from the geographical heart of his occupation (Gen. 4:12). The phrase "a fugitive and a vagabond" is a Hebrew participle consisting of two similarly sounding syllables conjoined by a conjunction, and implies "homeless wanderer" (TEV). The term "earth" encompasses the entirety of the planet. The phrase is translated variously, but all encapsulate three key aspects: (i) Cain's future is devoid of a place to call his own, (ii) he is destined to always be on the move, and (iii) he will wander all over the world.[22]

(5) Enforcement

In Genesis 4:16, the account of Cain's banishment is succinctly documented: "Then Cain went out from the presence of the Lord and dwelt in the land of Nod, on the east of Eden." Without remorse or repentence, Cain embarked on a journey eastward, departing from God's presence, and settled in the land of Nod, a place symbolizing wandering and impermanence.[23]

Cain's trajectory diverges from his parents' exile from Eden. While Adam and his wife were sent away by God, Cain takes it upon himself to venture further, seeking to establish a society devoid of God's presence. While his parents had come out of Eden with faith in God in their hearts, Cain forsook his relationship with God, adopting a nomadic existence driven solely by material pursuits.

Cain is referred to in Solomon's Ecclesiastes 10:3 without being mentioned by name: "But when the unrighteous [Cain] departed from her [wisdom] in anger, he also perished in the anger that had slain his brother." Eve was defeated in her search for wisdom outside of God, and Cain was destroyed because he did not listen to God's words and acted according to his own stubbornness,

---

manslaughter, Israel established cities of refuge where the killer could flee to save their life. See Num. 35:12, 22-25; Deut. 19:4-7; Josh. 20:2-3, 5, 9.

22 Reyburn, 116.

23 In English, the term "land of Nod" signifies a place of sleep, which is why the Today's English Version avoids using this expression. Refer to the following for translation issues related to the land of Nod (*'eretz-nôd*). Ibid., 119.

rejecting instruction provided personally by God, the source of wisdom. The New Testament speaks of Cain as belonging to the wicked (1 John 3:12) and puts him at the forefront of the ranks of those who perished, including Balaam and Korah (Jude 1:11).

(6) Mitigation

God granted Cain's plea protesting against the divine verdict. Responding with compassion, God safeguarded Cain's life by bestowing upon him a protective sign and issuing a promise of retribution sevenfold for anyone who might seek to end Cain's life (Gen. 4:13-15). While a possible interpretation could envision the sevenfold vengeance as encompassing the demise of Cain's slayer and six individuals from the perpetrator's kin, that interpretation is not plausible given God's character; rather, the expression is likely a poetic portrayal of God's comprehensive justice, leaving no aspect of retribution unaddressed.[24]

God did not take Cain's life, despite his lack of remorse and his future as the progenitor of a godless society fraught with immense suffering. Instead, God safeguarded Cain, preserving his existence and allowing him to continue experiencing the blessing to be fruitful and multiple.

Tragically, this mercy was later perverted by Lamech, Cain's descendant, who twisted it to justify and exalt his own violent actions, as depicted in Genesis 4:24. This distortion marks the apex of violence within the Cainite lineage, reflecting a deeply troubling trend. This era became defined by escalating violence, a time when retribution becomes customary and God's intervention in judgment becomes imperative.

4. Flood

(1) Period of Grace

The Flood account in Genesis 6–9 begins with the fulfillment of God's blessing: "Now it came to pass, when men began to multiply on the face of the earth" (Gen. 6:1). Although sin entered the earth, God did not remove from man the blessings of fruitfulness and multiplication that He had bestowed upon him in the beginning (Gen. 1:28). When the earth was so filled with sin that it was no longer unacceptable to God, God still granted mankind a period of grace of one hundred and

24 Wenham, *Genesis 1-15*, 109. See Ps. 12:7[6]; 79:12; Prov. 6:31; and Isa. 30:26 regarding the completeness symbolized by the number seven in the Bible.

twenty years (Gen. 6:3). While some interpret this period as a cap on human lifespans,[25] this notion is contradicted by the existence of individuals in Genesis, such as those mentioned in Genesis 11:10-32, who lived beyond this timeframe. Instead, this period serves as a window of opportunity—a temporary reprieve—granted by God to those who faced his impending judgment.[26]

During this time, Noah, a preacher of righteousness, diligently constructed the ark, and God exhibited unwavering patience: "the Divine longsuffering waited in the days of Noah" (1 Pet. 3:20; 2 Pet. 2:5).

(2) Crime

Genesis 6:2 and 4 offer a glimpse into the transgressions prevalent in the pre-Flood era. The "sons of God" were captivated by the allure of the daughters of men, leading them to take wives according to their desires. These unions gave rise to individuals who achieved renown and prominence.

The descendants of Cain had constructed a secular civilization, utilizing force to establish dominance; conversely, the lineage of Seth, born to Adam after Abel's demise, had fostered a faith-based community that invoked the name of Yahweh. As the years passed, however, the righteous descendants of Seth deviated from their spiritual convictions through intermarriage with the wicked descendants of Cain, resulting in a loss of their moral influence in the world. The term "Nephilim" often interpreted as "giants" in English translations, could also signify "those who are depraved," from its association with the term "napal".

These individuals were known for their might and were "men of renown" (Gen. 6:4). The narrative sequencing of the genealogies of Seth (Gen. 4:25-26) and the pre-Flood people (Gen. 6:1-4) emphasizes the exaltation of names, by placing the word "shem" ("name") at the end of section. The once-faithful Sethite community, which had called on the name of Yahweh, now sought to exalt their own names. This elevation of personal fame contributed to an age marred by lawlessness, violence, and sin, overshadowing the exaltation of Yahweh. The decline of the godly lineage ushered in a

---

25 Joseph Blenkinsopp, 'P and J in Genesis 1:1-11:26: An Alternative Hypothesis,' *Fortunate the Eyes That See: Essays in Honor of David Noel Freedman in Celebration of his Seventieth Birthday*, ed. Astrid B. Beck et al.(Grand Rapids, MI: Eerdmans, 1995), 9; Mathews, Genesis 4:27-11:26, 334-335; Laurence A. Turner, *Genesis*, A New Biblical Commentary (Sheffield: Sheffield Academic Press, 2000), 44; Claus Westermann, *Genesis: A Practical Commentary*, Text and Interpretation (Grand Rapids, MI: Eerdmans, 1987), 44.

26 Richard M. Davidson, 'Flood, The,' *Baker Theological Dictionary of the Bible*, ed. Walter A. Elwell (Grand Rapids, MI: Baker Books, 1996), 262; Hamilton, The Book of Genesis: Chapters 1-17, 269; Carl Friedrich Keil and Franz Delitzsch, *Pentateuch*, trans., James Martin, vol. 1 (Grand Rapids, MI: Eerdmans, 1949), 136; E. A. Speiser, *Genesis*, Anchor Bible (Garden City: Doubleday & Co., 1964), 46.

period bereft of hope for moral and spiritual rejuvenation. This verse underscores that the suffering in the world stems not merely from the proliferation of evildoers, but primarily from the apostasy of God's own people.

(3) Investigation

The concept of investigative judgment is evident in Genesis 6:5-12, where the Hebrew verb "ra'ah" ("to see") is used to describe God's observation. In Genesis 6:5, God's "sight" signifies a process of examining the facts and preparing for subsequent action.[27] Faced with the pervasive sinfulness of the world, God made the decision to cleanse his creation through a cataclysmic event.

In this context, Noah emerges as a righteous figure recognized and favored by God within the framework of the investigative judgment. Genesis 6:8 states that Noah found grace in the eyes of the Lord. The use of neo-anthropomorphic expressions such as "see," "lament," and "grieve" in Genesis 6:5-6 emphasizes that God engages in judgment with intellect, emotion, and volition. his judgment is not mechanical; instead, it demonstrates an intelligent understanding of events and a resolute determination to address the situation. God actively evaluates the circumstances and employs his faculties to assess the righteous and the wicked; through this process of investigation, God determines appropriate consequences for the unrighteous and salvation for the righteous.

God's investigative judgment was global. Various expressions in the text emphasize the global scope of this judgment, such as "the earth" (Gen. 6:5, 6, 11), "on the earth" (Gen. 6:7), and "all flesh" (Gen. 6:12, 13).

"Then the Lord saw that the wickedness of man was great in the earth, and that every intent of the thoughts of his heart was only evil continually" (Gen. 6:5). God's original purpose in creating humanity was completely undermined. The pursuit of evil became the prevailing ethos and lifestyle of mankind (Gen. 6:12). The focal point of the investigative judgment centers on the spiritual and moral condition of humanity. The terms used, such as "evil" (Gen. 6:5), "corrupt" (Gen. 6:11, 12), and "violence" (Gen. 6:11), illustrate this deteriorating state.

This feature sets the Genesis Flood account apart from other flood narratives in the ancient Near East. Unlike those accounts, where the gods capriciously decided to annihilate humanity without moral or spiritual justification, the Genesis account highlights the deep moral decay and spiritual degradation that led to divine intervention. For instance, in the Epic of Atrahasis from the High

27 Sarna, 47.

Babylonian period, the gods resolved to exterminate humans due to their "noise." Although some interpretations suggested that this "noise" indicated defiance or rebellion against the gods, recent research suggests it simply referred to the clamor of a growing population, devoid of any moral wrongdoing or political uprising.[28]

The Creator takes center stage in the process of investigative judgment. Statements like "sorry that He had made man on the earth," "I will destroy man whom I have created from the face of the earth," and "I am sorry that I have made them" (Gen. 6:6-7) underscore that the Almighty Creator would now be exercising his sovereign authority for the purpose of uncreation. However, despite the impending judgment that would overturn the work of creation, God's gaze remained fixed on the righteous individuals who8stood apart from the prevailing wickedness. Not one righteous person escaped his notice.

"But Noah found grace in the eyes of the Lord" (Gen. 6:8).

Noah was not a being from the supernatural realm, but a human who led a daily life within a household (Gen. 6:10). Before the Flood judgment, God's grace had readied a righteous and blameless individual of that era to journey with Him.

(4) Sentencing

In Genesis 6:13-22, God's verdict of judgment upon the world was delivered, accompanied by precise instructions to Noah for the construction of the ark, which would serve as a means of salvation for both mankind and various creatures. The proclamation extended to "all flesh" under the heavens and "all flesh in which is the breath of life," (Gen. 6:13, 17). All human beings and all other living entities, save for aquatic life, were destined for obliteration. This proclamation invokes the name of the Elohim, the Creator of the physical universe (Gen. 6:13, 22).

The original Hebrew text underscores "the end" (*qetz*) in the phrase "The end of all flesh has come before Me" (Gen. 6:13). "End" (*qetz*) is an eschatological term and appears for the first time in this verse, receiving very strong emphasis.

---

28 Rainer Albertz, 'Das Motiv für Die Sintflut im Atramhasis-Epos', *Mythos* im *Alten Testament Und Seiner Umwelt: Festschrift für Hans-Peter Muller Zum 65. Geburtstag*, ed. Armin Lange et al., Beihefte Zur Zeitschrift für Die Alttesta mentliche Wissenschaft, 278 (Berlin; New York: Walter de Gruyter, 1999), 9; Richard J. Clifford, 'Review of Mythos im Alten Testament Und Seiner Umwelt: Festschrift Für Hans-Peter Müller Zum 65. Geburtstag by Hans-Peter Muller', *Catholic Biblical Quarterly* 62 (2000): 782; Hans P. Müller, 'Das Motiv für Die Sintflut: Die Hermeneutische Funktion Des Mythos Und Seiner Analyse', *Zeitschrift für die Alttestamentliche Wissenschaft* 97 (1985): 295-316.

During the investigation, God reveals that the judgment of "sweeping away" will take the form of a flood (hammabul) (Gen. 6:17).[29] "Hammabul" does not mean just any flood, but is a technical term that refers to Noah's Flood. Because of the unique and unprecedented of the Great Flood, the author of Genesis divides pre-Abrahamic biblical history based on this event (Gen. 9:28; 10:1, 32; 11:10).

In Psalm 29, written by David around the 10th century B.C., God's judgment against pagan idolatry is linked to the Flood, illustrating God's absolute sovereignty over the entire world (Ps. 29:3, 10). Notably, the locations mentioned in Psalm 29 that are subject to God's judgment lie beyond the borders of Israel. Lebanon and Sirion (also known as Mount Hermon) lie to the north, while the Wilderness of Kadesh refers not to Kadesh Barnea (Num. 13:26; 20:1), in the southern Negev region where the Hebrews wandered during their wilderness journey, but to a region on the eastern side of Mount Lebanon near Syria. This highlights God's role in both protecting his people and punishing idolaters.

When comparing Revelation 13 and 14, it becomes evident that the ultimate beneficiaries of God's eschatological salvation are those who steadfastly resist succumbing to the beast's global coercion to engage in idolatry and instead remain devoted solely to God the Creator. A crucial connection to the account of the Flood in Genesis 7:11 is established in Revelation 14:7, where the phrase "springs of water" is employed, evoking "the fountains of the great deep" in the Genesis narrative (Gen. 7:11).[30]

What a comfort it is for us to realize that embedded within God's judgment sentence is a profound promise of salvation, in the form of the ark of refuge and the covenant of life (Gen. 6:18)! Whereas the declaration of impending destruction is encapsulated in a single verse (Gen. 13), the narrative that follows unfolds to encompass the meticulous construction of the ark and the preparations for salvation (Gen. 6:14-22; see verse 17). God had prepared a way for the salvation of mankind and all other living beings. The destiny of the earth hinged upon the steadfast obedience of

29 The term "hammabbul mayim" ("flood") from Genesis 6:17 is rendered as "floodwaters" in the NKJV and NIV, and by the NASB as "the flood of water." The second term, *mayim*, is seen by Gesenius as a later gloss, while Davidson and Bandstra view it as an apposition and post-modifier respectively, translating "*hammabbul mayim*" as "flood, waters." See GKC §131k n2; Dav §29b; Bandstra, 368.

30 Just as Psalm 29 distinguishes between false worship and true worshipers, the three angels' messages in Revelation 14 distinguish between false worship and true worship based on the worship of the Creator. Such distinctions that take place outside the book of Genesis imply that a significant factor contributing to the flood judgment in Genesis was the corruption of God's people (the descendants of Seth), who had become idolaters. As a primary factor in the suffering of the end times, the apostle Paul pointed to those who love other things more than God, stating, "having a form of godliness but denying its power. And from such people turn away" (2 Tim. 3:5; see 2 Tim. 3:1-4).

Noah, who faithfully heeded and followed each of God's commands (Gen. 6:22).

(5) Enforcement

Genesis 7:1-24 describes the implementation of divine judgment. Prior to the execution of this judgment, God had Noah and his family to find refuge within the ark, and ensured the preservation of the creatures that carry the potential for future life by ushering them into the ark. The sweep of the Flood's devastation encompasses all living beings (Gen. 7:4), emphasizing their divine origin and status as creations of God. This includes the diverse array of creatures that traverse the earth, from birds and cattle to wild animals and humans. "[A]ll flesh...that moved on the earth" (Gen. 7:21), "[a]ll in whose nostrils was the breath of the spirit of life" (Gen. 7:22)—whose survival depended on the mechanisms of life instilled by God—were destroyed. By consistently referring to the beings subject to destruction in connection with the Creator God, the text demonstrates that God's enforcement of his judgment is an act of uncreation of the order of life.

God's instruments for executing judgment included the rain, the flood, the fountains of the great deep, and the windows of heaven (Gen. 7:4, 6, 11). Over the span of forty days and nights, relentless rain cascaded from the heavens, leading the water to reach a staggering height of fifteen cubits above the earth's loftiest peaks. Within this deluge, only Noah and his companions, sheltered within the protective confines of the ark, were able to elude the torrential force of destruction (Gen. 7:12, 17, 19, 20, 24). The mechanics of water's flow, adhering to the gravitational pull from higher to lower elevations, reinforce the portrayal of a worldwide and all-encompassing cataclysmic event.

As the judgment unfolded, Noah's righteousness served as the bedrock of salvation. Amidst the tumultuous upheaval that engulfed the entirety of the heavens and the earth, God provided unwavering protection and guidance to his chosen people by safeguarding the ark within the throes of these extreme conditions.

(6) Mitigation

In the culmination of the Flood account, God's ultimate action is not one of retribution, but of remembrance. "Then God remembered Noah, and every living thing, and all the animals that were with him in the ark" (Gen. 8:1). God remembered! In stark contrast to the feeble deities of the ancient Near East, who were powerless in the face of cataclysmic events, God emerges as a steadfast sanctuary for Noah and every living creature who had been sheltered within the ark amidst the overwhelming deluge.

In the renewed earth, only those who had survived the Flood remained. God blessed them with the ability to multiply and flourish on the newly recreated land (Gen. 8:17; 9:1, 7). Through his act of re-creation, God established a physical environment conducive to the proliferation of his creatures. He achieved this by sending the wind to dissipate the waters (Gen. 8:1), akin to the separation of the waters in the original creation (Gen. 1:2); by having the waters recede (Gen. 8:13, 14), mirroring the division of waters on the earth's surface (Gen. 1:9-10); and by causing plants to grow anew, symbolized by the appearance of an olive leaf (Gen. 8:11), resembling the creation of plant life in the beginning (Gen. 1:11-12). Moreover, God commanded the living creatures to exit the ark (Gen. 8:17), paralleling his mandate for the multiplication of animals in the initial creation (Gen. 1:21-25; 2:19). By instituting the prohibition against murder, God established a moral framework that upholds the sanctity of life. He also provided humanity with a stable and blessed abode by making a covenant never to devastate the earth and its inhabitants again through a flood (Gen. 9:5-6, 8-16). This covenant serves as a divine assurance of safety and continuity for both humans and the natural world.

The pinnacle of the literary composition within the Genesis Flood account is found in Genesis 8:1-5. This section magnificently underscores the central theme of God's salvation during the phase of mitigation.[31] Amidst the cataclysmic deluge, Noah and his fellow occupants of the ark found security and refuge as a result of God's remembrance and care.

Upon recreating the earth, God followed the process of the original creation. The rainbow is a perpetual emblem of God's enduring mindfulness towards his creations (Gen. 9:15, 16).

God laid aside his divine weaponry and suspended a "keshet" ("bow") in the clouds (Gen. 9:13).[32]

5. Babel

The Tower of Babel incident, recounted in Genesis 11:1-9, marked a significant turning point for humanity—the dispersion and confusion of languages. While the Flood judgment reshaped

---

31 Bernhard W. Anderson, 'From Analysis to Synthesis: The Interpretation of Genesis 1-11', *Journal of Biblical Literature* 97 (1978): 23-39; Umberto Cassuto, *A Commentary on the Book of Genesis: Part 2, from Noah to Abraham, Genesis Vi9-Xi32*, trans., Israel Abrahams (Jerusalem: Magnes, 1964), 30-33; Robert E. Longacre, 'The Discourse Structure of the Flood Narrative', *Annual Meeting Seminar Papers, Society of Biblical Literature* (Missoula, MT: Scholars Press, 1976), 235-262; William H. Shea, 'The Structure of the Genesis Flood Narrative and Its Implications', *Origins 6* (1979): 8-29; Gordon J. Wenham, 'Coherence of the Flood Narrative', *Vetus Testamentum* 28 (1978): 336-348.

32 "Keshet" (qešet) means both "bow" and "rainbow."

the physical world, the events in Shinar triggered a profound transformation in the intellectual and cultural realms of human existence, leaving a lasting impact on mankind's history and development.

(1) Period of Grace

Despite the enduring effects of the Flood on the earth's ecosystem (Gen. 8:22), God's promise to humanity to be fruitful, multiply, and fill the earth remains intact (Gen. 1:28; 9:1). Following the Flood, mankind migrated eastward and continued to communicate in a common language that had been shared since creation.

"Shappah" ("language"), originally means "lips." Lips are organs that were created by God and were intended to be used to glorify the Creator. Instead, mankind chose to misuse this very gift and collectively rebel against God.

(2) Crime

The construction of the city and tower on the plain of Shinar is intricately woven with the narrative of mankind's dispersion as depicted in the genealogies of Genesis 10. The builders' intentions were far from virtuous. In their audacity, they sought to defy God's command to scatter and repopulate the earth (Gen. 9:1, 11:4). Much like the people in the days of Noah, their ambitions were geared towards elevating their own name (Gen. 6:4, 11:4). Their aspirations bore a distinctly religious character. The term "Babel," rooted in Akkadian, translates to "Bab-ili" ("Gate of God"), or "Bäb-ilani" ("Gate of the Gods"). The Ziggurats (ziggurratu in Akkadian) were temples that were referred to as the gateways to heaven. These individuals linked their monumental tower to the temple and referred to these structures as "e-temen-an-ki," signifying "house of the foundation of heaven and earth." In their grand design, the builders of Babel sought to position their realm as the epicenter of the entire world.

The builders of Babel distrusted God's promise that He would not destroy the world again with a flood and aspired to build a tower that would reach heaven and protect them from a possible flood. The spirit of Babel is disbelief in God. The execution of such an ambitious construction endeavor naturally necessitated the rise of an authoritarian ruler. The Hebrew term "habah" (Gen. 11:3, 4), often translated as "Come" in English versions of the Bible, carries an undertone of compelling one's will, urging a neighbor to comply with a specific purpose.

At the core of this rebellion stands Nimrod, the grandson of the ungodly Ham and the son of Cuz (Gen. 10:6-12). Nimrod is portrayed as a skilled and fearless hunter who earned distinction before

Yahweh (Gen. 10:9), and he rose to prominence as a builder of an empire, most notably associated with the city of Calah, believed to be represented by the archaeological site Birs Nimrud.

Regarding Nimrod's identity, some consider him as a figure inspired by Mesopotamian deities like Ninurta[33] or Marduk,[34] or akin to legendary heroes of Mesopotamian lore such as Gilgamesh or Lugalbanda. However, the more likely interpretation is that he was an actual historical figure. Potential contenders include Sargon of Agade (ca. 2340-2284 BC); Tukulti-Ninurta I of Assyria (ca. 1234-1197 BC); and Naram-Sin (ca. 2334 to 2154 BC), Sargon I's grandson. Naram-Sin's extensive rule over the Near East during the close of the third millennium BC left behind a rich collection of writings and legendary tales. his titles of "king of the four corners of the world" and "strong man" bear a resemblance to the description of the "mighty one" (*gibbör*) in Genesis 10:8. Naram-Sin's demise is said to have been tragic, attributed to his defiance of the gods. The Hebrew name "Nimrod" (*nimröd*) could potentially be a linguistic play on words, reflecting both "marad" meaning "rebellion" and "Naram-Sin." [35]

(3) Investigation

God Himself intervened in the situation, as depicted in Genesis 11:5. God's immediate assessment is captured through the Hebrew verbs "ra'ah" ("to see") and "yarad" ("descend"), which succinctly convey God's judgment on humanity's audacious pride. Regardless of how high mankind constructs a tower in an attempt to touch the heavens, such endeavors can never elevate them to the realm of God. In fact, the insignificance of these efforts is underscored by the fact that God Himself must descend from his exalted position. This emphasizes the stark contrast between human aspirations and divine reality, highlighting the limitations of human achievements in comparison to the divine nature.

---

33 Ninurta was the god of the ancient city of Nippur, the oldest city of Sumer, and is identified with the deity Ningirsu, the son of the god Enlil. Often depicted with a bow and arrow, sickle and sword, Ninurta is associated with war and agriculture. In Sumerian-Babylonian mythology, Ninurta protects the kings of Assyria in war and hunting; this led Von Soden to identify this god with Nimrod. Richard S. Hess, *Studies in the Person al Names of Genesis 1-11* (Kevelaer: Verlag Butzon & Bercker, 1993), 74.

34 In Sumerian, Amar Utu, meaning "solar calf," was a storm god and the patron deity of Babylon. According to the epic creation poem of the Akkadians, the Enuma Elish (Tablets VI and VII), the gods assigned fifty names to Marduk, in a divine assembly. These names granted him the power to exercise all functions, determining the fate of heaven, earth, the realm of gods, and the world of humans. Benjamin R. Foster, 'Epic of Creation (1.111): Enuma Elish', *The Context of Scripture: Canonical Compositions from the Biblical World*, ed. William W. Hallo et al..(New York: Brill, 1997), 400-401.

35 Sarna, 73.

Through observation and investigation, God affirmed that the current state of human affairs would be lasting (Gen. 11:6). Despite God's efforts, the inherent rebellion against God's authority persisted within the human heart. The shared language among the rebels had facilitated their ability to exert significant influence over humanity, to the extent that if their ambitions are allowed to persist unchecked, it could lead to the eternal destruction of mankind.

(4) Sentencing

The triune God's swift and decisive intervention is aptly captured in the term "Come" (*habà*) in Genesis 11:7. This term paradoxically mirrors the rebels' repeated use of the same term in Genesis 11 verses 3 and 4. This portrayal starkly highlights humanity's direct defiance of God's authority. Despite mankind's audacious confrontation, God's divine will prevails unconditionally in all situations.

The Trinity agreed to confound mankind's language, thereby disrupting communication among the rebels. The Creator, God Himself, who had formed human lips and bestowed language upon them, chose to disrupt the very system of language.

(5) Enforcement

The confusion of languages effectively halted the construction of the rebellious cities, as detailed in Genesis 11:8-9. Consequently, the ambitions described in verses 3-4 were utterly frustrated. In narrating this event, the author of Genesis employed a deliberate play on words. The city's name was changed to Babel, signifying "confusion," rather than retaining the intended "Gate of God" meaning as Bab-ili or "Gate of the Gods" as *Bab-ilani*. Human pride was humbled and brought low.

The Hebrew word for 'to crowd' is 'b'll;b', bälal, the root b-l-l, Gen. 11:7, 9 and the verb is *nablâ*, 'let us congest' in Genesis 11:7, which is the 'rebenim' in Genesis 11:3. *Lebenim* the first three letters of the bricks are written in reverse order. nbl (L-B-N) is inverted to lbn (N-B-L) The main building material of the builders of the city of Babel became completely useless by divine intervention. Even though the whole world opposes God's will, God must fulfill his good will. There can be no force in the entire universe that can stop the progress of God's sovereign work of redemption.

The Hebrew term for "to confuse" is "balal" originated from the root b-l-l; Gen. 11:7, 9). In Genesis 11:7, it was rendered as "na'blah" (*nablâ*), meaning "let us confuse." This relates to the term "lebenim" ("bricks") that was used in Genesis 11:3: The first three letters of the term for "bricks" were reversed, from (l-b-n) to (n-b-l). By divine intervention, the primary building material of the city of Babel was rendered utterly useless. Even in the face of universal opposition to God's will, He remained committed to fulfilling his divine purpose. There exists no power in the entire universe capable of impeding the progress of God's sovereign work of redemption.

(6) Mitigation

In the face of collective rebellion, God chose not to bring harm to human life. Despite their spirit of rebellion, humanity remained the recipient of God's blessing. They were scattered across the earth, in line with the blessings of fruitfulness and multiplication bestowed upon them at the time of creation (Gen. 1:28; 11:9). Amidst a world mired in confusion about God's character, and with mankind seemingly without hope, God intervened by calling Abraham. Immediately after the Babel incident, God's plan unfolded through the genealogy of Shem and Terah, the ancestors of Abraham, who would become the bearer of blessings to all nations (Gen. 10:10-32). While mankind was dispersed, it was not a scattering devoid of hope, for God's divine purpose was still at work.

6. Sodom and Gomorrah

Sodom and Gomorrah were prominent cities of Canaan. These cities, together with Adma and Zeboim, faced divine judgment through the agency of fire, with Sodom particularly serving as their representative (Gen. 10:19; 14:2, 8; Deut. 29:23; Jer. 49:18; 50:40). Positioned in the Jordan plain, Sodom boasted abundant water sources and fertile beauty, reminiscent of the paradise-like Garden of Eden, Yahweh's own garden (Gen. 13:10; cf. Gen. 2:8, 9).

The narrative of God's judgment and subsequent salvation in Sodom holds a broader significance, paralleling themes of the Second Coming as presented in Luke 17:28-29

(1) Period of Grace

The people of Sodom were provided with the opportunity to encounter God's message of salvation through interactions with Abraham and Lot. Lot, a devout man who feared God, resided among them as a resident (Gen. 13:10-13). When Lot was captured during a conflict in which many Sodomites were taken captive, Abraham intervened to rescue his nephew. Abraham led a successful mission to liberate the captives and recover the plunder taken from Sodom and Gomorrah. Despite their wickedness and grave sins (Gen. 13:13), the people of Sodom experienced the grace and salvation of the Almighty God, the Supreme Ruler of the heavens and earth (Gen. 14:19, 22). Even as the sins of the residents of Sodom and Gomorrah reached a point of culmination that warranted impending destruction, Abraham interceded on their behalf (Gen. 18:22-33).

(2) Crime

The depth of the Sodomites' depravity is detailed in Genesis 19. When the two angels of judgment, sent by God, arrived in Sodom, the inhabitants attempted to commit heinous and perverse sexual crimes. In Genesis 19:4, the Sodomite men, referred to in Hebrew as ("men of the city," "men of Sodom"), demonstrated a complete disregard for their moral conscience and failure to recognize the divine nature of the heavenly visitors. They saw the angels only as objects to be subjected to sexual abuse.

Sodom was a dangerous and unwelcoming place for outsiders. When Lot attempted to prevent the Sodomites from harming the heavenly visitors, they responded by saying, "This one came in to stay here, and he keeps acting as a judge; now we will deal worse with you than with them" (Gen. 19:9). This was how they treated Lot, who had been living among them; to whom they owned their lives and property; whose daughters were engaged to be married to Sodomites; and who addressed his fellow Sodomites as "my brethren". Despite his efforts to integrate, Lot's status remained that of a resident foreigner. The Hebrew Scriptures emphasize the phrase "he keeps acting as a judge." This is a significant phrase that links to the theme of divine judgment present in Genesis 18. Lot's role was to awaken their consciences by confronting their evil actions, prompting them to recognize the impending judgment of God. However, their consciences had become so calloused and deadened that Lot's words failed to stir a sense of morality within them. Instead, they reacted with irrational hostility, demonstrating how deeply entrenched their wickedness had become. Attempts to do good only seemed to further enrage them.

Lot's sons-in-law exemplify the Sodomites' attitude toward truth, righteousness, and divine judgment. When Lot warned his sons-in-law about the impending destruction of Sodom, they responded by treating it as a joke: "But to his sons-in-law he seemed to be joking" (Gen. 19:14). The Hebrew word "chahak", which means "to laugh," takes on a negative connotation in this context. The term "mechahek" is used, indicating a sense of despising or ridiculing.

Despite having individuals of moral stature like Abraham and righteous figures like Lot in close proximity, the Sodomites had shut their hearts off from God, the righteous Judge. They disdainfully ridiculed the message of impending judgment, demonstrating their complete rejection of divine guidance and moral accountability. The sin of incest committed by Lot's two daughters after their escape from the city's destruction further illustrates the irreversible moral decline of Sodom. This act is reflective of the corrupt mindset prevalent in the city, showing how deeply the Sodomites' values had deteriorated (Gen. 19:30-38).

In subsequent Scriptures, the sins of Sodom are identified as including adultery, lying, strengthening the hands of evildoers so that no one turns back from their wickedness (Jer. 23:14); pride amidst abundance, neglecting the poor, haughtiness, engaging in abominable practices before God (Ezek. 16:49-50); and fornication and pursuing unnatural desires (Jude 1:7). The fallen kingdom of Judah was compared to Sodom in terms of its moral decay (Isa. 1:10; 3:9; Jer. 23:14; Lam. 4:6; Ezek. 16:46, 48, 49, 53, 55, 56). Capernaum, a city where Jesus performed miracles but was not received, is portrayed as being even more susceptible to judgment than Sodom (Matt. 10:15; 11:23-24; Luke 10:12). In the book of Revelation, the beast that emerges from the abyss kills two witnesses of God, and the location where the Lord was crucified is metaphorically referred to as a spiritual Sodom (Rev. 11:8).

(3) Investigation

Yahweh, accompanied by two angels, arrived to investigate the sins of Sodom and Gomorrah (Gen. 18:1-2, 20-22; 19:1). Yahweh declared, "Because the outcry against Sodom and Gomorrah is great, and because their sin is very grave" (Gen. 18:20). The term "cry" or "outcry," represented by the Hebrew word "zakah" derives from the verb "za'ach", which is used in the Old Testament when a person in extreme distress appeals to God for salvation (see, e.g., Exodus 2:23; Judges 3:9, 15; 6:6, 7; 10:10; 1 Samuel 7:8, 9; 1 Chronicles 5:20; 2 Chronicles 18:31, Psalm 22:6). This verse underscores the gravity of the wickedness and cruelty of the Sodomites, highlighting the serious nature of the sins that the society had embraced. The lack of even ten righteous individuals in the city contributed to its inevitable downfall (Gen. 18:32).

The two angels arrived in Sodom during the evening and were welcomed by Lot. However, within a short span of time, the city was engulfed by chaos, with men from all around converging on Lot's house to commit sexual violence against Lot's visitors. It did not take long for the situation to escalate into a desperate and collective attempt at homosexual rape. Sodom, characterized by its swift inclination towards sinful behavior, had become a place where human dignity could no longer be upheld. The breaking down of Lot's door and the aggressive attempt to enter marked the end of the period of grace (Gen. 19:9).

(4) Sentencing

The recurring references to the Sodomites as great sinners before Yahweh and the magnitude of the outcry against them serve to underscore the impending judgment that could not be avoided (Gen. 13:13; 18:20; 19:13). The angels, who had witnessed the grievous wickedness, pronounced the judgment. In response, Abraham posed a question, asking whether the Lord would destroy the righteous along with the wicked. He advocated against the destruction of the righteous together with the wicked (Gen. 18:23).

The term "sapah," translated as "to destroy," carries the meanings of "to sweep away, annihilate, burn utterly." As Sodom faced condemnation and imminent destruction by the fire of brimstone, the righteous Judge of the world distinguished between the righteous and the wicked. Although Sodom was destined to be consumed by the fiery judgment due to the lack of even ten righteous individuals in the city, not a single righteous person was lost in that judgment.

The angels first extended the opportunity for salvation to the righteous. Lot was tasked with leading those who belonged to him out of the city, and only then would the angels proceed with the city's destruction (Gen. 19:12-13). It is important to note that the angels did not execute judgment based on their own authority; rather, they acted in accordance with Yahweh's command (Gen. 19:13). Having directly witnessed the magnitude of the outcry against Sodom before Yahweh, the angels ensured that the judgment would be executed with complete justice and without any misjudgment.

(5) Enforcement

God intervened to "delive[r] righteous Lot,,.who was oppressed by the filthy conduct of the wicked" (2 Pet. 2:7). However, Lot's initial decision to settle in Sodom came with its own tragic consequences. As Lot's wife looked back as they fled the city, she was turned into a pillar of salt, symbolizing the consequences of her disobedience (Gen. 19:26). Lot's hesitation in fleeing the city cost him his wife's life (Gen. 19:15, 16, 18-20). his deliverance despite his lack of decisiveness in the face of destruction was solely a result of God's mercy and his remembrance of Abraham (Gen. 19:29). Lot's deliverance occurred against all odds due to this great divine mercy.

Sodom, Gomorrah, and the surrounding cities faced a devastating judgment from God in the form of a fiery rain that rained down from heaven (Gen. 19:24). This catastrophic event served as a force of nature, much like the floodwaters in the account of the Flood, to bring about divine judgment. The word "himtir" ("to rain"), used in the earlier Flood narrative, was used again in depicting the destruction of Sodom by fire. The Sodomites, like the people at the time of Noah, were so morally depraved as to be beyond all help. The entire city, along with its inhabitants and the abundant crops that had been their pride, was completely overturned and destroyed (Gen. 19:25). The rising smoke from the ruins, akin to the smoke from a furnace, served as a visible testimony to the world, displaying the consequences of sin and the severity of God's judgment. This event demonstrated that the God who judges the world is alive and active in holding humanity accountable for its actions (Gen. 19:18).

The account of the judgment of Sodom and Gomorrah culminates with the perspective of Abraham. Abraham had hosted the God of judgment in Hebron (Gen. 18:1), and when the fiery judgment of sulfur began to unfold, he could only witness the destruction from a distance. Standing in the early morning on the heights where he had fervently wrestled with God, Abraham observed the devastating events as they unfolded some forty miles away (Gen. 19:27-28).

(6) Mitigation

While there were not even ten righteous individuals found in the city, the entirety of Sodom's residents was not obliterated; instead, Lot was mercifully delivered from destruction. Yet, Lot's subsequent life bears witness to the repercussions of his choices. Unfortunately, his proximity to the sinful city had lasting and detrimental effects. Through his eldest daughter, the nation of Moab was born, and through his younger daughter, the Ammonite nation emerged. Lot's continuous association with the wicked environment significantly impacted his moral character (2 Peter 2:8), ultimately leading to his fading into the background of biblical history. Although his life was spared, it was not without a heavy cost. his life serves as a vivid testament to the grave consequences that can arise from dwelling in the midst of sin.

PART V

Grace and Salvation

Chapter 13 | Salvation

The Bible is essentially the story of God's salvation. Within the book of Genesis, this divine salvation unfolds through a collection of relatable stories that offer clear insights. Through the lives of patriarchs, the foundational principles of the Reformation—faith alone and grace alone—are vividly illustrated. These principles are not mere theological concepts but are manifest in the lived experiences of these patriarchs, revealing salvation as a profound blessing bestowed upon God's covenant people. Embedded within the pages of Genesis are accounts of a faithful remnant who encountered salvation firsthand, providing early glimpses of God's ongoing revelation. This divine salvation is intrinsically linked with the concept of walking in harmony with God and thereby participating in the new creation.

Genesis primarily focuses on earthly events and interactions rather than delving into explicit discussions of salvation or the afterlife. However, even within its temporal narratives, there are subtle indications that offer glimpses of profound spiritual truths, such as the account of Abraham's willingness to sacrifice Isaac (Gen. 21:12; 22:5; Heb. 11:17-19). This episode serves as a faint shadow of the future resurrection faith that would come to fruition.

The salvation depicted in Genesis, though rooted in earthly contexts, holds spiritual significance and provides valuable insights into the ultimate salvation promised in God's glorious kingdom. By examining the stories in Genesis, we can glean spiritual lessons and parallels that shed light on the broader theme of eternal salvation. In this chapter, we will examine what the Genesis accounts have to teach us about eternal salvation.

1. Salvation by grace

(1) Adam

Adam's transgression led to a rupture between humanity and God, ushering in death; however, even in the depths of this darkness, God chose to visit humanity (Gen. 3:8-9). Amidst the shadows of mortality, God arrived with the proto-evangelium (Gen. 3:15), the path to life that God provided in his infinite grace. In the absence of God's presence, humanity would have been hopeless. Salvation finds its footing solely in God's profound love for sinners.

The proto-evangelium is a proclamation that Jesus Christ, the seed of the woman, will attain salvation for humanity's sake. Within Jesus Christ, mankind can achieve victory over Satan, obtain eternal life, and recover the lost paradise.

The clothing of skin that Adam and Eve received from God exemplifies his abundant love for humanity. He bestows upon us the everlasting righteousness of the Lamb of God, who removes the sins of the world. This contrasts with human righteousness, which can quickly wither and fade like fig leaves.

(2) Enoch

The genealogy of Adam (Gen. 5) begins with the blessed creation of God and concludes with the statement, "So all the days of ... were ... years; and he died" (Gen. 5:5, 8, 11, 14, 17, 20, 27, 31). Although the patriarchs typically lived close to a thousand years, their lives concluded in death, with the exception of Enoch.

Concerning Enoch, who was the seventh generation from Adam, it is written: "Enoch lived sixty-five years, and begot Methuselah. After he begot Methuselah, Enoch walked with God three hundred years, and had sons and daughters. So all the days of Enoch were three hundred and sixty-five years. And Enoch walked with God; and he was not, for God took him" (Gen. 5:21-24). Enoch's translation into heaven provided a glimmer of hope that the earth was not the permanent resting place for humanity. He demonstrated that separation from God due to sin is not humanity's inevitable destiny, through his close walk with God in his daily life. The phrase "God took him" underscores that the initiative for eternal salvation comes from God Himself.

The Hebrew name of Enoch, Hanok (*hánôk*), is derived from the Western Semitic root "hanak" (*hnk*), which means "to begin, to introduce." This name holds significant meaning. While the son of Cain bearing this name is associated with the establishment of the first city on earth,[1] Enoch, a descendant of Seth, through God's gracious guidance, holds a different legacy. He was the first to enter the eternal heavenly city prepared by God, serving as a precursor and introducing the way for mankind. Enoch's life illuminated the path of hope for those who were wandering in the shadowy

1 It is possible to linguistically associate "Enoch" with the term "Unug," which is another name for "Uruk,"one of the greatest cities of Mesopotamia. K.A. Kitchen suggests that this geographic designation could phonetically relate to the Hebrew name "Enoch." Hess, 39.

valley of death, highlighting the possibility of redemption and eternal communion with God.

In the genealogies presented in Genesis 4-5, both Enoch and Lamech appear as the seventh-generation descendants of Adam within the genealogies of Seth and Cain, respectively. A striking contrast emerges between Enoch's extraordinary ascension to heaven and the escalating violence within Cain's genealogy, exemplified by Lamech's boastful words (Gen. 4:23-24). Enoch's unique experience serves as a powerful testament that, regardless of the pervasive wickedness in the world, God has the ability to safeguard his people from succumbing to sin. This lesson offers profound comfort and encouragement to God's followers, especially in the last days, when they will face challenges and strive to maintain their faithfulness, ultimately ascending to heaven. Enoch's narrative stands as a resounding affirmation that God is alive, actively rewarding those who diligently seek Him (Heb. 11:5-6).

(3) Noah

Concerning Noah, the Scriptures declare, "But Noah found grace in the eyes of the Lord" (Gen. 6:8). In this passage, a significant term emerges for the first time in the Bible: "hen" (*hën*), meaning "grace." In Hebrew, this word conveys the concept of "favor" or "grace," and the underlying verb, "hanan" ("to be gracious, to confer a favor"), signifies an "active acceptance and positive favor" in the context of a personal relationship. This active favor involves a deliberate commitment to assist the impoverished, provide sustenance to the hungry, offer hope to the despairing, and extend rescue to those in dire circumstances.[2]

At the backdrop of Genesis 6:8 is God's impending judgment upon sinful humanity during the time of the Flood. The destiny of Noah's contemporaries is juxtaposed with that of Noah himself. In the realm of judgment, favor takes on the role of salvation and deliverance. The notion that "a man cannot extend grace and simultaneously hold anger" holds true; the presence of grace cannot harmonize with a disposition of judgment.[3]

A favorable disposition is revealed through one's face. The Old Testament metaphorically equates favor with "face" (Ps. 119:58; Dan. 9:13; Zech. 7:2; Mal. 1:9). Similar to Enoch, Noah also enjoyed a close communion with God, walking in his presence (Gen. 5:24; 6:9). This intimate relationship served as Noah's salvation. Through their profound connection, God revealed to Noah the means of escaping judgment and surviving the cataclysmic flood, and remembered Noah in the midst of the flood (Gen.

---

2 D. N. Freedman, J. R. Lundbom, 'hanan', TDOT 5:23-24.

3 Ibid., 24.

6:13-22; 8:1). This recurring theme of God's remembrance (Gen. 8:1), highlighted in the structural framework of the Flood account using the cross-codification method,[4] underscores his one-sided protection, care, and grace that ultimately led to Noah, his family, and the creatures being saved.

(4) Abraham

The account of Abraham is a narrative marked by a series of crises and divine interventions that lead to salvation. From the moment Abraham responded to God's call to journey forward into an uncertain future, his path was punctuated by challenging situations. For instance, he deceived first the Pharaoh of Egypt and later Abimelech, the king of Gerar, into believing that Sarah his wife was his sister, and surrendered her to these individuals for a certain period (Gen. 12:10-20; 20:1-18). Another crisis arose due to his nephew Lot's unwise choice to settle in Sodom, a city steeped in iniquity, which resulted in Abraham's involvement in an interregional conflict against powerful monarchs of his time (Gen. 14:1-24). In the midst of these trials, God intervened to save his faithful servant. He brought plagues upon the households of both Pharaoh and Abimelech to protect Abraham, and issued a warning to Abimelech through a vision (Gen. 12:17; 20:3; cf. Gen. 20:7). Melchizedek, the king of Salem, acknowledged that God had granted Abraham the victory (Gen. 14:20).

In the narrative of Abraham, the term "hen" ("grace") is mentioned in Genesis 18:3 and 19:19. These accounts center around celestial beings visiting Abraham. During the occasion when Abraham hosted Yahweh's guests, God revealed to him the forthcoming birth of Isaac and disclosed the impending judgment upon Sodom. God's promise of a son to Abraham and Sarah was an act of sheer grace, especially as human hope had dwindled, such that Sarah even laughed at the prospect. Furthermore, God displayed his gracious nature by attentively considering and accepting Abraham's repeated intercessions on behalf of the people of Sodom.

In Genesis 19:19, Lot, placing his trust in God's grace, implored the angels of judgment for mercy, and his plea was met with the granting of permission to escape to Zoar. This passage marks the initial usage of the word "hesed," meaning "lovingkindness," in the Bible. Although his plea was honored, Lot's failure to fully adhere to the given instructions resulted in unfortunate consequences.

The most profound demonstration of salvation through grace in the narrative of Abraham is illustrated in his willingness to offer his son Isaac as a burnt sacrifice on Mount Moriah, as depicted in Genesis 22. This serves as a prefiguration of God's boundless love for humanity, ultimately culminating

---

4 Anderson: 23-39; Cassuto, A Commentary on the Book of Genesis: Part 2, from Noah to Abraham, 30-33; Longacre, 235-262; Shea, 8-29; Wenham, 'Coherence of the Flood Narrative', 336-348.

in the sacrifice of his own Son, Jesus Christ, on the cross for the redemption of sinners (Rom. 5:8).

(5) Jacob

Upon Jacob's return to his homeland of Canaan from Padan Aram, he found himself facing a daunting threat from his brother Esau. Esau's refusal of Jacob's attempt at reconciliation and his approach with four hundred men to seek vengeance left Jacob feeling "greatly afraid and distressed" (Gen. 32:7). Jacob's heartfelt prayer is recorded in Genesis 32:9-12, providing a glimpse of a genuine spirit of prayer. In his prayer, Jacob tenaciously clung to God's grace, interpreting all of God's promises as expressions of divine grace.

He reinterpreted the phrase "I will be with you" in Genesis 31:3 as "I will deal well with you" (Gen. 32:9[10]), using the word "hetib" meaning "to be good to." Rather than simply re-evoking God's earlier promise from Bethel that he would have many descendants, Jacob claimed the promise God had made to Abraham at the time of Abraham's sacrifice of Isaac as his own: the declaration "I will bless you greatly" is conveyed as "I will truly treat you well. In this moment, Jacob's feelings of unworthiness before God's grace (hesed) and truthfulness (emet), along with material blessings, are apparent (Gen. 32:10[11]). However, faced with the imminent threat of the destruction of his entire family, Jacob found himself clinging to God and seeking his grace as his only source of hope and refuge.

Jacob found God's grace in the promise, "I will… make your descendants as the sand of the sea, which cannot be numbered for multitude" (Gen. 32:12[13]).

The term "hetib", translated as "to be gracious," signifies "to treat well" or "to do good." In the original Hebrew, the fundamental form "yatab" signifies "good." Despite Jacob's unjust treatment of his brother, God treated him well. Grace entails God responding to evil not with retaliation but with goodness. God stands by sinners, accompanying them on their journey and bestowing abundant blessings upon them.

Jacob did not place his reliance on his own merits but rather on the promises that were made to him and his forefathers, Abraham and Isaac. In his plea for his life, he demonstrated his complete dependence on God's favor. Wrestling with God at the Jabbok, he proclaimed, "I will not let You go unless You bless me" (Gen. 32:26), a testament to his complete reliance on God's goodness. This incident led to the naming of the place as "Peniel," which means "The Face of God," signifying the triumph of faith.

In this pivotal moment, Jacob, who had solely God as his hope and clung to his grace, was shown mercy by God. God softened Esau's heart that very night. Jacob, recognizing God's hand at work in his reconciliation with Esau, perceptively remarked, "I have seen your face as if I had seen the face of God, and you were pleased with me" (Gen. 33:10). When Jacob, having grappled face-to-face with God, encountered his previously wrathful brother, he ascertained from Esau's countenance that there was no intent to harm him. Esau's visage, once bearing murderous resentment, had been transformed into the merciful countenance of God. By the grace of God, Jacob's life was spared.

(6) Joseph

Joseph's life serves as a profound example of the transformative power of God's grace even in the depths of despair. Despite facing a near-death experience, Joseph was rescued from harm's way and ultimately found himself sold into Egypt. This latter unfortunate event turned out to be in accordance with God's providential plan (Gen. 37:20, 22, 27). This divine orchestration laid the foundation for Joseph's role as a savior to not only the nation of Israel but also to all other surrounding nations.

Throughout his trials, Joseph was consistently the recipient of God's favor. In the household of Potiphar, an Egyptian official and chief of Pharaoh's court, Joseph found favor and was entrusted with weighty responsibilities (Gen. 39:4). Even when he was unjustly imprisoned, the chief jailer recognized Joseph's exceptional character and granted him favor within the prison walls (Gen. 39:21). The incident involving Potiphar's wife posed a grave threat to Joseph's life, yet he managed to escape death's clutches. Despite his wrongful imprisonment, Joseph displayed exceptional leadership skills and was eventually placed in charge of all the prisoners (Gen. 39:20-23). his journey, marked by divine grace, resilience, and unwavering trust in God, showcases the remarkable impact of God's favor even in the face of adversity.

In every trial that Joseph encountered, he not only survived but also thrived. The key factor behind his resilience and success was the undeniable presence of Yahweh with Joseph (Gen. 39:2, 21, 23). During a period of profound global crisis, marked by seven years of devastating famine following seven years of abundance, Joseph's exceptional insight and wisdom were recognized by Pharaoh himself. Within the grandeur of the Egyptian palace, Joseph emerged as a man uniquely guided by the Spirit of God, positioning him as the world's savior during those tumultuous times (Gen. 41:38).

The divine directive for Abraham to be a source of blessing to all nations found its fulfillment through the life of Joseph. When revealing his true identity to his brothers, Joseph conveyed that God had orchestrated his journey to Egypt as a means of rescuing their lives from crisis and safeguarding their descendants throughout the world (Gen. 45:5, 7). This moment holds immense redemptive significance, as it signifies that God's providence intervened to prevent the obliteration of the Israelites—forebears of Jesus Christ, the seed of the woman—during the seven years of famine. Through the grace of God, Joseph's actions ensured the salvation not only of himself and his family but also of numerous nations and the entire global community.

Joseph's narrative is replete with deeply poignant moments that underscore the providential guidance of God's grace. This divine favor extends beyond mere crisis intervention, encompassing the intricate preparation of individuals for distant futures and the bestowal of blessings upon all humanity. As Genesis draws to a close with Joseph's story, the book unambiguously attests to the comprehensive salvation of the entire world through God's grace.

God hates sin and loves sinners. Just as Joseph's brothers were held accountable for their transgressions, the nation of Israel likewise faced consequences for their sins. For a span of three days, Joseph's brothers were incarcerated (Gen. 42:17), and Simeon's captivity endured until his brethren's return (Gen. 42:24; 43:23). Benjamin stood on the precipice of enslavement in Egypt (Gen. 44:17), and their father Jacob teetered on the brink of sorrowful descent into the realm of death (Gen. 44:29, 31). However, when Joseph witnessed his brothers' penitence and complete transformation through the words of Judas, who acted as an intermediary, he wholly forgave them, reconciled with them and rescued the family of Israel from the famine. Similarly, when Israel, the covenant-bearing people, strayed from God's will, they would be ensnared by a curse (Deut. 28:20-68); yet, upon their repentance, God would extend his mercy and present them with a fresh opportunity for renewal. The cycle of Israel's apostasy, penitence, and divine salvation, recurring in the book of Judges, serves as an emblematic demonstration of this pattern.

When Solomon offered a prayer to God subsequent to the construction of the temple, it centered on the themes of divine forgiveness and restoration (1 Kings 8:22-53). Amid national turmoil and upheaval, Israel encountered widespread devastation, yet God's commitment to the nation endured. He provided for their return from Babylonian captivity; he revived an entire nation as an expression of his grace.

Despite its imperfections, the Church remains the recipient of the Lord's boundless affection. Throughout history, the church has encountered trials and tribulations, yet it has never been subjected to irrevocable divine judgment. None of the seven churches depicted in Revelation 2-3 were forsaken by the Lord. On the contrary, the church of Laodicea, fraught with flaws and seemingly bereft of commendation, was bestowed with an unparalleled gift. The words of Revelation 3:20 resound as a testament to this grace: "Behold, I stand at the door and knock. If anyone hears My voice and opens the door, I will come in to him and dine with him, and he with Me." In Jesus Christ, an unwavering source of hope eternally resides.

2. Salvation by faith

In the realm of salvation by faith, which constitutes the very heart of Christianity, the terms "faith" or "believe" are infrequently found in the book of Genesis. Nonetheless, Hebrews 11—a chapter dedicated to faith—encompasses a roster of illustrious figures from Genesis, including Abel, Enoch, Noah, Abraham, Isaac, Jacob, Sarah, and Joseph. This list spans 22 verses, a majority of the chapter's 40 verses (Heb. 11:1-22).

Genesis, while not explicitly delving into theological discussions on faith, adeptly unveils the essence of genuine faith through the lives of its emblematic characters. Faith, in its essence, is lived out through one's daily life. Within Genesis, faith in God is directly mentioned only in Genesis 15:6: "And he believed in the Lord, and He accounted it to him for righteousness." The Hebrew root of "believe," refers to faith only when used in the Hiphil form, *hēmîn* (it does not have this connotation when used in the Qal form). *Hēmîn* refers not merely to an intellectual affirmation but rather reliance and trust. When oriented toward God, belief encompasses not solely the veracity of God's utterances, but embraces the full spectrum of divine attributes—truth, benevolence, love, justice, holiness, consistency, and every facet that defines God in his entirety.[5]

(1) Adam

Hebrews 11 effectively unveils fundamental facets of faith, drawing upon attributes found in the lives of the forebears of faith in Genesis. Though the initial section of this discussion on faith omits the mention of Adam, the quintessence of Adam's faith lies in his belief in the Word of God (Heb. 11:3). Adam directly received divine discourse from God regarding the profound design of the cosmos and the foundational underpinning of his existence. The utterances of God bore an inherent creative potency, each pronouncement ushering forth existence itself, all of which manifestations were pleasing in God's sight. For Adam, God's Word transcended mere communication; it was a matter of life and death. When Adam violated the divine command, his disbelief brought death into the world. Life does not hinge upon one's arduous endeavors to uphold physical well-being, but

5 E. Pfeiffer, 'Glaube Im Alten Testament', Zeitschrift für die alttestamentliche Wissenschaft 71 (1959): 151-164. Cf. Joseph P. Healey, 'Faith (Old Testament)', ABD 2:745.

rather finds its essence in the steadfast embrace of God's Word.

(2) Abel

Abel believed that paradise and eternal life would be restored to mankind through the sacrificial system initiated in Eden. That Edenic institution testifies that God has prepared measures for the restoration of mankind. Salvation came about not by the design of man, but was made available through a redemptive decision involving self-sacrifice on the part of God. Salvation begins with the acceptance of the sincerity of God's love for man. Salvation becomes present in our lives through obedience, which gratefully accepts the way of salvation that God has provided. Abel offered a better sacrifice than Cain, who presented his merits before God, and his martyrdom testifies to the fact that absolute faith in God is more precious than life itself (Heb. 11:4).

(3) Enoch

Enoch's reward of ascension was a result of his vibrant relationship with God. True faith that pleases God goes beyond mere religious rituals; it involves walking closely with God in everyday life. This kind of relationship with God was a blessing enjoyed by humanity in the Garden of Eden before the Fall, and despite the sin-filled world, it remains attainable. Enoch exemplified this by continually being aware of God's presence in every moment of his life.

Enoch's ability to walk with God presupposes a fundamental belief in the existence of God. This relationship is fulfilled when comes to truly believe that God desires humanity's well-being and happiness, that He values companionship over ritual sacrifices, and that the ultimate purpose of the sacrificial system is to facilitate a meaningful encounter with Him (Heb. 11:5-6).

The ultimate reward that the Lord's people can receive from God is the opportunity to be transferred to heaven. Enoch's ascension serves as a reminder to humanity that this earthly life is not the final resting place; rather, the gates of eternal heavens are wide open for all to see. Walking with God encompasses a holistic experience that involves the entirety of one's being—body, soul, and spirit. Eternal life and salvation are not abstract philosophical concepts; rather, they are tangible realities that human beings can experience and embrace. Salvation is not an illusion but a practical, day-to-day reality within the human community.

(4) Noah

Noah received a divine warning from God about the impending worldwide judgment that would take place after a hundred and twenty years. Despite the enormity of this prophesied event, Noah maintained a profound personal confidence in God's word and dutifully followed every instruction given to him (Gen. 6:22; 7:16). his unwavering trust in God's guidance and his faithful execution of God's commands were counted as righteousness in the sight of God. As a result of his obedient faith, Noah became an heir of righteousness, inheriting the promise of a renewed world (Gen. 6:9; Heb. 11:7).

Noah's faith also extended beyond his personal sphere. his resolute commitment to building the ark and obeying God's instructions ensured the salvation of his household. This underscores the profound truth that genuine faith is not confined to individual matters but extends its influence to impact and benefit one's family members as well (Heb. 11:7).

(5) Abraham

Abraham responded faithfully to God's call, embarking on a journey to the Promised Land. This land, however, existed primarily within the realm of God's promises, requiring Abraham to live as a sojourner among the Gentiles. Isaac and Jacob, Abraham's descendants, similarly resided in the Promised Land without fully possessing it, yet their unwavering faith in the promise endured. Joseph, on his deathbed, left a testament for the Israelites, directing them to carry his remains to Canaan, a testament to his unshakable faith in the promise despite its unfulfilled state.

This same principle extends to our hope in the Second Coming of Christ. While its manifestation may not transpire during our lifetimes, we, as believers, can live as citizens of two realms. Amid the transient nature of earthly existence, we embrace the approaching kingdom with exultant joy, even if we are regarded as strangers in this temporal domain (Heb. 11:8-9, 13-16, 21-22).

The wondrous birth of Isaac and Abraham's obedient readiness to offer this cherished child on Moriah profoundly bolstered his faith. These encounters made him vividly realize that He served the God who turned the unattainable into reality and was even able to resurrect the dead (Heb. 11:17-19).

Genesis 15:6. Genesis 15:6 had a significant influence in the New Testament's understanding of faith. Before delving into the New Testament references, it is important to examine Abraham's faith as presented in the Genesis passage. The accounts of Abraham's faith are marked by trials and tests, underscoring the theme of testing (Gen. 15:6).[6]

Abraham's divine calling encompassed the assurance of land, descendants, and blessings, yet initially these promises seemed implausible. Even though Abraham did not possess even an acre of the Promised

6 Healey, 745-746.

Land, the entire expanse before him was pledged as the inheritance for his lineage (Gen. 13:14-15, 17). When Sarah's ability to bear children had waned, the assurance of a son emerged as a promise. The offspring that would emerge from her would multiply like the earth's dust and stars of the sky (Gen. 13:16; 15:4-5; 16:1). The declaration that Abraham, a wanderer, would be a source of blessing to all nations appeared unattainable (Gen. 12:2-3). Of the three promises, the narrative of Abraham's journey chiefly centers on Isaac, the promise whose fulfillment became tangible in Abraham's lifetime.

When Abram took matters into his own hands and obtained Ishmael through Hagar, Yahweh directly appeared to him, renaming him Abraham and Sarai, Sarah, and in due time fulfilled the promise through the birth of Isaac (Gen. 21:1-7). This sequence of events persistently tested the genuineness of Abraham's faith in God. Despite Genesis 15:6 affirming Abraham's faith, subsequent occurrences raise questions about the completeness of his belief. Because of a lack of faith, Abraham took Hagar as a concubine. This same dearth of faith led Abraham and Sarah to inwardly laugh when God Himself visited and promised to provide Isaac (Gen. 17:17; 18:12). Abraham's spiritual condition was such that he was not ready to embrace miracles that surpassed human logic. Nevertheless, God tolerated their incredulity, reiterating with clarity that his promise would indeed come to pass by declaring, "Is anything too hard for the Lord?" (Gen. 18:14; cf. Gen. 17:19, 21).

The Genesis account does not record the two individuals' responses to God's assurance. However, Hebrews 11:11 informs us that Sarah's ability to conceive was made possible through her faith in the promise.

After the birth of his son, Abraham underwent a profound transformation in his faith. Having witnessed God's miracles, he embraced the notion that nothing was beyond God's capabilities. Yet he was to face his greatest and most rigorous trial yet when God commanded him to offer Isaac as a sacrifice on Mount Moriah. This pivotal moment tested Abraham's faith to the utmost, compelling him to internalize the crucial lesson of unwavering trust in the face of apparent contradictions between God's words and promises regarding Isaac.

God's intervention had previously brought life to Sarah's barren womb, which led Abraham to have faith that even in the face of death, Isaac, the heir of the promise, would experience a resurrection. This ultimate act of faith encompasses the entire spectrum of believers' faith as demonstrated throughout Genesis. It includes Adam's trust in the Word and creation, Abel's obedient faith, Enoch's experiential faith in the living God, and Noah's faith in inheriting a renewed world. Abraham's faith was carried forward by his descendants—Isaac, Jacob, and Joseph—and was eventually inherited by the nation of Israel. The church, Abraham's spiritual legacy, also looked to him as a model. Abraham's faith radiated blessings to all of humanity, as he became the patriarch of all those who believe (Gal. 3:7-9, 14).

The New Testament frequently alludes to or directly references Genesis 15:6 to emphasize the distinction between righteousness based on works and righteousness based on faith (Rom. 4:3, 9, 22; Gal. 3:6; James 2:23; Heb. 11:12). These verses utilize Genesis 15:6 as a foundational basis for refuting the idea of achieving righteousness through one's own efforts and instead establishing the concept of righteousness by faith.

In the book of Genesis, the term "righteous" (*tsaddîq*) refers to someone who has passed judgment and is consequently saved (Gen. 6:9, 7:1, 18:23, and 20:4). The concept of righteousness is closely tied to the impending judgment of God. During this judgment, humanity will be divided into the righteous and the wicked, each facing either salvation or destruction. Thus, the illustration of God's recognition of Abraham's faith as righteousness in Genesis 15:6 directly correlates with the New Testament's overarching theme of salvation through faith.

In the context of Genesis 15:6, several key insights about righteousness by faith are revealed:

(1) Righteousness is based on a relationship with God. In the phrase "he believed in the Lord [Yahweh]," the verb "hemin" ("believed") signifies a deep relationship of reliance and trust in God. The object of "hemin" was Yahweh. Abraham's close bond with God earned him the designation "a friend of God" (Rom. 4:17, 20-22; James 2:23).

(2) God is the source of righteousness. Abraham's act of trust was recognized and credited by God as righteousness (Rom. 4:5).

(3) Righteousness is a gift from God. Righteousness was not a reward for Abraham's deeds. God accepted Abraham's belief in God and bestowed righteousness as a gift (Rom. 4:2-5).

(4) The righteous obey God's Word. A trusting relationship with God is exemplified through faith in his promises and obedience to his commands. Since God's Word reflects his character, those who intimately trust in Him, like Abraham, demonstrate their faith through obedience. Faith and works are inseparable (Gen. 15:9-10; 22:9-12, 16-18; James 2:21-24).

(5) God's righteousness is made available to all of humanity. Abraham's justification occurred prior to his circumcision, illustrating that God's righteousness is extended to the uncircumcised Gentiles (Rom. 4:9-12).

(6) God's righteousness has an evangelistic nature. As God made Abraham a blessing to all people, the righteousness he received becomes an invitation to salvation for all. It bears an evangelistic aspect, emphasizing God's inclusive plan for humanity's redemption (Rom. 4:16; Gal. 3:6-9).

Chapter 14 | The Covenant

The covenant holds a significant place within biblical theology, with some Old Testament scholars, such as Walther Eichrodt, even regarding it as a central concept.[1] Notably, some scholars assert that the entire framework of the Bible revolves around the concept of the covenant. M.G. Krein, in particular, supported this perspective by closely examining ancient Near Eastern treaties and their relevance to the biblical understanding of covenant.[2]

1. Etymology and meaning of "berit"

The etymology of the term "covenant" has been linked to three Akkadian words: "birîtu," which refers to "shackles, clamps" (Weinfeld), "birit," meaning "middle" (Noth), and "barû," signifying "more than" (Kutsch).[3] Among these, *birîtu* is often considered the most fitting etymology, as regardless of its linguistic origin, the essence of a covenant is the binding together of two parties.[4] Covenants can take place between individuals or between God and humanity.

The Hebrew term for "covenant" is "berit". It appears 27 times in the book of Genesis, out of a total of 286 times in the Old Testament. Notably, Genesis 17 features the highest frequency of its usage in the entire Old Testament, with 13 occurrences. The second most frequently used chapter is Leviticus 26, with 8 occurrences, followed by Genesis 9, which employs it 7 times.[5] Thus, intensive use of the term is particularly prominent in the book of Genesis.

---

1 Walther Eichrodt, *Theology of the Old Testament*, The Old Testament Library, 2 vols (Philadelphia: Westminster Press, 1961). For works of other theologians who conducted significant scholarship on the covenant, see Gerhard F. Hasel, *Old Testament Theology: Basic Issues in the Current Debate* (Grand Rapids, MI: Eerdmans, 1991), 138, n. 107; Henning Reventlow, *Problems of Old Testament Theology in the Twentieth Century*, 1st ed. (Philadelphia, PA: Fortress Press, 1985), 126-128}

2 Meredith G. Kline, *The Structure of Biblical Authority* (Grand Rapids, MI: Eerdmans, 1972).

3 Gordon J. McConville, '*berit.*', *NIDOTTE* 1:747.

4 J. Arthur Thompson, 'Covenant (OT)', *ISBE* 1:790

5 Gen. 6:18; 9:9, 11, 12, 13, 15, 16, 17; 14:13; 15:18; 17:2, 4,7 (2 times), 9, 10, 11, 13 (2 times), 14, 19 (2 times), 21; 21:27, 32; 26:28; 31:44.

Throughout Genesis, we encounter various covenants, including the Creation Covenant, the Adamic Covenant, the Noahic Covenant, and the Abrahamic Covenant. These covenants form the foundation for later covenants such as the Mosaic Covenant, the Davidic Covenant, and the New Covenant established through Jesus Christ. A thorough understanding of the covenants in Genesis enables us to grasp the profound significance of both the old and new covenants.

2. Creation Covenant

(1) Biblical evidence for existence of the Creation Covenant

The Creation Covenant refers to the relationship God established with his creatures from creation. Although the term "covenant" is not explicitly mentioned in Genesis 1–5, it would be a mistake to assume that the covenant is absent from the creation account. In fact, there are various biblical passages that strongly suggest the presence of a covenant within the context of creation.

1) Genesis 6:18

"But I will establish My covenant with you; and you shall go into the ark—you, your sons, your wife, and your sons' wives with you" (Gen. 6:18). This is the first instance in which a covenant is explicitly mentioned in the Bible. Following the Flood, God did indeed follow through on his promise here and establish a covenant with Noah (Gen. 9:1-17). The Hebrew term used in the text, "wahakimoti" ("I will establish") conveys the idea of affirmation of an existing covenant, rather than execution of a new covenant.[6] In Genesis 9, God was renewing the ancient covenant that he had entered into with Adam. Whereas that initial covenant had been between God and Adam, the first human, the reaffirmed covenant was with Noah, the new Adam. The allusion to a preexisting covenant in Genesis 6:18 points to a divine relationship that has been established based on the fact of the creation.[7]

While the term "covenant" may not be explicitly present in the creation account, the covenantal relationship between God and his creation is implicitly revealed. The Noahic Covenant can

---

6 Bruce K. Waltke and Cathi J. Fredricks, *Genesis: A Commentary* (Grand Rapids, MI: Zondervan, 2001), 136. The Hiphil form of "kum" ("to stand up, rise") signifies "endorsing or establishing [a covenantal relationship]" (*hëqîm*). The Hebrew term "karat" (*krt*) etymologically implies "initiating or making [a covenantal relationship]." Leonard J. Coppes, '*qwm*', 793.

7 William J. Dumbrell, *Covenant and Creation: A Theology of Old Testament Covenants* (Nashville, TN: Thomas Nelson, 1984), 32.

be understood as a reaffirmation of this foundational covenant, emphasizing God's ongoing commitment to his creation.

2) Hosea 6:7

"But like Adam they transgressed the covenant; there they dealt treacherously with Me" (Hos. 6:7). The prophet Hosea, through the words of this verse, draws a parallel between the Israelites and Adam in the context of breaking the covenant. Hosea's prophetic message revolves around the Israelites' unfaithfulness and their breach of the covenant relationship with God. This was symbolically reenacted through Hosea's own marriage to Gomer, a prostitute, which serves as a powerful symbol of Israel's unfaithfulness to God.

3) Jeremiah 33:20-21

"Thus says the Lord: 'If you can break My covenant with the day and My covenant with the night, so that there will not be day and night in their season, then My covenant may also be broken with David My servant, so that he shall not have a son to reign on his throne, and with the Levites, the priests, My ministers'" (Jer. 33:20-21).

In this passage from Jeremiah, the prophet emphasizes God's unchanging and steadfast covenantal love for the nation of Israel. He uses the example of God's covenant with the day and night, which is established in the natural order of creation, to illustrate the enduring nature of God's covenants: "And God saw the light, that it was good; and God divided the light from the darkness. God called the light Day, and the darkness He called Night. So the evening and the morning were the first day" (Gen. 1:4, 5). The law of nighttime and daytime that God established at creation was part of the Creation Covenant; further, the cycle of the Sabbath, which is a sign of the Creation Covenant, is measured in accordance with this night-day covenant.

The three examples above are the direct utterances of God Himself. God intends for us to perceive his acts of creation as a covenant.

(2) The two objects of the Creation Covenant

The testimony of the prophets mentioned above points out that there are two objects that God makes the object of the covenant in the founding covenant. According to Hosea, the object is humanity, and according to Jeremiah, it is nature. Man and nature are intimately related to God by virtue of the Covenant of Creation. The fate of man and nature depends on God, the Creator, who is the owner of the covenant. The entry of sin into the world seriously damaged the order of creation, causing upheavals in the natural world and causing man to become profoundly corrupted, but the covenant of creation was not removed. Through Jesus Christ, God will make mankind a new creation and will make all things new. Through Jesus Christ, God still holds all things and mankind.

The testimonies of the aforementioned prophets highlight that the Creation Covenant is directed at two objects. One such object is humanity, as indicated by Hosea, and the other is nature, as attested by Jeremiah. Humanity and the natural world are intricately linked to God through the Covenant of Creation. The destiny of both humanity and nature rests upon God, the Creator, who is the covenant's owner. The intrusion of sin into the world profoundly disrupted the order of creation, leading to disturbances in the natural realm and the corruption of mankind. Nevertheless, the Creation Covenant remained intact. Through Jesus Christ, God intends to fashion a new creation out of humanity and renew all things. By means of Jesus Christ, God's dominion continues over all things and mankind.

(3) The image of God

"Then God said, 'Let Us make man in Our image, according to Our likeness; let them have dominion over the fish of the sea, over the birds of the air, and over the cattle, over all the earth and over every creeping thing that creeps on the earth.' So God created man in his own image; in the image of God He created him; male and female He created them. Then God blessed them, and God said to them, 'Be fruitful and multiply; fill the earth and subdue it; have dominion over the fish of the sea, over the birds of the air, and over every living thing that moves on the earth' (Gen. 1:26-28).

When God created man, He established a covenant relationship with humanity. The text outlines the unconditional terms of the Creation Covenant, which was the purpose of man's creation.[8] In the ancient Near East, the term "image" (*tselem*) referred to a representation of the gods through sculptures or idols.[9] However, human beings were created not only in the likeness of God, but also as blessed beings who serve as representatives of God and embody his authority over creation. This covenant encompasses the responsibilities of stewardship, and God's command in Genesis 1:28 is often referred to as the cultural mandate.

8 Eugene H. Merrill, 'Covenant and the Kingdom: Genesis 1-3 as Foundation for Biblical Theology', *Criswell Theological Review* 1 (1987): 303.

9 Westermann, *Genesis 1-11: A Commentary*, 146-147.

The cultural mandate involves more than just population growth and development; it encompasses the protection of nature and the responsible use of resources. It is a significant blessing bestowed upon humanity by God, granting us the privilege to participate in the ongoing process of creation and stewardship.

(4) Sabbath

"Thus the heavens and the earth, and all the host of them, were finished. And on the seventh day God ended his work which He had done, and He rested on the seventh day from all his work which He had done. Then God blessed the seventh day and sanctified it, because in it He rested from all his work which God had created and made" (Gen. 2:2-3).

The Sabbath serves as a powerful reminder that the heavens, the earth, and all that exists are the result of God's creative work. It testifies to his role as the ultimate Creator and Lord of all things. When humanity acknowledges God's absolute sovereignty over the entire universe, it enables us to fulfill our role as responsible stewards of creation.

God instituted the Sabbath, which is a sign of the Creation Covenant, as part of the covenant that governs the order of day and night. Through observing the Sabbath, humans can deepen their covenant relationship with the Creator, manifesting reverence for Him and discovering unparalleled joy in obedience.[10]

(5) Tree of the Knowledge of Good and Evil

"And the Lord God commanded the man, saying, 'Of every tree of the garden you may freely eat; but of the tree of the knowledge of good and evil you shall not eat, for in the day that you eat of it you shall surely die'" (Gen. 2:16-17). The Creation Covenant underscores that mankind is God's creation and that assurance of life depends on their obedience to the Creator. The command regarding the Tree of the Knowledge of Good and Evil is a key element of the Genesis Covenant, as it outlines the terms for securing life.

Human beings are not independent entities with autonomous existence. While they possess dominion over all things, they are not on par with God; rather, they are under the authority of the Creator who brought them into being. This hierarchical relationship within the created order is an inviolable principle that humans must never transgress. Obedience is the key to life.

---

10 Gerard Van Groningen, 'Covenant', *Baker Theological Dictionary of the Bible*, ed. Walter A. Elwell (Grand Rapids, MI: Baker Books, 1996), 125.

The concept of the image of God partially conveys that humans act on behalf of God and represent Him; however, humanity does not want to be under God's rule.[11] This was the beginning of mankind's tragedy.

(6) God Who blesses

The Creation narrative consistently presents God's blessings towards humanity. God fashioned humans in his own image (Gen. 1:26-27). He ordained the sanctified Sabbath as a source of blessing (Gen. 2:1-3). God transformed the dust of the earth into a living soul (Gen. 2:7). He endowed on humanity the splendors of Eden (Gen. 2:8, 15). By bringing forth the animals for Adam to name, God established Adam's dominion over them (Gen. 2:19-20). Additionally, God provided Adam with a companion, enabling the joys of family life (Gen. 2:18, 20-25).

Throughout this process, God's benevolent intentions towards humanity are encapsulated in three Hebrew words, which translate to "God blessed them" (Gen. 1:28; cf. Gen. 5:2). God's purpose for humanity is one of blessing, not condemnation. The Covenant of Creation stands as a pact of blessing, ensuring mankind's eternal life and happiness.

3. Adamic Covenant

The Adamic Covenant pertains to God's covenant with Adam subsequent to his transgression (Gen. 3:14-19). Under this covenant, the serpent, which led humanity astray, is cursed to crawl on the ground. Women are destined to experience pain at childbirth, while men are fated to toil strenuously due to the earth's unproductivity. Notably, within the Adamic covenant, God presented the inaugural gospel, commonly referred to as the proto-evangelium (original gospel).

(1) Seed of the woman

"I will put enmity between you and the woman, and between your seed and her Seed; He shall bruise your head, and you shall bruise his heel" (Gen. 3:15). The Hebrew text accentuates the supernatural antagonism between the serpent and the woman, as well as between their respective descendants, by positioning the term "enmity" at the forefront of the sentence.

Good and evil are incompatible. There is an inherent conflict between Satan and Christ. In the

11 Merrill: 304.

context of humanity's vulnerability to the influence of Satan, this supernatural animosity provides the prospect of salvation. God is resolute in not permitting his people to remain under the dominion of Satan. Ultimately, God will overcome Satan and deliver his people from bondage. The enmity placed by God reaches its pinnacle in the triumphant arrival of 'the man,' a representative figure among the descendants of the woman.[12]

Christ, the seed of the woman, initially dealt a decisive blow to the serpent's authority through his sacrificial death and subsequent resurrection on the cross. "Inasmuch then as the children have partaken of flesh and blood, He Himself likewise shared in the same, that through death He might destroy him who had the power of death, that is, the devil" (Heb. 2:14) However, the complete realization of this victory will happen in the future. The promise remains that "the God of peace will crush Satan under your feet shortly" (Rom. 16:20). In the ultimate culmination, God will cast the devil into the lake of fire and brimstone following the millennial period, leading to the devil's eternal destruction (Rev. 20:10).

Describing the Messiah as the seed of the woman may appear inconsistent with the male-dominated genealogies commonly found in the Bible. While Moses did not explicitly elaborate on how it was that the Messiah would descend from a woman, the prophecy in the book of Isaiah, often referred to as the fifth Gospel, foresaw the miraculous virgin birth of the Messiah: "Therefore the Lord Himself will give you a sign: Behold, the virgin shall conceive and bear a Son, and shall call his name Immanuel" (Isa. 7:14). In accordance with this prophecy, "when the fullness of the time had come, God sent forth his Son, born of a woman" (Gal. 4:4). The Messiah was supernaturally conceived in the womb of Mary by the power of the Holy Spirit (Matt. 1:20, 23, 25).

The triumph of the gospel of God is certain. God Himself foretold its victory by pronouncing a curse upon the serpent: "So the Lord God said to the serpent: 'Because you have done this, you are cursed more than all cattle, and more than every beast of the field; on your belly you shall go, and you shall eat dust all the days of your life'" (Gen. 3:14). This curse pronounced upon the serpent is symbolic of the fate of those destined to be defeated. It signifies their submission and defeat, akin to conquered princes who bow down and place their faces to the ground as a sign of subjugation before the victor's throne.[13] The very serpent that had tempted Adam and Eve in the Garden now lies in the dirt, judged by God. This image foreshadows Satan's ultimate destiny of defeat and destruction.

---

12 Walter Kaiser, *Old Testament Theology* (Seoul, Word of Life, 1982), 109.

13 Kaiser, 108; William L. Moran, *The Amarna Letters*, English-language ed. (Baltimore: Johns Hopkins University Press, 1992), 100:33-44, n. 8. Cf. Ps. 72:9; Isa. 49: 23; Mic. 7:17.

The genealogies presented in the *Tôlĕdôt* sections of Genesis are focused on tracing the lineage of the Messianic family, from which the Messiah will come. The Messianic lineage is rooted in the characters of Genesis, such as Adam, Noah, Seth, Abraham, Isaac, and Jacob. Within this lineage, Jacob prophetically declared that Judah would play a significant role as an ancestor of the Messiah. He proclaimed, "The scepter shall not depart from Judah, nor a lawgiver from between his feet, until Shiloh comes; and to Him shall be the obedience of the people" (Gen. 49:10). This prophecy found fulfillment in the line of David, and ultimately in the Messiah, a descendant of David (Mark 1:1).

(2) Succession of the Adamic Covenant

Although the Adamic Covenant was conceived within the shadow of judgment, the radiance of God's grace still shines through it, much like a rainbow following a rain shower. God ordained for mankind to continue to enjoy the blessings of fertility (Gen. 1:28; 3:16) and land (Gen. 1:28-29, 3:17-19), as well as spiritual blessings (Gen. 2:3; 3:21), that He had bestowed at the time of creation. However, fulfillment of the cultural mandate would now be accompanied by suffering and toil.[14] The presence of this mandate even after the fall underscores the enduring nature of mankind's covenant relationship with God, wherein humanity continues to bear the image of God despite their transgression.

The aim of humanity's cultural mandate is the ultimate restoration of the paradise lost in Eden—a renewal akin to a new creation. However, this monumental task remains unattainable, regardless of the depth of human passion and effort, given the specter of mortality that looms over mankind: "For dust you are, and to dust you shall return" (Gen. 3:19). Yet, a remarkable transformation occurs—a new humanity and a new world emerge—owing to God's fulfillment of his flawless purpose throughout history, achieved through the incarnation, crucifixion, and resurrection of the promised Seed of the Woman.

(3) Expression of hope for the Messiah

Adam expressed the hopes he placed in the Seed of the Woman through the new name that he gave his wife. Initially, upon greeting her following her creation, he had named her "Woman" (Gen 2:23). However, as he comprehended the pivotal role her descendants would play in the restoration of life, his perspective shifted. She embodied the hope of life. "And Adam called his wife Eve,

---

14 Merrill, 302.

because she was the mother of all the living" (Gen. 3:20). "Hawah" means "life."

Meanwhile, God fashioned garments of skin for Adam and his wife (Gen. 3:21). Just as innocent animals were sacrificed to provide covering for their newfound shame, Messiah would offer Himself as the ultimate sacrifice on the cross to justify sinners. The animal sacrifices that mankind offered to God after their expulsion from Eden served as a prefiguration of the Lamb of God who would eventually bear the sins of the world (John 1:29).

4. Noahic Covenant

After the Flood, God established the Noahic Covenant with Noah, a covenant often referred to as the Noahic Covenant (Gen. 9:1-17). The Hebrew term for covenant, "berit", appears seven times in Genesis 9:9-17 (Gen. 9:9, 11, 12, 13, 15, 16, 17), following its earlier mention in Genesis 6:18. The Noahic Covenant embodies the realization of God's promise to Noah as initially stated in Genesis 6.

The Noahic Covenant is God's pledge to refrain from annihilating the world through another flood, symbolized by the appearance of a rainbow as a sign of this promise. God granted humans the consumption of animals for sustenance but instructed them not to consume blood and prohibited the taking of human life. Through the Noahic Covenant, God established the assurance that both humanity and all living creatures would persist on Earth following the catastrophic Flood.

(1) Renewal of the Creation Covenant

God communicated with Noah and his sons, as stated in Genesis 9:1 and 8. However, the scope of the Noahic covenant extends to encompass all of humanity and every living creature: "behold, I establish My covenant with you and with your descendants after you, and with every living creature that is with you: the birds, the cattle, and every beast of the earth with you, of all that go out of the ark, every beast of the earth" (Gen. 9:9-10). This covenant serves as a reaffirmation of the Creation Covenant.

When examining Genesis 8:22–9:7 as a precursor to the covenantal promises found in Genesis 9:8–17, a distinct linguistic parallel between the latter and the creation narrative emerges, particularly in relation to Genesis 1 (compare Gen. 9:1 and 1:28; Gen. 9:2-3 and 1:29, and Gen. 9:10 and 1:20-25).[15] These parallels highlight themes of fruitfulness and multiplication; dominion over creation; land; and relationship with God. Just as God blessed all living things in the initial act of creation, He

---

15 McConville, '*berit*', *NIDOTTE* 1:748.

extended his blessings to mankind, all living creatures, and the Earth as their habitat in the aftermath of the Flood (Gen. 9:1, 7, 9-11, 17).

God's command to abstain from consuming the blood of animals and the establishment of a penalty for shedding human blood (Gen. 9:4-6) were designed to ensure peace and harmony in the post-Flood world. This reflects that God's original intention for his creation was peace. The rainbow ("bow, rainbow"), placed in the clouds as a symbol of the covenant (Gen. 9:13, 14, 16), represents God's decision to set aside his bow for battle"[16] for the sake of peace. the bow used for battle. Through this covenant, God seeks to restore and sustain a relationship of love, affection, and friendship between Himself and humanity.William Hendricksen, The Covenant of Grace, rev. ed. (Grand Rapids, MI: Baker, 1978), 18.[17] This friendship has the nature of forgiveness (Jer. 31:31-34; Rom. 11:27), and represents an intimate bond in the form of a covenant, lovingkindness or unchanging love.[18]

God referred to the covenant as "My covenant" (*bürîtî*, Gen. 6:18; 9:9, 11, 15, 17). This highlights the active role of God as the initiator of the covenant relationship. It is God who takes the initiative in establishing and renewing the covenant through the creation and re-creation. The unbroken thread of God's covenant against the backdrop of the "creation-anti-creation-re-creation" serves as a testament to the unwavering and steadfast love that the Lord has for his creation. This enduring love forms the foundation for understanding the history of humanity as a history of redemption and salvation.

(2) God Who remembers

"Then God remembered Noah, and every living thing, and all the animals that were with him in the ark" (Gen. 8:1). In the narrative of the Flood, the covenantal love of God for his creation is poignantly expressed through the Hebrew terms "zakhar", meaning "to remember" (Gen. 8:1; 9:16). God remembered Noah, his covenant partner, and all living beings sheltered within the ark with him amidst the cataclysmic deluge. Post-Flood, God affirms, "I will…remember the everlasting covenant" (Gen. 9:16). The gravest crisis a human being can encounter is God forgetting. Isaiah

---

16 Francis Brown, S. R. Driver, and Charles A. Briggs, 'tvq', *A Hebrew and English Lexicon of the Old Testament, with an Appendix Containing the Biblical Aramaic Based on the Lexicon of William Gesenius* (=BDB) (Oxford: Clarendon Press, 1951).

17 William Hendricksen, *The Covenant of Grace*, rev. ed. (Grand Rapids, MI: Baker, 1978), 18.

18 Ibid. Deut. 7:9; 2 Chron. 6:14; Dan. 9:4.

54:7-10 conveys that hope endures for Israel because God recalls the covenant of peace, just as the world had hope through his remembrance of the Noahic covenant.[19] This essence of the covenant is encapsulated in the phrase "God remembered," portraying the covenant as a manifestation of God's self-imposed obligation.[20] Within the covenant, God assumes the burden of redemption and furnishes the means of salvation. The sacred bestowals, including the sanctuary, the Ten Commandments, the Holy Spirit, the new birth, and spiritual gifts, stem from God's divine providence, rather than being the intellectual constructions of human religious thinkers. [21] The invitation extends to all to grasp the priceless gift of grace offered unconditionally.

The Seed of the woman was destined to appear on earth as a progeny of Shem, one of Noah's sons. God was invoked as "Yahweh, the God of Shem" (Gen. 9:26). Shem emerged as the recipient of the covenant, one who had received God's distinctive favor. The offspring of Shem were chosen to be devoted adherents of the one true God, serving as a wellspring of salvation.[22]

5. Abrahamic Covenant

Abraham was a descendent of Noah, of the lineage of Shem (Gen. 10:21-31; 11:10-32). The Abrahamic Covenant is encapsulated within Genesis 12:1-3; 15:1-5; and 17:1-14. Genesis 12:1-3 chronicles Abraham's divine summoning, within which are embedded an array of special divine assurances. Chief among them is an encompassing missionary call, devised to rescue a fractured world in the aftermath of the Tower of Babel. This covenant extends an invitation to all nations, ushering them into the embrace of God's redemptive gospel.

(1) Genesis 12

In Genesis 12:1, God told Abraham to depart from three things. During antiquity, when origin

19 Rolf Rendtorff, 'Noah, Abraham and Moses: God's Covenant Partners', *In Search of True Wisdom: Essays in Old Testament Interpretation in Honour of Ronald E. Clements*, Journal for the Study of the Old Testament Supplement Series (Sheffield, England: Sheffield Academic Press, 1999), 132-133.

20 E. Kutsch, '*berit*', *TLOT* 1:265.

21 For a discussion of the theological significance of the covenantal structure of the history of salvation, see Thomas E. McComiskey, *The Covenants of Promise: A Theology of the Old Testament Covenants* (Grand Rapids, MI: Baker Book House, 1985).

22 Johann Peter Lange, Tayler Lewis, and Abraham Gosman, *A Commentary on the Holy Scriptures: Genesis* (Bellingham, WA: Logos Research Systems, Inc., 2008), 337.

and familial bonds held paramount significance, relinquishing one's "country," "family," and "father's house" equated to forfeiting the bedrock of one's identity and security.[23] The imperative form "lek-leka", which is exclusively employed in this verse, literally translates to "go to you." This wording conveys that this odyssey involves forsaking all earthly entanglements and embarking on a voyage towards self-discovery. Through a resolute severance from past entwinements,[24] Abraham stood poised to discover his true self and forge a personal relationship with his God.

Abraham's calling was unequivocally centered on God. In Genesis 12:1-3 and 7, the phrase "I will…" showcases an incomplete verb in the promise form, expressed in the first-person singular, used five times.[25] This signifies the unfolding of God's initiative in Abraham's life, compelling him to act in accordance with the Divine Word, as evidenced by his relocation in accordance with God's command and his construction of altars.[26]

God's call, constituting the scaffolding of Abraham's existence, unfurls in threefold promises. Firstly, the promise of land is reiterated across Genesis 12:1, 7; 13:15, 17; 15:8; and 17:8. Secondly, the pledge of offspring resounds through Genesis 12:2, 13:15, 16; 15:5; 17:4-6, 17:16; 18:18; 21:13; and 22:17. Thirdly, the commitment to bestow blessings reverberates in Genesis 12:2, 3; 18:18; and 22:17-18. This tripartite pledge encompasses a rich tapestry of promises for Israel (descendants and land) and international blessings.

This overarching framework aligns seamlessly with God's plan for a new creation, arising as redemption after the narrative of humanity's falterings in Genesis 1-11. The most pronounced focal point within this calling lies in the cascade of blessings, prominently featured five times in Genesis 12:2-3.[27] This heralded the inception of a watershed moment in the history of redemption, wherein humanity, previously ensnared in the shackles of Adam's Fall, would be ushered into a realm of

---

23 Gordon J. Wenham, *Exploring the Old Testament: The Pentateuch*, vol. 1 (Seoul: Scripture Union Korea, 2007), 75.

24 The preposition "lu" used in "lek-luka" carries the meaning of "separating, taking leave of." See Nahum M. Sarna, Genesis, ed. Nahum M. Sarna, The JPS Torah Commentary, vol. 1 (Philadelphia, PA: The Jewish Publication Society, 1989), 88.

25 The divine promises of God to Abraham, expressed in the Hebrew imperfect verb forms of first person, can be seen in the calling and obedience of Abraham. They are as follows: (i) "I will make you" (Gen. 12:2); (ii) "I will bless you" (Gen. 12:2, 3); (iii) "I will make your name great (Gen. 12:2); (iv) "I will give you" (Gen. 12:7).

26 Sidney Greidanus, *Preaching Christ from Genesis: Foundations for Expository Sermons* (Grand Rapids, MI: William B. Eerdmans, 2007), 142.

27 Charles T. Fritsch, *Genesis*, ed. Balmer H. Kelly, The Layman's Bible Commentary, vol. 2 (Atlanta, GA: John Knox, 1959), 53.

blessings through Abraham, a new Adam.[28]

"You shall be a blessing" (Gen. 12:2) resounds as an imperative, reflecting God's direct appeal to Abraham to become a conduit of blessing to humanity through unwavering fidelity to his commands. Abraham's profound interaction with the Divine would serve as a means for humanity to enjoy the gift of renewed comprehension and direct experience of God's presence.

"And in you all the families of the earth shall be blessed," as stated in Genesis 12:3, serves as a stark contrast to the endeavors of humanity exemplified by the construction of the Tower of Babel. The Tower symbolized their pursuit of self-security and aggrandizement. Even though God's blessing was already being realized—the population had grown such that there were approximately seventh tribes on the earth at that time (Gen. 10:1-32; 11:10-32), humanity had fallen into a state of deep spiritual depravity. Rather than glorify God, they were only interested in making a name for themselves (Gen. 11:4). Ultimately, their languages were confused and they were dispersed throughout the earth. It was in this period of crisis that Abraham emerged as a pivotal figure. He was to not only enjoy God's blessings personally, but to become a conduit of blessings to all nations. What the nations could not achieve through their organizational prowess, God was bestowing through his grace.[29] In Abraham's calling, we find one of the earliest accounts of global evangelism.[30]

Abraham's decision represented the decision of the nation of Israel. God chose one man, and through him one nation, and through that nation one Savior. He is in the course of fashioning one family, global in its reach, that ardently worships that Savior.[31] Genesis 15 and 17 intricately detail the birth of the nation of Israel and the assurance of a designated homeland where they will establish their residence.

(2) Genesis 15

Genesis 15 contains a covenant that God made with Abraham in a vision, at a time when the fulfillment of God's promise to make his descendants as numerous as the "dust of the earth" (Gen. 13:16) appeared delayed. In this iteration of the promise, God promised Abraham that his descendants would be like the stars in the sky, and Abraham believed in Yahweh (Gen. 15:5, 6).

This chapter depicts Abraham in his role as a prophet. He saw a "mahazeh" ("vision"), and

---

28 Robert Alter, *Genesis: Translation and Commentary* (New York, NY: W. W. Norton & Company, 1996), 50.

29 Kaiser, 115.

30 Ibid., 121.

31 Rendtorff, 131.

received divine revelation of future events (Gen. 15:12-21). Based on this experience, Abraham was later referred to as a prophet when God spoke to Abimelech the king of Gerar in a dream (Gen. 20:7).

It is important to remember the covenantal background against which the prophecy was given, and Abraham faith credited to him for righteousness (Gen. 15:6). Being in a covenantal relationship requires unwavering trust in God, who never forgets. Despite any apparent delay in the realization of the covenant, God can be trusted to fulfill his promises. The people of the covenant are the people of the prophecy.

Covenants are inherently forward-looking, driven by the anticipation of a future that is firmly rooted in God's Word, and it is God Himself who brings this envisioned future to fruition. Genesis 15:12-20 serve as a testament to a history governed by God's sovereign control. God unequivocally announces his intent to enact justice upon Egypt for its enslavement of the Israelites (Gen. 15:14). Moreover, God reaffirms his pledge to bestow the land currently occupied by the Canaanite nations—stretching from the river of Egypt to the Euphrates—as an inheritance for the descendants of Abraham (Gen. 15:18).

When God entered into the covenant with Abraham, He passed through the pieces of the sacrificial offerings, manifesting Himself as a burning torch (Gen. 15:17). The cutting of the offerings symbolized a reciprocal pledge, signifying that the person who broke the covenant would endure a fate akin to that of the sacrifice itself. Notably, in this instance, only God traversed through the divided offerings, with Abraham not taking part. This arrangement underscores the covenant's unilateral character,[32] emphasizing that it is initiated and upheld solely by God.

The subsequent events, such as the Exodus from Egypt and the expansion of Israel's territory, would be effected under God's sole responsibility. Israel's emergence as a nation, their settlement, and territorial acquisition were not attributable to their own might, but instead resulted from God's distinct favor and his steadfast commitment to the promises made to their forefathers (Deut. 7:6-8).

(3) Genesis 17

In Genesis 17, we find God initiating yet another covenant with Abraham, this time involving his very body. Whereas previous covenants had been based on symbolic imagery—descendants as numerous as the dust of the ground and the stars in the sky—the Genesis 17 covenant centered

32 P.R. Williamson, 'Abraham', *Dictionary of the Old Testament: Pentateuch*, ed. T. Desmond Alexander; David W. Baker (Downers Grove, IL.: InterVarsity Press, 2003), 10.

around the rite of circumcision, where the covenantal relationship would be physically manifested in the bodies of Abraham and the men of his household. Circumcision served as a visible sign, indicating their identification as people of the covenant through their faith. Additionally, those who underwent circumcision were called upon to serve as witnesses to God's covenant with the world.

This emphasizes that the most significant representation of the covenant is humanity itself, rather than celestial bodies or earthly elements. The covenant's essence is not confined to the cosmic or material realms; rather, it is embodied in the physical sign of circumcision on the human body. Furthermore, its transmission to the world relies on those who carry it within their hearts and live it out in their lives. Ultimately, the fulfillment of the covenant is accomplished through the faithful obedience and testimony of those who are part of it.

God's revelation to Abram and Sarai marked a significant transformation in their identities and roles within the covenant. In Genesis 17:5, God changed Abram's name, which means "High Father," to Abraham, signifying his new role as the "Father of the Multitude." Similarly, Sarai's name, meaning "My Princess," was changed to Sarah, meaning "Princess" in a broader sense. These new names carried a deep covenantal faith, symbolizing the bearers' destiny to become not only the ancestors of Israel but also the spiritual forebearers of the Church of God, representing spiritual Israel and bringing blessings to the entire world.

Genesis 18 further provides insight into the unfolding of this covenant. It foreshadows the birth of Isaac and highlights Abraham's intercession for Sodom, pointing to the eventual emergence of Israel as a holy and priestly nation mediating the gospel (Gen. 18:22-33; Ex. 19:6). Although Israel would ultimately fail in fulfilling this role, Jesus would fulfill this calling perfectly. Jesus, through his Church, which serves as the royal priesthood and the holy kingdom of God, extends his reach to all corners of the earth, gathering people from diverse backgrounds to worship and serve God (1 Pet. 2:9).

The significance of a name goes beyond a mere label; it reflects a person's character and destiny. In the case of Abraham, his name became intertwined with God's covenant, signifying his role and identity within it. To mark this momentous occasion, God further disclosed the precise timing of Isaac's birth: "But my covenant I will establish with Isaac, whom Sarah shall bear to you at this set time next year" (Gen. 17:21).

At long last, the son of the covenant was born: "And the Lord visited Sarah as He had said, and the Lord did for Sarah as He had spoken" (Gen. 21:1). God is faithful to fulfill his promises. He is the one who brings to pass what He declares. The birth of Isaac stands in stark contrast to the story of Hagar and Ishmael. Ishmael's conception was a result of human effort driven by fleshly desires, but Isaac's birth was a fulfillment of God's promise (Gal. 4:23). Isaac's birth carries a profound lesson about righteousness through faith and the true freedom that faith brings. It demonstrates that God's promises are fulfilled according to his Word, not through human manipulation or effort.

Sarah's attainment of motherhood may be likened to a resurrection from the dead, and was the direct outcome of the extraordinary power wielded by the Creator—He who formed the stars as well as the innumerable grains of sand in the sea (Heb. 11:11-12). Even though Sarah's womb had seemingly been devoid of life, God, the very originator of the cosmos, through his divine utterance brought forth the wondrous phenomenon of birth. This was brought about by faith, not by deeds. Divine covenants always entail the realization of God's singular grace through supernatural events. The attainment of salvation within this covenant requires an unwavering, absolute trust in the Creator God.

(4) Genesis 22

In Genesis 22, we encounter a pivotal moment that tests the depth of Abraham's faith in the fulfillment of the covenant. This chapter centers on Abraham, the bearer of the covenant name, facing an excruciating trial. Unlike in previous moments of weakness, Abraham here displayed a resolute faith as he offered his beloved son Isaac—the very embodiment of the covenant—as a sacrifice unto God.

As Abraham's outstretched hand held the blade over Isaac, prostrate on the alter, Abraham gave up all human hope of fulfillment of the covenant. his hope now lay exclusively within the realm of the divine, in the Creator God who bestows life upon the dead. Abraham's sacrifice was an embodiment of self-relinquishment and absolute reliance and submission to God, who fulfills his covenants. This awe-inspiring event, set against the backdrop of Mount Moriah, serves as an exquisite emblem of the eternal covenant, which would be realized on Calvary's hill. The temple, eventually erected upon this hallowed ground, stood as a tangible testament to the lessons embedded within the covenant of salvation.

In the wake of Abraham's victorious obedience, a cascade of blessings unfurled. God told Abraham that his lineage would burgeon into a multitude, possess the gate of their enemies and become a blessing for all nations of the earth (Gen. 22:16-18).

Abraham's unwavering obedience to God's command, even to the point of willingness to sacrifice his own son, serves as a foreshadowing of the ultimate act of obedience and sacrifice fulfilled by Jesus Christ. Abraham's name is placed at the very beginning of the genealogy of Jesus Christ with which the New Testament opens: "The book of the genealogy of Jesus Christ, the Son of David, the Son of Abraham" (Matt. 1:1).

6. The Patriarchs' Faith in the Covenant

Abraham took deliberate steps to ensure that the covenant would exclusively run through Isaac's descendants, by sending away all of the children of his second wife Keturah to the East (Gen. 25:1-6). Following Abraham's passing at the age of one hundred and seventy-five, God reaffirmed the covenant with Isaac and Jacob (Gen. 26:3-4; 28:13-14).

Abraham's acquisition of the cave of Machpelah in Hebron holds special significance in the context of the Promised Land. The sacred resting place of Abraham's beloved companion, Sarah, is located there (Gen. 23:19). Abraham himself was laid to rest in this hallowed ground (Gen. 25:9), and Jacob was also interred here (Gen. 49:29; 50:12-13). The legacy of this covenant-bound lineage endured, with Joseph requesting on his death bed that his remains should be laid to rest in the Promised Land when the Israelites left Egypt (Gen. 50:25; Ex. 13:19; burial in Sechem, Josh. 24:32). This account shows that Abraham's faith in the covenant was passed down to the children of Israel. Exodus and the books that followed show this covenant being achieved within the history of Israel.

The ancient yearning for the Promised Land serves as a source of encouragement for present-day believers to cultivate a similar longing for their ultimate heavenly abode. The patriarchs placed their faith in God's covenant and desired to be interred in the land of promise. Yet, our destiny surpasses earthly confines, as we are destined for an eternal residence in the heavenly Promised Land. This everlasting dwelling is affirmed by Jesus, the covenant's descendant, who tenderly pledged, "I go to prepare a place for you...that where I am, there you may be also" (John 14:1-3).

Chapter 15 | The Law and the Sabbath

1. Meaning and Function of the Torah

In Hebrew, the term for "law" is "torah", derived from the root verb "hora" (Hiphil of *yarah*) which means "to teach" or "to instruct." In the Old Testament, the term *torah* is used approximately 220 times and is used to convey (i) teachings, lessons, or instructions to be learned and followed; (ii) commands that are to be obeyed; and (iii) guidance and instruction on how to conduct oneself in specific circumstances.[1]

"Torah" is also the name of the first part of the Hebrew Scriptures, known as the Pentateuch, which comprises the books of Genesis, Exodus, Leviticus, Numbers, and Deuteronomy. Every seven years, during the Feast of Tabernacles, all the people of Israel were to gather together to hear a reading of the Torah and learn to "carefully observe all the words of this law" (Deut. 31:10-12). Kings were commanded to keep a copy of the book of the law by them and read and observe those laws throughout their lives (Deut. 17:18-20).

The Torah serves an educational purpose. It is meant to be heard, learned, observed, and acted upon (Deut. 5:1). While the word "laws" evokes laws, commands, and statutes, the Pentateuch encompasses both narratives and legal regulations. Deuteronomy utilizes the word "torah" in various contexts, both for storytelling and judicial matters (Deut. 4:8; 17:18; 27:3; 31:9). The term "Torah" isn't confined to a single literary style; rather, it encompasses the entirety of these books.

The collections of laws within the Pentateuch are intricately woven into the fabric of the stories they accompany.[2] The remarkable history of God's interactions with his people—showing his faithfulness in the face of repeated apostasy by the Israelites—is presented in an unbroken manner, encouraging readers to place their trust in God and keep his commandments (Psa. 78:3-8). Keeping the law is not burdensome but rather a blessing and a pathway to success (Josh. 1:8; Ps. 1:2-3; Neh. 8:10-18). Moreover, the Torah in a broader sense extends beyond the Pentateuch to encompass the

---

1 M. J. Selman, 'Law', *Dictionary of the Old Testament: Pentateuch*, ed. T. Desmond Alexander, David W. Baker (Downers Grove, Ill.: InterVarsity Press, 2003), 498.

2 Ibid., 500.

entire Old Testament. God, as the inspiration behind both the Old and New Testaments, uses the stories and commands within Scripture to provide doctrine, reproof, correction, and instruction in righteousness, so "that the man of God may be complete, thoroughly equipped for every good work" (2 Tim. 3:16-17).

The Torah, in its narrow sense, serves as a legal framework to regulate conduct. Judaism identifies 613 precepts within the Pentateuch. The core of the law is encapsulated in the Ten Commandments, which were "written with the finger of God" (Ex. 31:18) and establish the foundational principle for the ethical life of mankind. These commandments are referred to in the Pentateuch as "asheret haddeberim," meaning "Ten Words" (Ex. 34:28; Deut. 4:13; 10:4). This evokes parallels with the "Wayomer Elohim", the ten words that brought into being the physical world (Gen. 1:3, 6, 9, 11, 14, 20, 24, 26, 28, 29). God is the creator of both the material and spiritual realms, and his Word forms the foundation for the existence of the world and humanity.

2. The Law in Genesis

(1) The Law in Creation

All things came into existence by the creation commands of Genesis 1—"let there be," "let them be for," "let...abound with," "let...bring forth"—and God bestowed upon human beings the cultural command (Gen. 1:28). As biological beings, humans are bound to obey the laws of the material world that God has established. Additionally, as spiritual beings created in the image of God, they are compelled to obey the spiritual and moral laws ordained by God.

The law is virtuous and imbued with divine blessings. God's law has the pivotal role of upholding the meticulously crafted world that sprung forth from the creation commands in accordance with God's good will. The Creator Himself, who sculpted humanity's existence, bequeathed this law so that mankind could fulfill the cultural mandate to propagate and thrive under a benedictory mantle. At its core, the inaugural commandment on good and evil was a proclamation that obeyance to God's Word leads to eternal happiness. As long as man acknowledges the supremacy of God and embraces the role of stewardship, man can lead a holy life that reflects the holiness of God. The Sabbath, a hallowed celebration harkening back to the very commencement of creation, attests to the holiness of the Creator's moral character and the purpose of the divine laws, which is to bestow blessings upon creation (Gen. 2:3).

The law is eternal. At the time of creation, mankind was given a cultural mandate, and God's

Word as the principle of life and existence will last eternally even in the age of the new heavens and the new earth. Just as there was a simple commandment distinguishing good from evil before the giving of the Ten Commandments, so in the new era, mankind will continue to live under the law of love—to love God and love one's neighbors, which is the spirit underlying the Ten Commandments. God's law will be written in the hearts of mankind, not merely inscribed in stone.

(2) The Ten Commandments in Genesis

Genesis 26:5 testifies that God's law existed before Mount Sinai: "because Abraham obeyed My voice and kept My charge, My commandments, My statutes, and My laws." The Hebrew word for "laws" in this verse is torah. In Genesis, we can find traces of the Ten Commandments as they existed prior to codification on Mount Sinai, as follows.

First Commandment. Monotheism is evident in the creation account. God, the Absolute Sovereign who creates all things through his Word, is the only one who deserves to be worshipped. Abraham was blessed by Melchizedek in the name of Yahweh, the Most High God, Lord of heaven and earth (Gen. 14:19; cf. Gen. 14:22). After Jacob returned to the land of Canaan, he returned to Bethel and worshiped. The object of his worship was exclusively the God who had providentially guided his path (Gen. 35:1-4).

Second Commandment. Ancient societies widely worshipped the sun, moon, stars, animals, vegetation and other natural things and phenomena. All of these were all created by God. The creation account is a refutation of polytheism. After receiving his calling, Abraham "built an altar to Yahweh" wherever he traveled within the idolatrous land of Canaan, and his altar became a testimony to the God in Whom he believed (Gen. 12:7, 8; 13:4, 18). Jacob carried out a reformation in his household, throwing out man-made pagan images and returning to God (Gen. 35:2-4).

Third Commandment. Lamech, a descendant of Cain, used the protection God had bestowed upon Cain to proclaim his own vengeful intentions, thus abusing God's grace and, indirectly, taking God's name in vain (Gen. 4:24). He instilled in his descendants the tradition of vengeance by making revenge an obligation.[3] The world became so full of violence that God lamented his creative work.

Fourth Commandment. Genesis 2:1-3 reveals the origin of the Sabbath. By deliberately emphasizing the number of the Sabbath—seven—the book highlights the sanctity of the Sabbath.

Fifth Commandment. God chose Abraham to lead his children and household in accordance

---

3 Hughes, *Genesis: Beginning and Blessing*, 114.

with the Word of God (Gen. 18:19), and Isaac was obedient to his godly father, even to the point of surrendering himself to be bound up as a sacrifice (Gen. 22:9-11). God, in response, bestowed on Abraham and Isaac the blessings of abundance and might as well as the promise of a Messiah. This is in line with the nature of the fifth commandment, which is the first of the Ten Commandments to be accompanied by a promise (Gen. 22:17, 18; cf. Ex. 20:12; Eph. 6:2).

Sixth Commandment. The first murder in human history took place between brothers, and God pronounced judgment upon Cain for the killing of his brother Abel (Gen. 4:8-15)

Seventh Commandment. The city of Sodom faced God's judgment due to the sin of homosexuality (Gen. 19:1-10). Joseph resisted the advances of Potiphar's wife because of his fear of Yahweh (Gen. 39:7-9).

Eighth Commandment. Jacob restituted Laban for stolen livestock (Gen. 31:39). Joseph's brothers protested their innocence regarding theft to Joseph (Gen. 44:8).

Ninth Commandment. Abraham faced a crisis when he deceived the rulers of the land regarding his wife, Sarah, by claiming she was his sister. God intervened and protected his servants in these instances (Gen. 12:11-20; 20:1-10).

Tenth Commandment. Jacob and Rebekah, driven by covetousness for the blessing of the firstborn, deceived Isaac and orchestrated a situation in which Jacob received the blessing intended for Esau (Gen. 27). This act had profound consequences, and Rebekah was never again able to see Jacob.

The Ten Commandments are a love of love that serves as a foundation for humanity to lead lives of peace and happiness. The first four commandments are centered on the love for God, while the subsequent six focus on loving one's fellow human beings (Matt. 22:35-40; Mark 12:28-31; Luke 10:25-28). The Ten Commandments are inherent within the blessing of God's command to "be fruitful and multiply." By honoring God and parents, by not murdering, by not engaging in adultery or theft, by not bearing false witness and refraining from covetousness, we uphold the very foundations of human existence. These commandments, inherent in the fabric of God's creation, represent universal values that govern humanity. Going against these principles constitutes sin and leads to the erosion of human life. The Ten Commandments are intrinsically tied to the principles of creation, exemplified in the words "Wayomer Elohim", "God said". The Sabbath commandment, which is a part of the Ten Commandments, testifies that its authority emanates from the Creator God.

3. The Sabbath in Genesis

The Sabbath was instituted by God at the time of creation. Genesis demonstrates the Sabbath faith in various manners, such as through the use of the creation paradigm in the account of the great Flood and the prominent use of the number seven.

The number seven is among the most symbolically important numbers in the Bible. It appears in nearly six hundred verses. This sacred number was revered in various Semitic cultures. Some interpret this phenomenon as stemming from the lunar calendar's composition of four sets of seven days, or based on the seven celestial bodies (sun, moon, and five planets). However, the theologically sound interpretation is that the number seven's sanctity originates from the weekly system ordained at creation.

In Genesis, the number seven is referenced in various contexts, including seven days (Gen. 2:2, 3; 7:4, 10; 8:10, 12; 31:23; 50:10); seven-fold (Gen. 4:15, 24); seven years (Gen. 29:18, 20, 27; 41:26, 27, 29, 30, 34, 36, 47, 53, 54); multiples of seven (Gen. 4:24; 5:12, 31; 11:26; 46:25, 27; 50:3); seven things (beasts: Gen. 7:2, 3; 21:28, 29, 30; 41:2, 3, 4, 18, 19, 20, 26, 27; heads of grain: Gen. 41:5, 6, 7, 22, 23, 24, 26, 27; persons: Gen. 46:25); and seven bows (Gen. 33:3).

(1) Creation and the Sabbath (Gen. 2:1-3)

The creation account in Gen. 1:1–2:3 is constructed with deliberate use of the perfect number seven and its multiples. The first verse of Genesis consists of seven words, while the second verse contains twice that number, totaling fourteen words. Notably, the seventh paragraph corresponds to the seventh day of creation. Moreover, the seventh day is positioned in the middle of three consecutive sentences, each comprising seven words (note that the number three is used to emphasize): "And on the **seventh** day God ended his work which He had done, and He rested on the **seventh** day from all his work which He had done. Then God blessed the **seventh** day and sanctified it, because in it He rested from all his work which God had created and made" (Gen. 2:2-3).

Next, let's delve into the content of the creation account. Within it, we find seven of God's absolute commands that facilitate the existence of creation: "Let there be light," "Let there be a firmament," "Let the waters be gathered together into one place," "Let the earth bring forth grass," "Let there be lights in the firmament," "Let the waters abound with an abundance of living creatures," and "Let the earth bring forth the living creature."

Furthermore, in the first paragraph of Genesis 1:1-5, the words "light" (*'ôr*) and "day" (*yôm*) appear a combined total of seven times. The phrase "God saw that it was (very) good" appears seven times (Gen. 1:4, 10, 12, 18, 21, 25, and 31). Moreover, the words "earth" (*eretz*) and "heavens" (*shamaim*) appear twenty-one times. The term "God" (*elohim*) is mentioned thirty-five times, which is five times seven.[4]

The theological meaning of the Sabbath as revealed in the text is as follows.

1) The Sabbath belongs to the created order.

Genesis 2:2 states, "on the seventh day God ended his work which He had done." Given that the heavens, the earth, and all that they contain were created in six days, it may be assumed that the seventh day has no relevance to God's creative work. This led to variations in translation. The Greek translation, the Septuagint Version, implies completion by saying that the creation was finished on the "sixth day" (ἐνn τῇ ἡmέrᾳ τῇ ἕkτῃ, *en te hemera te hekte*), while the Korean version vaguely translates it as "when the seventh day came."

However, the Hebrew Scriptures explicitly state "on the seventh day" which was accurately reproduced in the King James Version and New King James Version. What God did on the seventh day was to establish the Sabbath through the act of resting. The Sabbath acted as a full stop to the creation week—with the Sabbath, creation reached its completion.

2) The Sabbath belongs to the divine order.

The Sabbath is under divine authority, being uniquely sanctified, set apart, and blessed by God. While it spans a 24-hour period like any other day of the week, it is exclusively infused with divine blessings and holiness. This distinction is a result of God, the transcendent Creator, bestowing upon the seventh day the significance of both blessing and holiness.

3) God rested on the Sabbath.

What God did on the Sabbath was rest. In Genesis 2:2, the Hebrew noun "shabbat", meaning "Sabbath," was not utilized; instead, the verb "shabat" was employed to convey that God "rested." This verb appears in Genesis 2:2, 3 and Genesis 8:22, signifying "to rest" or "to finish." The Sabbath signifies the cessation of labor. By observing rest on this day, God provided humanity with an example, highlighting the importance of rest as an integral aspect of the created order.

---

4 Cassuto, *A Commentary on the Book of Genesis: Part 1, from Adam to Noah*, 14-15.

4) The Sabbath is the anniversary of creation.

The rationale behind the Sabbath is expounded in Genesis 2:3, which states: "because in it He rested from all his work which God had created and made." The fourth commandment of the Ten Commandments explicitly underscores the importance of the Sabbath as a commemoration of the creation's anniversary (Ex. 20:11).

5) The Sabbath was given to mankind.

The Sabbath is not limited to the Jewish people; it was instituted for all of humanity at the time of creation. As beings made in the image of God, humans are called to observe a day of rest, mirroring God's own example.

6) The Sabbath is a holy day.

The Sabbath is a day set apart by God Himself. God's inherent attribute of holiness imparts sanctity to the Sabbath, making it a day that stands apart from the rest. The Sabbath is a "holy of holies" within the realm of time.

7) The Sabbath is a time for humans to experience God's holiness.

The concept of holiness is a quality unique to human beings, who possess intelligence and spirituality, setting them apart from animals or plants within the realm of creation. The sanctification of the Sabbath is specifically directed towards humanity among all living creatures. God's rest on the Sabbath was not due to weariness; rather, He set aside one day to spend with mankind. Through Sabbath worship, humans can engage with God and cultivate a sense of holiness, enabling them to live each day as beings dedicated to sacred communion with Him.

8) The Sabbath is an eternal institution that can never be abolished or destroyed.

In commemoration of his creation, God did not appoint a physical structure made of gold, silver, or any other material object that could be susceptible to human destruction. Instead, He ordained the intangible concept of time, something beyond human control or manipulation. The Sabbath stands as a perpetual institution, enduring as long as the earth itself, functioning as a dual celebration of both creation and redemption. It serves as a testament to the roles of God as both creator and redeemer, providing a timeless testimony through the ages.

9) The Sabbath had an evangelistic character.

The Sabbath invites mankind to partake in the abundant blessings and holiness of God. Sabbath draws near to mankind on a weekly basis, urging them to revel in the richness of God's creation and salvation. God, the generous king, orchestrates a grand feast and graciously invites all to partake (cf. Matt. 22:3; Luke 13:29).

10) The Sabbath gives man a sense of belonging as a child of God.

The Sabbath stands as a testament that humanity's origin is not rooted in the lower life forms of evolution, but rather in the loving embrace of a caring and intentional creator.

11) The Sabbath frees us from the crime of idolatry.

By deepening our faith in the creator of all, the Sabbath serves as a safeguard, preventing us from succumbing to the folly of worshiping man-made idols. By fostering a reliance on the providence of the Creator, it shields us from idolizing material pursuits such as wealth, fame, and power.

12) The Sabbath encourages believers to be stewards.

The Sabbath inspires a sense of gratitude towards the abundant blessings bestowed upon us by God. Through this sacred day of rest, we acknowledge that God reigns supreme over all aspects of existence. This recognition prompts us to remember that our possessions, skills, and opportunities are divine gifts, entrusted to us by God. We thereby come to embrace responsible stewardship within our families, churches, communities, and the broader world.

(2) Cain (Gen. 4:3, 15)

In the story of Cain and Abel, the number seven is employed in Genesis 4:15, which states: "And the Lord said to him, 'Therefore, whoever kills Cain, vengeance shall be taken on him sevenfold.'" Before delving into the significance of this passage in connection with the Sabbath, it is worth examining Genesis 4:3, which subtly hints at the observance of the Sabbath.

The term "mikketz yamim" in Genesis 4:3, which introduces the story of Cain and Abel, literally translates to "at the end of the days." Throughout Genesis 1-4, the term "yom", which means "day," is used in various ways, including to refer to: (i) twelve-hour period (Gen. 1:5, 14, 16, 18); (ii) twenty-four-hour periods (Gen. 1:5, 8, 13, 14, 19, 23, 31; 2:2, 3); (iii) unspecified period of time (Gen. 3:14, 17); (iv) time when an event occurred (Gen. 2:4); (v) a certain time of the day (Gen. 3:8);

and (vi) today (Gen. 4:14).[5]

Genesis 4:3 narrates an event that transpired one day after Cain and Abel had matured sufficiently to offer sacrifices to God independently. The text does not provide explicit details about the exact time of the offering, but the phrase "end of the days" could allude to the conclusion of a year, the Sabbath (which is the conclusion of a week), a fasting day in which one was to remember mankind's apostasy, [6] or the end of the agricultural season for that year.[7] Alternatively, it might be an idiomatic expression indicating the initiation of an action after an unspecified period of time.[8]

It cannot be conclusively determined that the sacrifices were offered on the Sabbath, although that does remain a possibility. As the progenitors of humanity departed from Eden, they carried with them the institutions of the Sabbath and of sacrificial offerings. A division emerged within the community of God's people, resulting in Abel becoming a martyr for his righteous worship, while Cain committed murder and distanced himself from God's presence. The act of worship continues to hold significant importance, especially in the context of the last days (cf. Rev. 13:15; 14:7, 9-12).

In order to prevent a vicious cycle of retribution, God granted Cain a protective sign, declaring that anyone who harmed him would face sevenfold punishment (Gen. 4:15). This act of divine mercy resonates with the blessings of the Sabbath in the human experience. The number seven, representing the blessing of rest, is consecrated by God as a safeguard for sinners. This blessing bestowed upon Cain upon his departure from God underscores that the promise of fruitfulness and multiplication remains in effect even after sin's entrance (Gen. 1:28). God's providential care continues to shield human prosperity.

Moreover, God's sign served as evidence of the existence of God the Creator to the descendants of Cain. Enoch, the seventh generation from Adam, fulfilled the role of an evangelist to these descendants (Gen. 5:21-24; Jude 14-15). Enoch's unique destiny as one who walked with God and was transported to heaven to live with God shows that God sent the best messenger he could provide to the fallen line of Cain. God demonstrated that even for sinners, there is hope and the possibility of turning to God the Creator through his grace.

5 Ronald F. Youngblood, *The Book of Genesis: An Introductory Commentary,* 2nd ed. (Grand Rapids, MI: Baker, 1991), 44.

6 Matthew Henry, *Matthew Henry's Commentary on the Whole Bible: Complete and Unabridged in One Volume* (Peabody, MA: Hendrickson, 1991).

7 Lange, Lewis, and Gosman, *A Commentary on the Holy Scriptures*, 255-256; Wenham, Genesis 1-15, 103.

8 Reyburn, 106.

(3) Lamech, a descendant of Cain (Gen. 4:24)

Lamech, of the seventh generation from Adam within the lineage of Cain, was at the forefront of those who tried to undermine Enoch's message. After taking the life of a young man who had wounded him, he boastfully composed a song that propagated a tradition of vengeance by blood: "If Cain shall be avenged sevenfold, then Lamech seventy-sevenfold" (Gen. 4:24). While Genesis 4:15 contains God's own words, Genesis 4:24 is a personal expression of audacious arrogance. Lamech assumed a position akin to God's and instituted a world order governed by brute force. This shift disregarded the value of life, which the Sabbath safeguarded, and ushered in a sinister era characterized by the prominence of the Nephilim or "fallen" beings (Gen. 6:4).

Similarly, a clear contrast between God and Lamech becomes apparent when one compares Genesis 2:2-3 and Genesis 4:24. These two passages employ the terms "shebi'ih" ("seventh") and "shebau" ("seven") a total of three times. Concerning the concept of rest, God who has meticulously provided everything for humanity extends an invitation to partake in rest and peace solely through faith. (Heb. 4:3-4, 9-11). In stark contrast, Lamech's declaration implies that individuals are responsible for creating and maintaining their own rest and peace through their own strength. This worldview, marked by self-reliance and self-idolization, eventually led to the devastating deluge of the Flood.

(4) Lamech, Noah's father (Gen. 5:29, 31)

Noah's father, another Lamech, holds a unique distinction. He welcomed a son into the world and named him Noah, signifying "comfort" (Gen. 5:29), and "lived seven hundred and seventy-seven years and died" (Gen. 5:31). The number 777 features three occurrences of the sacred number seven, mirroring the divine pattern of creation. This Lamech's desire for a world marred by sin to be transformed into a realm of genuine rest through his son found partial realization in Noah, a new Adam.

(5) Noah (Gen. 7-8)

The number seven is prominently featured in the account of the Flood. Noah safeguarded life within the ark by bringing in seven pairs of clean beasts and birds (Gen. 7:2, 3). Seven days following Noah's entry into the ark, the deluge commenced (Gen. 7:4, 10). Subsequent to the subsiding of the waters, the ark came to rest upon Mount Ararat on the seventeenth day of July (Gen. 8:4). Noah then patiently waited for seven more days to ascertain if the waters had receded before dispatching the dove (Gen. 8:12, 14).

Noah was a man of unwavering faith and obedience, diligently following all that God had commanded him (Gen. 6:22; 7:5, 9, 16). God, who established the Sabbath as a commemoration of creation, provided for the institution of the week to be revealed within the flood account. Jaubert has calculated the date (including the day of the week) of Noah's flood using the calendar from the Jubilee Book (ca. second century B.C.), which is based on a year of 364 days. According to his analysis, each date corresponds with a specific day of the week. For example, the first day of each year consistently falls on Wednesday, the commencement of the latter part of the creation week. Just as creation dawned on Sunday, the week's initial day, the great flood of Genesis 7:11 commenced on a Sunday. Just as God finished his creative work on Friday, the ark, which had floated around on the waters searching for a harbor of rest, finally came to rest on a Friday. On Wednesday, a day of new beginnings that inaugurated the latter half of the creation week, the mountaintops appeared (Gen. 8:5), the waters dried up (Gen. 8:13) and the people came out of the ark (Gen. 8:14).[9]

Building upon Jaubert's hypothesis, Wenham uncovered another significant insight within Genesis 7-8. The devastating phase of the Flood concluded on a Friday (Gen. 7:12), and mirroring God's creative pattern, Noah embarked on a fresh endeavor every Sunday (Gen. 8:6, 10, 12; cf. Gen. 7:10, 11). This underscores Noah's righteous adherence to Sabbath observance.[10] Noah's faithful observance of the Sabbath was closely tied to his close relationship with God (Gen. 6:9; cf. Gen. 6:22; 7:5, 9, 16; 8:18). Noah's exemplary conduct serves as a model for the saints of the latter days, who are called to keep the commandments of God and the faith of Jesus (Rev. 14:12).

(6) Abraham (Gen. 21:23, 28-31)

Upon witnessing that God was with Abraham, Abimelech entered into a peace agreement and requested an oath from Abraham: "swear to me by God" (Gen. 21:23). To symbolize this covenant, Abraham set apart seven ewe lambs (Gen. 21:28-30). In Hebrew, the terms "seven" and "oah" share a common origin. Abraham deliberately selected the number seven as a representation of the covenant and as a testament of his commitment to God.

The significance of the number seven—which vividly reveals Abraham's faith in God, the "possessor of heaven and earth" (Gen. 14:22) and "judge of all the earth" (Gen. 18:25)—is closely tied to the concept of the Sabbath, which commemorates the anniversary of creation. In honor of this

9 Annie Jaubert, 'Le Calendrier Des Jubilés Et Les Jours Liturgiques De La Sem aine', *Vetus testamentum* 7. (1957): 33. 참조, Wenham, *Genesis 1-15*, 180.

10 Wenham, *Genesis 1-15*, 180.

covenant, Abraham named the place Beer-sheba, meaning "Well of Oaths" (verse 31).

(7) Jacob (Gen. 29:18, 20, 27, 30; 33:3, 46:27; 50:3, 10)

On his way to escape from his brother Esau, Jacob experienced God at Bethel and renewed his devotion to God. Afterwards, he arrived at the home of his uncle Laban. Here his seventh-day faith was expressed in his longing for Rachel and his service to Laban, which caused him to regard the seven years as days (Gen. 29:18, 20). Jacob's offer to serve seven years instead of the three or five years is a reflection of his Sabbath faith. Laban's decision to celebrate Jacob and Leah's wedding for seven days suggests that there was a seven-day weekly system during those times. Afterwards, Jacob again served Laban for seven years for Rachel (Gen. 29:27, 30). Like Jacob, who regarded seven years as but seven days because of his love, God's people should show their love for the Lord with fervent devotion through Sabbath observance.

When Jacob returned from Mesopotamia to Canaan, he bowed seven times to Esau, who came to meet him (Gen. 33:3). According to the Amarna letters from the kings of Palestine to the king of Egypt in the 14th century B.C., the king of the vassal state bowed seven times at the feet of the king of the suzerainty. Artamanya, the ruler of Siribašani, demeaned himself by likening himself to a dog, saying that he prostrated himself seven times plus seven times at the feet of his lord the king (EA 201).[11] The number seven was a special symbol used in ancient times to completely humble oneself and seek the favor of the other. Jacob called Esau "my Lord" and pleaded for grace, saying that seeing Esau's face was like seeing "the face of God" (Gen. 33:5, 8, 10, 11). Sabbath faith leads to total reliance on God's grace of salvation and forgiveness.

The Sabbath faith led Jacob to form a community of seventy, which would become the ancestors of Jesus Christ, the one who would bring true rest to the whole world (Gen. 46:27). Jacob died at the age of one hundred and forty-seven years old (3×7×7=147) (Gen. 46:27). Following a seventy-day period of mourning, his body was taken to Canaan, and after Joseph had mourned for Jacob for seven days, he was buried in a cave in the field of Machpelah (Gen. 46:27; 50:3, 10).

(8) Joseph (Gen. 41; 46)

The number seven changed Joseph's destiny. He interpreted Pharaoh of Egypt's dream about the seven fat cows and seven lean cows, the seven plump ears of grain and seven thin ears of grain,

11 Moran.

signifying the upcoming seven years of abundance and seven years of famine (Gen. 41:1-36 NKJV). The theme of seven is prominent throughout this narrative, appearing 29 times. The story unfolds in Pharaoh's palace, where a troubling dream torments Pharaoh. Egypt's soothsayers and wise men offer no relief. Summoned from prison, Joseph interprets the dream, revealing the impending seven years of plenty followed by seven years of severe famine. "And the dream was repeated to Pharaoh twice because the thing is established by God, and God will shortly bring it to pass" (Gen. 41:32). Through the wisdom of Joseph, an individual who had the Sabbath faith and put his reliance on the Creator God, the world was spared from widespread famine. God vividly employed the number seven, which symbolizes God's existence and power, in the context of bringing good news to this Gentile setting, where the human Pharaoh was idolized as a god.

Through Joseph, the nation of Israel was preserved during a period of drought. "All the persons of the house of Jacob who went to Egypt were seventy" (Gen. 46:27). The number seventy is ten times seven, holding significance in biblical numerology. The Pentateuch highlights the importance of the number ten, which is seen in the Ten Commandments (Ex. 20:2-17; Deut. 5:6-21), tithing (Lev. 14:20; Num. 18:21, 26; Deut. 26:12), and the design of the tabernacle and its utensils (Ex. 26:1, 16; 27:12; 36:8, 21, 12). In Genesis, there were ten patriarchs before and after the Flood (Gen. 5; 11:10-30), and both Abraham and Jacob tithed to God (Gen. 14:20; 28:22). The concept of ten righteous individuals influencing the fate of Sodom and Gomorrah also underscores the importance of this number (Gen. 18:32).

When combined with seven, the number ten symbolizes the remnant of God's people, Israel, who were divinely ordained to bring salvation and true rest to the world. God rescued this community of life, which had been entrusted with the most precious mission of all, from the troubled land of Canaan and sheltered this community for a time in Egypt, the center of civilization.

Chapter 16 | Sacrifices and Altars

Jesus' closest disciple, John, began following Jesus after hearing John the Baptist proclaim Him as "the Lamb of God who takes away the sin of the world" (John 1:29, 35-37). John later described Jesus as "the Lamb slain from the foundation of the world" (Rev. 13:8).[1] The gospel of the cross is ancient and spans back to the creation of the world. The book of Genesis introduces this gospel message through references to sacrifices and altars, and this theme is further illuminated in the book of Leviticus, which intricately develops the truth of the sanctuary.

1. The proto-evangelium (original gospel)

Upon mankind's fall into sin, God gave the prophecy of the rise of the "seed of the woman" who would ultimately triumph over the serpent for the salvation of humanity (Gen. 3:15). God further provided an object lesson for this original gospel, by killing sheep and using their skins to clothe Adam and Eve (Gen. 3:21). This act foreshadows the ultimate sacrifice of Jesus Christ, who would die on the cross to cover the shame of sin and to provide righteousness for repentant sinners. As described by Peter, Christ was "the lamb without blemish or spot," whose sacrifice was foreordained before the foundation of the world, proclaimed to mankind through the proto-evangelium and manifested through the cross (1 Pet. 1:19-20).

After mankind's fall, God placed cherubim and a flaming sword on the east side of the Garden of Eden to guard the way to the tree of life (Gen. 3:24). Adam was originally intended to provide a priestly service to God in Eden,[2] but this holy place was now guarded by cherubim. Later, cherubim were placed with their wings covering the mercy seat of the ark of the covenant, in the holy of holies

1 The phrase "ἀπὸ καταβολῆς κόσμου" ("from creation") from Revelation 13:8 can be connected to either "not written" or "slain" in the syntax of the Greek. See Rev. 17:8; Matt. 25:34; Eph. 1:4; 1 Pet. 1:19, 20.

2 Eden bears the image of a sanctuary, and tilling the land (*'abad*) was employed by the Levites in their service within the sanctuary (Num. 3:7-8; 4:23, 30, 47; 8:11, 19, 22; 16:9; 18:6, 7, 21, 23). Wenham, 'Sanctuary Symbolism in the Garden of Eden Story', 19-25.

(Ex. 25:22).

The flaming sword that turns every way signifies the presence of God. The Hebrew verb "shakan" ("to put") used in Genesis 3:24 has the same root as "shekinah", which refers to the glorious light of God's presence that dwelled among his people. This divine presence was displayed between the cherubim above the ark of the covenant. After their expulsion from paradise, God's people approached the entrance of Eden to offer sacrifices and worship God.

2. The sacrifices of Cain and Abel

That mankind bore the sacrificial system with them as they departed from Eden is illustrated through the story of the two brothers, Cain and Abel, in Genesis 4. God rejected Cain's offering of produce from the earth, while He accepted Abel's offering of the firstborn of his sheep along with its fat. This marked the first instance in the Bible where the term "sin" was associated with a sacrificial event.

"[S]in lies at the door. And its desire is for you, but you should rule over it" (Gen. 4:7). Here, the Hebrew term "hattat" conveys both the concepts of "sin" and "sin offering." Just as a wild beast crouches, ready to attack, sin can assail us. Yet, God has provided a sin offering for those with repentant hearts—the Lamb of God, Jesus Christ, who was sacrificed for the sins of the world. The shedding of his blood on the cross is essential for the remission of sins (Heb. 9:22).

Cain's misguided self-righteousness led to anger and ultimately the murder of his brother. This stands as a stark warning against the dangers of relying on one's own merit for salvation. As sinners, we must humble ourselves before God and our fellow humans, expressing love for one another as Christ loved us. True sacrifice should lead to reconciliation, a principle emphasized by Jesus in the Sermon on the Mount, where he addressed murder, sacrifice, and reconciliation with one's brother (Matt. 5:23-24). Cain's offering reflects the harmful spirit of seeking salvation through personal righteousness. One of the gravest sins that has ensnared countless individuals is the belief in salvation through human works. This not only severs relationships with our fellow human beings, as seen in Cain's actions, but also separates us from God.

3. Noah's burnt offerings

The first action Noah took upon disembarking the ark was to construct an altar to Yahweh. He gathered offerings from all the clean animals and birds and presented burnt offerings to God (Gen.

8:20-21).

The term "mizbeah", which translates to "altar," appears for the first time in the Bible in this context. Throughout Genesis, this word is exclusively used to refer to the altar dedicated to God. This altar symbolized a vow to God and was a way for Noah and his family to give thanks for their survival and commit to a life of wholehearted devotion in the renewed world. Although Eden had been lost and the pre-Flood world had vanished, Noah's family chose to offer themselves to God in the new creation, mirroring the communion that Adam and Eve shared with God in the Sabbath hours immediately after their original creation.

"And the Lord smelled a soothing aroma" (Gen. 8:21). The Hebrew word for "soothing" is "nihoah", and refers to a state of rest. In this context, it suggests that Noah's sacrificial act brought a Sabbath-like rest to God. After the turmoil caused by the wickedness of the pre-Flood era, Noah's voluntary act of devotion and worship provided God with a sense of peace and comfort. We, too, are invited to participate in God's rest through worship.

4. Abraham

Everywhere Abraham went, he left behind an altar to Yahweh that would stand as silent witnesses of his unwavering faith. As he journeyed through the land of Canaan, he built altars at Shechem (Gen. 12:7), in the region between Bethel and Ai (Gen. 12:8; 13:4), and in Hebron (Gen. 13:18). Abraham's altars commemorated God's appearance to him and were a sign of his faith in God's promises. Notably, they were constructed in response to his intimate conversations with God. Building altars and communicating with God, he lived as a sojourner in a foreign land.

Spiritual worship is characterized by walking closely with God and engaging in intimate communication with Him. This form of worship goes beyond mere rituals; it involves understanding God's will with our minds and obeying it with our entire bodies. Abraham serves as a prime example of such worship. Despite dwelling in the morally compromised region of Canaan, Abraham, unlike his nephew Lot, remained untainted by the prevailing spirit of his time. He discerned God's good, pleasing, and perfect will and acted upon it. Like Enoch and Noah, Abraham walked closely with God, leading to a deep relationship that earned him the title "my friend Abraham" from God (Isa. 41:8; James 2:23). Worship acts as a spiritual preservative against corruption. When genuine worship is abandoned, humanity tends to decay morally, and the world becomes engulfed in wickedness and sin.

Abraham was the first person to erect an altar in the land of Canaan. After God promised that this land would belong to his descendants, Abraham constructed an altar in Shechem (Gen. 12:7). Through this act, he anticipated the future when the Israelites would inherit the land and worship the Almighty on that very ground.[3] As time unfolded, Jacob acquired this land, and upon the Israelites' return to Canaan, they interred Joseph's remains there (Gen. 33:19; Josh. 24:32). It was in this sacred space that Joshua gave his farewell sermon and reaffirmed the people's covenant with God (Josh. 24:25). Abraham's unwavering faith bore fruit, as these events unfolded in the wake of his altar-building. With each altar we raise, we offer this earth as a domain for God's redemption, and in his benevolence, He shall ultimately restore the entirety of creation to his divine kingdom.

Yahweh instructed Abraham to present his cherished son Isaac as a burnt offering upon Mount Moriah. Abraham, demonstrating his unwavering obedience, carried out the directive. Just as Abraham was about to complete the offering, God intervened, preventing him from proceeding further, and commended Abraham for his unreserved submission. Abraham offered a burnt offering using the ram that God had prepared to take the place of Isaac (Gen. 22:2, 3, 6, 7, 8, 13). This incident helps us to gain a deep understanding of the love of God, who loved the world and sent his only begotten Son, Jesus Christ, to die for our sins.

The way of salvation that God has prepared for his children does not consist of the repetitive sacrifices of sheep, goats, or cattle that have been or will be offered by the Israelites throughout history. Instead, it is the Son of God who offered himself upon the cross. In a manner akin to Abraham's experience of receiving his son Isaac back from the brink of death, Jesus was resurrected as the "firstfruits of those who have fallen asleep," thereby flinging open the gateway to eternal life for all of humanity (1 Cor. 15:20). Abraham's faith in the resurrection—encapsulated in the words "the lad and I will go yonder and worship, and we will come back to you"—was rewarded with the divine provision in the form of a ram that God provided for himself (Gen. 22:5, 8, 13).

5. Isaac

Isaac had a direct encounter with God in Beersheba, where Abraham had previously called on "the name of the Lord [Yahweh], the Everlasting God." He built an altar there, called on the name of Yahweh, and pitched his tent (Gen. 21:33; 26:23-25). It is a beautiful example of faith that is sustained from generation to generation. It was here that Abraham planted a tamarisk tree and dug

---

3 Wenham, *Genesis 1-15*, 283.

a well, and Isaac met God in this place steeped with memories of Abraham. Sacrificial offerings served as a bridge between past and present, facilitating the transmission of faith from parents to children. Similarly, the practice of worship ought to be a cherished family tradition, one that bequeaths a religious legacy to future generations.

6. Jacob

As Jacob departed from Padan Aram and returned to Canaan, he and Laban established a covenant of non-aggression and erected a heap of stones to serve as a visible testament to their agreement. Subsequently, Jacob offered sacrifices and swore an oath invoking the name of the God his father Isaac revered, thus solidifying their compact (Gen. 31:53-54).

It is at this juncture that we encounter the Hebrew term "zebah", for "sacrifice," which is distinct from the burnt offerings that were entirely consumed by fire. This event marks the first usage of the term in the Bible, setting it apart from the burnt offerings previously described in Genesis (Gen. 8:20; 22:2, 3, 6, 7, 8, 13). Jacob presided over the sacrificial rite, and extended a portion of the offering to Laban's assembly, fostering unity through this shared act. By engaging in this offering, they solidified their accord with one another and ratified their covenant in communion with the divine.[4]

God would be the judge between them. The act of sharing sacrificial food served to bind all involved parties in a shared devotion to God. Analogously, Daniel and his three companions were resolute in their decision to abstain from consuming certain foods while residing at the Babylonian court because the food provided had been offered as sacrifices to pagan deities.

After Jacob's encounter with his brother Esau, he acquired a parcel of land in Shechem. There, he established a dwelling, erected an altar, and christened it "El Elohe Yisrael", signifying "God, God of Israel" (Gen. 33:20). This was the first altar he enacted after receiving the name Israel.

In Shechem, the family experienced a singular crisis. The son of the Hivite chief violated Dinah's honor, and Simeon and Simeon and Levi exacted a ruthless revenge for the rape of their sister. Following this violent retribution, Jacob sensed peril from neighboring peoples and chose to flee with his family. His destination was Bethel, a place where he had previously erected an altar to God while escaping from his brother Esau (Gen. 35:1). Revisiting this spot rekindled memories of days gone by, leading Jacob to construct another altar to God. God subsequently inspired fear among the

4 Reyburn, 744.

surrounding nations, rescuing Jacob's family from their dire predicament (Gen. 35:3, 7). The altar he raised was christened "El Bethel", meaning "God of Bethel." Like Jacob, we need sanctuaries of solace amidst life's crises. Recalling past experiences of salvation within our hearts serves as an enduring wellspring of encouragement. In order to achieve victory day by day, we must constantly cherish and revisit these memories of God's miraculous deliverance and give thanks to God for his past and continued guidance and care.

As Jacob traveled to Egypt in response to Joseph's invitation, he arrived at Beersheba and presented sacrifices to the God of his father, Isaac (Gen. 46:1). In response to this sacrificial act, God appeared to Jacob in a vision, offering him encouragement and a promise to lead Jacob's descendants back to Canaan, where they would flourish as a great nation. Throughout moments of adversity, God guided his people through the institution of sacrifices. Even today, our worship leads us to have a clear vision of our celestial abode and God's promises to bring us there.

The words "I will go down with you to Egypt, and I will also surely bring you up again" (Gen. 46:4) found literal fulfillment through the Israelites' exodus from Egypt under the leadership of Moses and their eventual conquest of Canaan led by Joshua. In a spiritual context, Jesus, having assumed the human form to journey alongside us, will rescue his covenant-bound followers from the metaphorical Egypt of sin, guiding them to their heavenly dwelling in the metaphorical Canaan.

Israel entered Egypt as a people that offered sacrifices to God. Their spiritual walk and revival would flourish so long as they continued to offer sacrifices to God in spirit and in truth. Regrettably, amid the polytheistic surroundings of Egypt, their worship gradually waned, and they drifted away from their sacred practices. The primary impetus for the eventual exodus was the restoration of their worship and devotion to God. Four centuries later, the call for liberation of the children of Israel resonated within the chambers of Pharaoh's palace: "The Lord God of the Hebrews has met with us; and now, please, let us go three days' journey into the wilderness, that we may sacrifice to the Lord [Yahweh] our God" (Ex. 3:4; cf. Ex. 3:18 5:8, 17; 8:8, 25-29; 10:25).

Chapter 17 | The Remnant

The remnant is an important concept in biblical theology, and refers to three groups of people. Firstly, it refers to the historical remnant who were survivors of past instances of calamity and upheaval. Secondly, there exists the faithful remnant, who have a sincere faith and true relationship with God. Finally, there is an eschatological remnant who will pass through the refining fires of judgment and endure the trials of the apocalyptic plagues at the end of history, ultimately emerging victorious to inherit the eternal kingdom.[1]

In the Old Testament, the Hebrew roots for the remnant are "sha'ar" ("to remain"), "palat" ("to escape, get away"), "malat" ("to run away, save"), and "yatar", "to remain", and the nouns "sarid" ("survivor") and yaharit ("one who remains") are also used.[2]

1. Genesis 7:23

Genesis 7:23 introduces the idea of the remnant for the first time in the Hebrew Scriptures. "Only Noah and those who were with him in the ark remained alive." The Hebrew root "sha'ar" ("to remain, be left behind)[3] is a predicate that refers to the theologically significant concept of remnant. The common thread in the emergence of the idea of the remnant in Scripture and extra-biblical

1 Gerhard F. Hasel, 'Remnant', *ISBE* 4:130.

2 The following Hebrew terms are used in the Bible to refer to the remnant:
(i) "sha'ar" ("to remain"), 226 times, 10 times in Aramaic. Gen. 7:23; 14:10; 42:38; Deut. 3:11; Num. 13:12.
(ii) "palat" (*plt*, "to escape, flee"), 80 times. Noun form "palit" ("refugee"). Gen. 14:13; 2 Sam. 45:20.
(iii) "malat" (mlṭ, "to flee, save"), 89 times. Developed from "palat" (*plt*). 2 Sam. 20:6; Judg. 3:29; 1 Kings 1:12; receive eschatological promise: Isa. 49:14-20; Joel 2:32 [MT 3:5]; Dan. 12:1.
(iv) "yatar" (*ytr*, "to remain"), 248 times. Noun form "yeter" (*yeṯr*, "that which remains"), Job 1:4; Num. 12:4; 23:12.
(v) Noun "sarid" ("survivor"), 28 times. Num. 10:20; Judg. 5:13.
(vi) Noun "aharit". Derivative of root "ahar" (*'hr*), "those who remain." Amos 4:2; 9:1; Ezek. 23:25—The survivors here experience complete destruction without any future hope. Ibid., 131.

3 Sang Hoon Park, 'rav', *NIDOTTE* 4:11.

sources is an interest in matters of life and death.[4] The term appears in Genesis 7:23 in the context of the threat of worldwide destruction.

2. Characteristics of the remnant from the perspective of judgment

In the context of judgment, the characteristics of the remnant can be described as follows:

First, the remnant is composed of God's people who experience his salvation amid divine judgment. In the immediate context of God's judgment, the Hebrew term "sha'ar", meaning "to remain, to be left behind," is used to mean the opposite of other Hebrew terms such as "gavah" ("to cease breathing, die," Gen. 7:21); "mut" ("to die," Gen. 7:22); and "mahah" ("to wipe out, erase, destroy," Gen. 7:23). These terms illustrate the stark consequences of judgment. All but the remnant faced the punishment of death; only the remnant was spared and survived the flood.

Second, the remnant serves as the seed of humanity, ensuring the continuity of human existence. While the concept of the remnant is closely linked to the cataclysmic nature of God's judgment, it carries both negative[5] and positive connotations. Anyway, in many cases the implication is positive. Despite the enormity of the cataclysm, the remnant survives as the basis of a renewed communal life.[6]

In the Flood, only a remnant, consisting of Noah and his family, survived. The renewal of the entire human race was made possible through this remnant mentioned in Genesis 7:23. This remnant serves as an intermediary, ensuring the continuation of human history after the catastrophic flood.

The surviving remnant contains the seeds of life required for the ongoing existence of humanity, safeguarding human life and ensuring its continuity for generations to come. The concept of the remnant serves as a link, connecting the historical human experience of the past to that of the present and future in an unbroken chain. While deeply rooted in significant past events such as Creation and the Flood, the theme of the remnant also points strongly toward the future. The important aspects to note are that the remnant were actually preserved, that they survived the catastrophic upheaval, and that continued human existence became possible through the remnant.[7]

4 Hasel, 'Remnant', 132.

5 In the midst of a tremendous upheaval experienced by the community, survival is extremely rare, as the following texts show: 2 Kings 21:13-15; Isa. 17:4-6; Jer. 8:3; Ezek. 15:1-8; Amos 3:12; 5:3; 9:1-4. See Lester V. Meyer, 'Remnant', *ABD* 5:670.

6 Ibid.

7 Gerhard F. Hasel, *The Remnant: The history and Theology of the Remnant Idea from Genesis to Isaiah* (Berrien Springs, MI: Andrews Univ Pr, 1972., 1972), 140-141.

Thirdly, the remnant plays a crucial role in upholding God's plan of salvation. The fulfillment of the original gospel faced a significant threat due to the occurrence of a global catastrophe. Despite this, God's promise regarding the seed of the woman (Gen. 3:15) persevered through the remnant—the seed of humanity. Given this spiritual function, the remnant functions as a close-knit spiritual community entrusted with the weight of God's salvific blueprint for all of humanity. The remnant constitutes a group of individuals who receive and faithfully uphold God's revelation.

Fourthly, the remnant functions as a community that upholds and safeguards God's covenant. The remnant is saved based on their covenantal relationship with God (Gen. 6:18). Importantly, the remnant is not confined to an individual; rather, it comprises a collective of individuals, like Noah and his family in the context of the Flood. This collective, formed by a plurality of individuals, embodies a covenantal community founded on faith. As a community that is consecrated to God, the remnant enjoys special divine protection in the midst of God's judgment. "Then God remembered Noah, and every living thing, and all the animals that were with him in the ark" (Gen. 8:1).

Fifthly, the remnant is a group of righteous people who are loyal to God and have a loving relationship with Him. God chose Noah because he was favored by God, because he was righteous, and because he walked with God (Gen. 6:8-9). Through the four repetitions of 'according to all that God commanded him' [Gen. 6:22; 7:5, 9, 16], the passage makes clear that a righteous man (Gen. 6:8) is one who obeys the Lord."[8] The righteous are those who have a right relationship with God. A right relationship with God, manifested through obedience to God, gives us the assurance of salvation from God's judgment.

Sixth, the remnant are saved, not by works of their own merit, but by the grace of God. Noah was saved by obeying God's command. Obedience, however, cannot be regarded as an act of personal merit. In the redemptive history of Israel, God's grace was manifested as follows:

The renewal of the remnant is based on the grace of God, not on their holiness.... God is the one who initiates the program of reconstruction and transplantation. Thus, restoration does not come simply as a result of choice (Garofalo, Sohn) or covenantal tradition (Roth, Braun, Lozano, Dube), but as a result of the holistic nature of God's character, the Lord's initiative, grace, forgiveness, and elective love.[9]

8 Park, 13.

9 Kenneth D. Mulzac, 'The Remnant Motif in the Context of Judgment and Salvation in the Book of Jeremiah' (Ph. D. diss, Andrews University, Seventh-day Adventist Theological Seminary, 1995), 375-376.

3. Other Remnants

Examples of the terms used to denote the remnant in the book of Genesis are as below:

1. Sha'ar ("*to remain*"). The soldiers of Sodom and Gomorrah who survived the attack of the Mesopotamian coalition (Gen. 14:10). Jacob divided his herd into two flocks in order to survive Esau's attack (Gen. 32:9). Benjamin was Jacob's surviving son by Rachel (Gen. 42:18). Ravaged by the great famine that struck the region, the people had nothing remaining but their bodies and farmland, which they surrendered to the king of Egypt (Gen. 47:18).

2. Palat ("*to escape*"). A derivative word, "happalit" ("one who escapes"), was used to refer to a survivor who brought news of the battle to Abraham (Gen. 14:13).

4. The remnant of the woman

"And the dragon was enraged with the woman, and he went to make war with the rest of her offspring, who keep the commandments of God and have the testimony of Jesus Christ" (Rev. 12:17). "Here is the patience of the saints; here are those who keep the commandments of God and the faith of Jesus" (Rev. 14:12).

Among the three groups of remnants described in the Bible, the concept of an "eschatological remnant" holds significant interest for many Christians. The foundational biblical passage supporting the idea of an "eschatological remnant" is Revelation 12:17. Revelation 12 provides insights into the ongoing cosmic struggle between Satan and Christ, originating in heaven and extending to earth. Within this context, the chapter reveals the historical timing of the remnant's emergence and outlines the distinguishing characteristics that identify them.

The appearance of the eschatological remnant takes place subsequent to the conclusion of the Dark Ages, a period that is part of the one thousand two hundred and sixty prophetic days and nights as foretold in the book of Daniel (Dan. 7:25; Rev. 12:6, 14). This remnant is characterized by their adherence to God's commandments and their testimony of Jesus Christ (Rev. 12:17; cf. Rev. 14:12, 19:10).

The book of Genesis foundational lessons regarding the concept of the remnant. By retracing the history of the great controversy outlined in Revelation 12, we arrive at the proto-evangelium and its promise of the seed of the woman. The Flood account in Genesis 6-9 is the first instance in the Bible that documents the presence of an eschatological remnant.

"And I will put enmity between you and the woman, and between your seed and her Seed; He shall bruise your head, and you shall bruise His heel" (Gen. 3:15). Revelation 12 uses the language and themes of Genesis 3 to provide an overview of how the proto-evangelium will be fulfilled.

(1) The remnant are a people ordained since the creation of the world. Linguistically, the two opposing forces from Genesis 3 reappear in Revelation 12 with identical characteristics and designations. A direct comparison of the original texts illustrates this clearly. The ancient "serpent" (*nahash*) that led humanity astray materializes as a menacing red dragon, threatening the remnant of the "woman" (*isha*) along with her "seed" (*zera*) (Rev. 12:9, 13, 17). Genesis 3 and Revelation 12 thus share a common cast of characters.

Retracing the trajectory of the Great Controversy to events preceding the age of persecution that spanned 1,260 years (Rev. 12:6, 14), we arrive at the time of Christ, when the dragon symbolically tried to swallow the child that the woman would give birth to. The woman's child was one "who was to rule all nations with a rod of iron" (Rev. 12:5; cf. Ps. 2:9). This verse traces its origins to the original gospel imparted to humanity in Eden: "her Seed...shall bruise your head" (Gen. 3:15). Remarkably, the Garden of Eden, where Satan initially corrupted mankind, became a battleground of defeat for Satan. Indeed, Satan had already suffered defeat in the hands of the archangel Michael in the war in heaven (Rev. 12:7-9).[10]

The proto-evangelium presents a figure who will ultimately bring an end to Satan's dominion on earth—the Seed of the woman. "But when the fullness of time had come, God sent forth his Son, born of a woman" (Gal. 4:4). Two millennia ago, Jesus died on the cross to "destroy him who had the power of death, that is, the devil" (Heb. 2:9, 14).

The "rest of her offspring" in Revelation 12:17 may also be translated as "the rest of her seed." The phrase "her seed" also occurs in Genesis 3:15. Both the Old Testament Hebrew Scriptures and the New Testament Greek Scriptures consistently use the word "her seed" (σπέρματος αὐτῆς).

Genesis and Revelation employ this common shared theological perspective of the Great controversy and employ the common term "her seed" to show that they are referring to the same person.

The "rest of her offering" (or "rest of her seed") in Revelation 12 did not suddenly emerge in the final days; its existence is rooted in the pages of history. This remnant has its origins in the seed

10 Michael means "Who is like God?" and refers to the archangel and supreme commander of God's army in the controversy between good and evil—i.e., Jesus Christ. See Dan. 10:13, 21; 12:1; Jude 1:9; Rev. 12:7.

of the woman promised in the proto-evangelium. Just as Jesus Christ's coming was foreordained before the foundation of the world but manifested in these last times, likewise, the remnant was chosen even before creation and manifested in the last days (1 Pet. 1:20; Eph. 1:4).

(2) The remnant emerged precisely at the divinely appointed moment. The seed of the woman referenced in Gen. 3:15 is embodied in two distinct roles within Revelation 12: the son of the woman and the remnant of her seed. These roles entail a profound mission to vanquish Satan and effect humanity's redemption within the grand tapestry of salvation history. Revelation 12 holds within it a "prophetic code," a key for discerning the identity of these figures. The appearance of the eschatological remnant is to follow a period of 1,260 days, a time of persecution and tribulation that is also referred to as "a time and times and half a time" (Rev. 12:6, 14). This prophetic timeline has ties with the book of Daniel.

In the book of Daniel, the prophecy of "a time and times and half a time" (Dan. 7:25) and the seventy-weeks prophecy (Dan. 9:24-27) are part of the prophecy of the two thousand three hundred days (Dan. 8:14), which is the prophecy with the longest time span in the Bible. The commencement of the two thousand three hundred days prophecy signaled the initiation of judgment preceding the Second Coming, heralding the advent of the glorious kingdom for the saints. With the fulfillment of this prophecy emerged the eschatological remnant.

The seventy weeks prophecy, which identifies the starting date (457 BC) of the two thousand three hundred prophecy, is focused on the redemptive work of the Messiah, the Seed of the woman. The Messiah's sacrificial death on the cross during the spring of 31 AD aligns with the midpoint of the final week of the seventy weeks prophecy, and fulfilled the prophecy of the original gospel, "And you shall bruise His heel" (Gen. 3:15). The year 1844 marks the end of the two thousand three hundred days, and is characterized by a restoration of Sabbath observance and the reemergence of a people of God who have the spirit of prophecy (Rev. 19:10). This people keep the commandments of God and the faith of Jesus, thereby satisfying the "theological code" for identifying the remnant. Just as Jesus Christ, the seed of the woman, was born of a woman in the fulness of time and through his crucifixion, vanquished him who had the power of death (Gal. 4:4; Heb. 2:14), so the remnant also emerged in the fulness of time to prepare this world for the Second Coming through the proclamation of the everlasting gospel (Rev. 14:6).

(3) The remnant is a victorious people. The book of Revelation resounds with the victorious narrative of the woman and her descendants. In Revelation 12, the woman shines with the radiance of the sun, symbolizing her victory over the forces of darkness, and has on her brow the "crown

of victory" (στέφανος, stephanos) (Rev. 12:1). The child, whom the dragon sought to devour, ascends to heaven and stands before God's throne, signifying his dominion over all nations with unyielding authority (Rev. 12:5). The woman is granted the wings of an eagle, allowing her to escape the serpent's grasp and find refuge in the safety of the wilderness (Rev. 12:14). Despite the dragon's wrath towards the remnant and its waging of war, the remnant steadfastly upholds the commandments of God and the testimony of Jesus Christ (Rev. 12:17; 13:15; 14:12). Ultimately, the seed of the woman, resembling the Son of Man, returns wearing a golden crown of victory (στέφανος, stephanos) and transports the remnant of the offspring to the heavenly realm (Rev. 14:14-16). "Then the King will say to those on His right hand, 'Come, you blessed of My Father, inherit the kingdom prepared for you from the foundation of the world" (Matt. 25:34).

Chapter 18 | Revelation

1. Words for Revelation

The English word "revelation" originates from the Latin word *revelare*, meaning "to remove the covering of, to reveal something that is hidden." In the biblical context, revelation centers on the Creator God, who actively unveils to humanity his power, glory, nature, character, will, ways, and overarching plan—essentially, revealing Himself so that mankind may come to know Him.[1] Theologically, revelation entails God communicating his intentions and designs for both himself and humanity through his spoken words, observable actions, and various other channels. Moreover, Jesus Christ serves as the ultimate and most comprehensive manifestation of God's revelation.[2] Throughout the Bible, a diverse range of phenomena tied to revelation are present. These include God's word, God's impactful interventions within history, divine appearances, prophetic dreams, natural displays of divine communication, revelations through Christ, revelations documented in the Gospels, and instances of eschatological manifestations.[3]

The New Testament contains specialized predicates for conveying the concept of revelation: ἀποκαλύπτω (apokalyptō), meaning "to reveal" or "to disclose by peeling off the veil," as well as "apocalypse" (ἀποκάλυψις, apokalypsis), meaning "revelation." The Old Testament, on the other hand, lacks a predicate that directly corresponds to revelation in a theological sense.[4]

Nevertheless, the Old Testament abounds with instances of God revealing Himself to humanity. No single Hebrew word can capture the entirety of phenomena related to divine revelation. Various

1 J. I. Packer, 'Revelation', New Bible Dictionary, (Leicester, England; Downers Grove, IL: InterVarsity Press, 1996), 1014.

2 Peter M. van Bemmelen, 'Revelation and Inspiration', Handbook of Seventh-Day Adventist Theology, Commentary Reference Series, Volume 12 (Hagerstown, MD: Review and Herald Publishing Association, 2000), 23.

3 Stephen N. Williams, 'Revelation', Dictionary for Theological Interpretation of the Bible, (London; Grand Rapids, MI: SPCK; Baker Academic, 2005), 678.

4 Carl Ludwig Wilibald Grimm, A Greek-English Lexicon of the New Testament, Being Grimm's Wilke's Clavis Novi Testament, (New York; Cincinnati, OH; Chicago, IL: American Book Company, 1889), 62.

verbs such as 'to show,' 'to see,' and 'to appear,' along with nouns that relate to God's word and visions,' collectively contribute to a deeper understanding of the Old Testament.[5] Words associated with anthropomorphism and theophony are used to point to God's revelation. These words have secular uses as well, and their theological or secular connotations are determined by the surrounding context.

In Hebrew, a verb that closely relates to revelation is "gala", meaning "to reveal" or "to take away." This term signifies the unveiling of something hidden, as exemplified in the experiences of Nebuchadnezzar (Dan. 2:19, Aramaic Peil form), Samuel (1 Sam. 3:21), and Daniel (Dan. 10:1). The phrase "things which are revealed" in Deuteronomy 29:29[28] refers to the law.

The most common terms for revelation are "amar", and "dabar", both meaning "to speak." Instances such as the following emphasize the auditory aspect of divine revelation: "God said" (Gen. 1:3; 6:13; Ex. 3:14; etc.); "Yahweh spoke to …" (Ex. 6:29; 25:1; Josh. 20:1; prophets, 2 Kings 21:10; Gad, a prophet of David, 1 Chron. 21:9; Menassah and his people, 2 Chron. 33:10); and "the word of the Lord that came to Jeremiah" (Jer. 47:1).[6]

Moreover, terms such as the following emphasize the visual aspect of revelation: "ra'ah" ("to see, appear, show"); "hazah" ("to see, see in a vision or dream, look at"); "ro'eh" ("seer"); "mareh" ("appearance, view, vision"); "hozeh" ("seer"); and "hazon" ("vision").

Finally, terms like the following are focused on the cognitive aspect of revelation: "yada" ("to know, cause to know, announce"); and "nagad" ("to cause to know, report, speak").

Most of the above terms appear in the book of Genesis. God "appeared" to mankind (Gen. 35:7. Abraham, Gen. 12:7; Isaac, Gen. 26:2; Jacob, Gen. 35:9); "came" (Gen. 20:3; 31:24[7]); "spoke" (amar: Noah, Gen. 6:13; Abraham, Gen. 12:1; Abimelech, Gen. 20:3; Isaac, Gen. 25:23; Jacob, Gen. 35:1. dabar: Noah, Gen. 8:15; Hagar, Gen. 16:13; Abraham, Gen. 17:3; Laban, Gen. 31:24; Jacob, Gen. 35:13); "showed" (Abraham, Gen. 12:1; Pharaoh, Gen. 41:28);and "made it known" (yada: Joseph, Gen. 41:39. Nagad: Jacob, Gen. 32:30; Pharaoh, Gen. 41:25).

As means of providing revelation, God uses his word, "visions" (Gen. 15:1), and dreams (Gen. 20:3; 31:11, 24; 37:5; 41:7; 42:9). God "walks" with mankind (Gen. 5:22, 24; 6:9) and employs "prophets" (Gen. 20:7).

---

5 Geoffrey W. Bromiley, 'Reveal; Revelation', ISBE 4:161.

6 van Bemmelen, 23.

7 Visitation in a dream is literally written as "came in a dream."

2. Based on Creation

God's ability to give revelations is based on the act of creation. God created humanity in the image of God (Gen. 1:27, 9:6). This establishes a fundamental connection between God and humans, as antitype and type respectively. There exists an inseparable unity and intimacy between the two.

The narrative of Creation underscores that the capacity for communication is rooted in the very nature of God. The phrase "Let us make" (*na'aseh*) in Genesis 1:26 presupposes the communicative essence inherent within the Trinity. God's desire to engage with humanity is subsequently expressed: "Let them have dominion" (Gen. 1:26). God communicated his purpose to his representative, and man comprehended it intellectually and acted upon it. Adam fulfilled his role as a steward of creation, cultivating the earth and assigning names to the creatures in accordance with the cultural mandate (Gen. 1:28; 2:15, 19).

One of God's creations, the tree of the knowledge of good and evil, becomes a symbol that articulates the divine-human relationship. Through God's revelation, material objects took on a spiritual and symbolic significance. Adam's identity and the purpose of his existence in the world were revealed through communion with God. Indeed, everything he encountered was a form of divine disclosure. The natural world constitutes God's creation and represents general revelation. However, the deeper meaning of things and the meaning of Adam's existence was unveiled through special revelation, achieved through communion with God.

God reveals himself to those who maintain a close relationship with him. This intimacy is exemplified in passages such as those depicting Enoch and Noah "walking with God" (Gen. 5:22, 24; 6:9). The relationship portrayed is one of profound closeness, akin to a father leading his small child by the hand such that the child walks with the father.[8] This is a form of revelation at its highest level. The parent-child relationship between God and humanity finds its roots in creation.

3. God takes the initiative

Revelation constitutes a unilateral communication from God to humanity. God, the ultimate sovereign over all of creation, determines the timing, recipients, and content of his revelations

8 J. H. Hertz, ed. The Pentateuch and Haftorahs Hebrew Text. English Translation and Commentary, 2nd ed. (London: Soncino Press, 1960), 26.

according to his divine will. The unpredictability of these moments does not preclude the possibility of God's revelation. Throughout history, instances of divine revelation have demonstrated this truth.

In the aftermath of Adam's fall, God extended his revelation of salvation, manifesting his presence even in the moment of human transgression (Gen. 3:8, 15). During Jacob's flight from his brother Esau, God imparted a renewed sense of purpose and comfort through divine revelation, healing his wounded heart (Gen. 28:12). The plan of redemption is orchestrated solely by God's guidance and governance, transcending human agency. The birth of the nation of Israel and the first and second advents of Jesus Christ are all events solely controlled by God. Divine revelations are not confined solely to individuals like Noah and Abraham, who were already aligned with God; God's communication extends to unexpected recipients such as Hagar, the Egyptian slave (Gen. 16:3), Abimelech, a Gentile king (Gen. 20:3), and Pharaoh, the ruler of Egypt (Gen. 41:25).

4. God's entry into human history

God, the Creator of history, enters into the history of mankind through revelation. God's intervention in history is revealed in the "I shall" passages of the Bible (Gen. 3:15; Gen. 6:7; Gen. 12:1).

Revelation is a promise. God's revelatory promises are fulfilled through God's providence and miracles. As promised, Jesus Christ, the seed of the woman, was born into this earth two thousand years ago. He came through a virgin conception, which is an impossibility from the human perspective. Impossibility is not a problem before God; the problem is rather mankind's lack of faith in the God who makes the impossible possible.

The Lord will return. Jesus described the historic salvation that would come as analogous to the Flood and judgment of Sodom and Gomorrah in the days of Noah and Lot respectively (Matt. 24:37, 38; Luke 17:26-29). A key lesson from both stories was that people believed the extraordinary events foretold by the prophets to be impossible and moved on with their daily lives, only to face sudden destruction. Just as the Flood was a worldwide event, so is the redemption and judgment of Christ. Salvation will be fulfilled within human history, but through supernatural means.

The one hundred and twenty years of grace in Genesis 6:3 bears witness to God's fulfillment of the events he has revealed within human history. When the time was ripe, God told Noah that the flood would begin in seven days; at the end of this time, he burst open the fountains of the deep and opened the windows of heaven to cover the world with a flood (Gen. 7:4, 10, 11). In the midst of the cataclysm, God saved Noah, who accepted and obeyed what God had revealed. Revelation is not just information. Revelation has to do with God's activity in the history of salvation.

5. Purpose of reconciliation and restoration

As a people of revelation, it is imperative that we remain aware of and attuned to historical occurrences that fulfill prophecy. Yet, of even greater importance is comprehending the intrinsic nature of God, whose desire is to save humanity. Instead of seeking the annihilation of a fallen humanity, God engaged with Adam directly after his fall to bestow upon him the proto-evangelium. In Noah's day, God extended a period of grace lasting one hundred and twenty years to the violent and morally corrupted society of that time. Following the incident at the Tower of Babel, when humanity became dispersed across the earth, bereft of true knowledge of God, Abraham received the divine call, one that was intended to elevate Israel as a beacon of blessing, illuminating the path for all nations.

What should not be overlooked in the account of the Flood is God's profound sorrow for his creation, alongside his severe judgment (Gen. 6:5-8; lament and grief). After the floodwaters abated, God was pleased with Noah's voluntary burnt offerings in the renewed earth (Gen. 8:21).

In the story of Sodom and Gomorrah, it is crucial to observe the depiction of God as one who actively sought grounds for sparing the city. He heeded Abraham's pleas for the city, endeavoring not to identify the largest contingent of righteous individuals, but rather the minimal number of the righteous to justify sparing the city (Gen. 18:22-33). God does not delight in punishment, but seeks reconciliation and restoration. Through revelation, we come to encounter God as a compassionate being who desires the salvation of all humanity. When we fail to recognize the loving heart of the Creator God, who extends his hand of salvation through revelation, the biblical revelations about judgment lead to despair, distrust, or distorted forms of legalism rather than inspiring trust in God.

Due to its exploration of human nature, purpose, and destiny, as well as its engagement with the matter of salvation, revelation holds immense significance that cannot be disregarded. It should not be reduced to mere informational content. As revelation is inherently tied to the identity of the one revealing, its recipients must acknowledge the personal nature of God. Moreover, it necessitates more than intellectual agreement; it calls for active response, including personal obedience, repentance, and transformed living.[9]

God granted revelation to Enoch with the purpose of cautioning an ungodly world and thereby offering salvation prior to the Flood (Jude 1:14, 15).[10] The eternal Jesus Christ, who was present in the Godhead at the time of the Flood, communicated the gospel to the people of the day through the Holy Spirit, seeking to turn unbelieving hearts to repentance (1 Pet. 3:19-20).

6. A personal encounter with God of communal significance

God's revelation is manifested on an individual level and centers around two key aspects: God's divine purposes and his chosen people.[11] God selects certain individuals to whom he will impart the revelation. This choice is a matter within God's absolute sovereignty; he selects whom he wants. In times of widespread spiritual and moral decline, like during Noah's and Abraham's eras, God singled out these individuals (Gen. 6:5; 11:9) as recipients of his revelations.

The significance of one person receiving divine revelation surpasses the value of an entire world without the revelation. The essence of true life lies not in sheer numbers, but in those who have been privileged with divine insights. The democratic principle that values numbers loses relevance in this context. Revelation is communicated by those who have encountered God face to face, who convey this message directly to humanity. Those who hear this message now have opportunity to themselves encounter the Lord. The entire world must be given this opportunity to hear the Lord's voice. Suppressing this voice is perilous, tantamount to muting the guidance to life. The integrity of divine revelation must remain unaltered and be proclaimed as originally intended by God. Distorting or confusing God's revelation invariably leads to his judgment.

A personal encounter with revelation profoundly transfers the recipient. In the act of revealing

---

9 Williams, 678, 680.

10 Jude 1:14-15 contains a quotation from chapter 1 verse 9 of 1 Enoch, a pseudepigrapha from around the first centry BC. Although the quote is from a non-canonical book, it was included under the inspiration of the Holy Spirit. Although according to the genealogy of Genesis 5:1-24, Enoch appears as the seventh in the line that begins with Adam, it appears the author deliberately cast Enoch as "the seventh from Adam" in order to use the number 7 to highlight Enoch's prophetic authority. The Book of Enoch repeatedly records Enoch as the seventh from Adam (1 Enoch 37:1; 60:8; 93:3). "Lord" in this context refers to Jesus Christ (Jude 1:4). The Seventh-day Adventist Bible Commentary, 7:708; Daniel C. Arichea, Howard Hatton, A Handbook on the Letter from Jude and the Second Letter from Peter, UBS Handbook Series (New York: United Bible Societies, 1993), 42; G. F. C. Fronmüller, Jacob Isidor Mombert, The Epistle General of Jude (New York,: C. Scribner, & Co., 1867), 23, 24.

11 Packer, 1014.

himself, God imparts a divine presence that necessitates a reciprocal commitment from the recipient. To align completely with the revelation, the individual must consecrate their entire being. Revelation imparts a lifelong purpose upon the recipient, who should live in harmony with its divine message. As revelation itself embodies eschatological significance, those who receive it are called to embody an eschatological existence—a life that reflects the ultimate fulfillment of God's plan. Noah, having received revelations about the future, could never revert to his former self. Similarly, Abraham's transition from Abram marked a definitive shift, as he responded to God's call with unwavering dedication. Both these men committed their lives to faithfully carrying out the Word of God.

When the recipient of revelation disregards their assigned mission, they subject themselves to the gravest consequence—the penalty of death. By neglecting their sacred duty, they bear the weight of responsibility for the lives lost due to their inaction.

7. Call for decisive action by humanity

God's revelation demands resolute action from humanity. It is not bestowed to satiate intellectual curiosity or foster individual pride in knowledge. Instead, it necessitates sacrifice. Noah's revelation demanded his financial resources, effort, toil, perseverance, and bravery. Revelation does not render individuals mere speakers; rather, due to its relevance to the fate of humanity, its profound significance warrants swift and resolute engagement.

God's revelation is often delivered privately but typically impacts the public sphere. God disclosed the impending global catastrophe to Noah. Those who received Noah's revelation and observed his construction of the ark were compelled to make a choice regarding their stance on his message.

8. Creating a community of faith

Because God's revelation holds significance for human society, those who resonate with it come together to establish a community of faith. Amidst the backdrop of God's global judgment, this assembly can be referred to as a remnant. The Genesis flood account yields profound theological understanding concerning the identity, purpose, and future of these faith communities in the final days.

God's initial revelation to Noah encapsulated the essence of his message: "The end of all flesh has come before Me" (Gen. 6:13). This concise statement provided Noah with guidance for his life's purpose. The entirety of Noah's identity, calling, and future, as depicted in Gen. 6:14 and onwards, can be understood through the lens of this singular verse.

The Hebrew term "ketz", meaning "the end," characterizes Noah's faith community. This community was inherently eschatological, taking on the hues of a future-oriented entity through God's revelation. This community existed within the tension of the "already" and "not yet." Even prior to the ultimate culmination, those touched by revelation sensed the imminent presence of the end times and inhabited an environment infused with eschatological significance.

For humanity, the important thing is to not simply belong to an eschatological community, but to embody an eschatological individuality. Operating as such, individuals can prepare for the impending end. The ongoing command to construct the ark and enter into it held deeper meaning for Noah, a meaning that only surfaced once he internalized the essence of "katz." An eschatological awareness propels a sense of urgency for evangelism, and prompts spiritual and ethical reformation.

The Hebrew phrase "kol basar", meaning "all flesh," serves as a poignant reminder that humanity is a finite and mortal creation, owing its existence to God, the Creator. This realization kindles the imperative of global mission. The faith community bears a divine mandate to redirect humanity toward its Creator. "All flesh" encompasses not only humans but also all living creatures. Noah, the new Adam and the remnant seed of mankind, assumed the task of rescuing humanity. He further safeguarded the "seed" (Gen. 7:3) of living beings, extending salvation to animals as well. This eschatological community of faith embodies humanity's hope—it is charged with the sacred mission of restoration and redemption for all creation.

PART VI

Beginning and End

Chapter 19 | Creation

The Bible begins with the magnificent declaration of Genesis 1:1—"In the beginning God created the heavens and the earth"—and ends with the promise of a new heaven and a new earth in Revelation 21:1. The redemptive journey that unfolds between the creation and re-creation encompasses a history of preservation, redemption, providence, judgment, and the second advent.[1] Prophecy, an integral facet of the history of redemption, originates from the very Creator who unveils the culmination from the outset. Given that creation marks the genesis of all existence and the redemption of humankind is within the grasp of the Creator, a precise understanding of the creation is crucial for accurately interpreting and applying the entirety of the Bible's salvific teachings.

Genesis, as its title implies, is a book about the creation. God is the creator of the heaven and earth, and the judge of the world. The Flood represents an instance of un-creation; in its wake, the world was recreated in accordance with the original order of the creation and once again bequeathed to humanity. God oversees and controls the progression of history, and intervenes providentially in the lives of the patriarchs so that they may partake abundantly in the history of redemption.

1. Why study creation?

One compelling rationale for delving into creation is the Bible's steadfast emphasis on this theme. As an example of this, the Book of Genesis commences with a resounding declaration of creation in its very first verse. Secondly, creation stands as a pivotal cornerstone for comprehending other theological tenets. Humanity, rather than being governed by celestial bodies, is a cherished creation of God, divinely nurtured under his providence. Thirdly, the creation functions to clearly distinguish Christianity from other belief systems and worldviews. Embracing the doctrine of creation provides protection from erroneous stances such as atheism, pantheism and idolatry.

1 Jong Keun Lee, *Hebrew Thinking*, 149.

Fourthly, creation theology fosters the assurance that authentic science is harmonious with biblical teachings.[2] Last but not least, belief in the creation imparts universal values, forging a shared bond with other human beings.

2. Creation from nothing

The verb "bärä" ("to create") used in the creation account conveys the generation of something entirely novel. In the Old Testament, this verb is used in the Qal and Niphal 38 times, while the noun form— "beri'ah" ("creation") is used only in Numbers 16:30. God is exclusively the subject of this verb. The fact that this verb is never used together with preexisting matter as the object underscores that God did not use preexisting matter in his creative acts. He forged existence ex nihilo, bringing forth matter and beings from nothingness. This creative process unfolded through his Word, which embodied his divine intent. God remains separate from the created realm, wielding absolute authority and sovereignty.

3. God created all of nature

The phrase "heaven and earth" as found in Genesis 1:1 is an idiomatic expression encompassing not only the celestial and terrestrial realms but the entirety of existence itself.[3] God is the originator of "all things" (Acts 17:24; 1 Cor. 8:6; Col. 1:16; Rev. 4:11), and the one "who created heaven and the things that are in it, the earth and the things that are in it, and the sea and the things that are in it" (Rev. 10:6; cf. Acts 4:24; 14:15).

4. God's creation is good

Genesis 1 repeatedly emphasizes that the created world was good (Gen. 1:4, 10, 12, 18, 21, 25, 31). The term "tov" refers to the moral goodness of the created order. The disruption of this goodness is attributed to sin, which undermined the harmonious order. The Savior God promises the restoration of a "new heaven and a new earth" (Rev. 21:1). It is crucial to note that God is not

2 Erickson, 392-394.

3 Ibid., 397.

responsible for the presence of evil and sin in the world. The dualistic separation between matter and spirit—positing that matter is evil while the intellectual realm is good—aligns with pagan Greek ideology and is refuted by biblical teachings.

5. One God

God's independent act of creation stands in stark contrast to the notion that the world originated through a divine conflict against multiple gods, as propagated by polytheistic traditions in the ancient Near East. While pagan cultures worshipped the celestial bodies, the Bible teaches that these were brought into existence by God Himself. God stands as the sole Creator and is deserving of exclusive worship and reverence.

6. Human beings as the chief concern of creation

Genesis 1:27 employs the verb "bara" three times, underscoring the idea that humanity represents the apex of God's creative work and that the entirety of creation has been advancing towards this pinnacle.[4]

7. Glorifying God as the purpose of creation

Creation culminates on the seventh day as God blesses and sanctifies it (Gen. 2:3). The Sabbath commandment directs attention towards the Creator. The account of the creation week concludes by centering awareness on God's state of rest. Human beings must not merely focus on the observable world but maintain a continuous awareness of the unseen Creator, living with the purpose of glorifying God through their stewardship of creation. In this role, humans act as conduits of blessing, serving as God's sacred ministers to the created world. Among all earthly creatures, humanity alone bears moral responsibility towards God.

4 LaSor, Hubbard, and Bush, *Old Testament Survey: The Message, Form, and Background of the Old Testament* (Grand Rapids, MI: Eerdmans, 1982), 77.

8. Foundation of other doctrines

All biblical doctrines find their roots in the person and actions of God as the creator, sustainer, restorer, and savior. God's creative work isn't a one-time event followed by disengagement; he continually upholds his creation. Even when sin threatened to destroy the world, God intervened as the restorer and savior, bringing the message of re-creation. The teachings encompassing creation, the fall, and redemption—spanning human origins, covenant, prophecy, redemption, the remnant, judgment, ecclesiology, sanctuary, and eschatology—originate from the Creator God's pursuit of restoring humanity to its blessed state.

God, the Creator, is also the Savior. The concepts of repentance, sanctification and glorification, as well as the hermeneutical method of interpreting the Bible through the lens of redemptive history, all hinge on a correct understanding of God as the Creator. God, the Creator, is also the Re-Creator. The promise of the Second Coming inspires anticipation for the time when the Creator, renewing all things, will grant a new heaven and earth.

The truth of the sanctuary offers hope that through Jesus Christ, the Lamb slain from the world's foundation, sin will be eradicated, and Eden's sanctuary will be reinstated. This restoration will lead to all people becoming priests of God, serving the Creator.

9. The patriarchs' faith in God the Creator

The promise of the seed of the woman following the Fall of humanity could only originate from God the Creator (Gen. 3:15). The incarnation and virgin birth, both events that transcend human understanding and the laws of natural science, are attainable solely through the agency of the Creator. The prophecy that "the virgin shall conceive and bear a Son" (Isa. 7:14) was achieved through the humility of a woman who declared, "Behold the maidservant of the Lord! Let it be to me according to your word" (Luke 1:38). In the fullness of time, Jesus, the culmination of the promise, was born through that woman (Gal. 4:4).

Adam, embracing God's promise, named his wife "Hawah" ("life"), signifying her role as the mother of all living beings (Gen. 3:20). The genealogy detailed in Genesis 5 underscores that God the Creator is the wellspring of human origin (Gen. 5:1, 2). The term "bara" does not recur in the book after Genesis 6:7,[5] yet the essence of the creation faith held by the patriarchs remains evident

5 The verb "barah" appears in Gen. 1:1, 21, 27(3 times) 2:3; 5:1, 2(2 times), and 6:7.

in their narratives.

The narratives of the patriarchs from Adam to Noah underscore the importance of experiential faith over mere theoretical knowledge of God the Creator. These individuals shared a profound and intimate communion with God. This relationship is vividly depicted by the verb "hithallek," which conveys the idea of accompanying and walking together. Enoch and Noah walked in close fellowship with the same Creator who had once strolled in the Garden of Eden, enjoying direct communion with Adam and his wife (Gen. 3:8; 5:22, 24; 6:9). Lamech's choice to name his son Noah is a reflection of his faith, signifying his desire to find solace amidst the Creator's impending judgment (Gen. 5:29).

Abraham was blessed by Melchizedek, the high priest of the Most High God, the Possessor of heaven and earth (Gen. 14:19). Abraham refrained from exploiting the misfortunes of the Sodomites for personal gain, acting in a manner that befitted his standing as a worshipper of this almighty God who was the possessor of all things (Gen. 14:22).

When sending his servant to find a bride for Isaac at Padan Aram, Abraham expressed his faith in "the Lord (Yahweh), the God of heaven and the God of the earth" (Gen. 24:3, 7). As Jacob invoked God's blessings upon Joseph, he addressed God as "the God of your father...the Almighty" and implored that God would bless Joseph "with blessings of heaven above [and] blessings of the deep that lies beneath" (Gen. 49:25).

The destruction of Sodom and Gomorrah, over which Abraham interceded for deliverance, was executed by God, the Creator, who exercises absolute sovereignty over the natural world (Gen. 19:24). Just as in Noah's time, God the Creator executed judgment in his role as the ultimate judge over sin (Gen. 6:5-7).

The genealogies presented in Genesis are a manifestation of the Creator's original command to "be fruitful and multiply." Through these genealogies, the Creator's intention for humanity's growth and multiplication is realized (Gen. 1:28). The accounts of the births of Israel's patriarchs and the subsequent formation of the nation of Israel serve to highlight the Creator's guiding hand throughout the history of redemption (Gen. 17:19; 25:23; 46:3; 48:19). Genesis commences with the narrative of the creation and records how God's promises to make Israel a great nation unfolded. It sets the stage for the events of Exodus, where those promises will begin to come into fruition. The book as a whole serves as a testament to the Creator God's active role in both the act of creation and the process of salvation.

Chapter 20 | Creation and Judgment

The Creator, holding absolute sovereignty, assumes the role of the ultimate judge over humanity's transgressions against the divinely appointed order and harmony of creation. This judicial aspect is evident in Genesis, notably in the narrative of the Flood, where the unfolding of the judgment scenes is intricately interwoven with the foundational principles of creation. Within these accounts, there is a notable linguistic and theological interplay that links the acts of creation and judgment.

1. Linguistic correlation

(1) Directives referring to creation

At the beginning and end of the great judgment, God himself uses creation-related vocabulary, including the following, to convey both the judgment and the defense rationale: "barah" ("to create"), "asah" ("to make"), and "betselem Elohim" ("in the image of God") (Gen. 6:7; 7:4; 8:21; 9:6; cf. Gen. 1:26-28).[1] Mankind's great wickedness led God to be sorry for creating them. In the judgment, living creatures are listed using the names and order indicated in the creation account (man-beast-creeping thing-birds, Gen. 6:7; 7:23; cf. Gen. 9:2).

The animals that are mentioned in the judgment context are ones that were also referenced in the creation narrative: animals, beasts (Gen. 1:24, 25, 26; 2:20; 6:7, 20; 7:2, 8, 14, 21, 23; 8:1, 17, 20; 9:10); creeping things, reptiles (Gen. 1:21, 24, 25, 28, 30; 6:7, 20; 7:8, 14, 21, 23; 8:17, 19; 9:2, 3); birds, Gen. 1:20, 21, 22, 26, 28, 30; 2:19, 20; 6:7, 20; 7:3, 8, 14, 21, 23; 8:17, 19, 20; 9:2, 10). Excluded from the judgment account were aquatic creatures including fish (Gen. 1:20, 21, 26, 28).

(2) Terms that refer to a global scope

The overarching and global nature of both the Creation and the Flood events is reflected in

1 Mathews, *Genesis 4:27-11:26*, 405.

the deliberate avoidance of specific place names in the terminology used. The term "earth" is not coupled with a particular geographical location.[2] Similarly, the term "sky" signifies the universal cosmic realm from which the floodgates were opened (Gen. 7:11; 8:2). The phrase "under heaven" is employed to depict worldwide devastation (Gen. 6:17; 7:19). This intentional usage of language serves to highlight the undoing of the creation order depicted in Genesis 1:8-9. The judgment of the Flood, in essence, marks an undoing of the state of creation and signifies the global collapse of the earth's ecosystems.

(3) Means to enforce judgment

The opening and closing of the "deep" in connection with the Flood (Gen. 7:11; 8:2) is closely linked with the "face of the deep" mentioned in Genesis 1:2, and denotes a return to the pre-creation chaos. With the closing of the "deep," the re-creation began.

(4) Order of re-creation reflects the seven-day creation week

The post-Flood re-creation in Genesis echoes the pattern of the original creation in Genesis 1,[3] as summarized below.[4]

(1) Before Creation. Just as God's Spirit hovered over the face of the waters before Creation, so after the Flood, God caused a wind to blow over the waters to prepare for \the new creation. Gen. 1:2, "earth," "deep," "Spirit of God" (ruach elohim), water = Gen. 8:1-2, "wind," "land," "water," "deep."

(2) Day 2. God divided the waters to establish the boundaries between the heavens and the earth. Gen. 1:6-8, "water," "heaven" = Gen. 8:2, "heaven."

(3) Day 3. God separated the dry land from the waters. God separated the dry land from the water. Gen. 1:9, "water," "land," "appear" = Gen. 8:3-5, "water," "tops of the mountains," "seen."

(4) Day 5. Birds fly again in the sky. Gen. 1:20-23, "birds," "above the earth" = Gen. 8:6-12,

2 *hä'ärec* is used 26 times in Genesis 1-2 and 46 in Genesis 6-9 without a limiting geographical reference. Gen. 1:1, 2, 10, 11(2 times), 12, 15, 17, 20, 22, 24(2 times), 25, 26(2 times), 28(2 times), 29, 30(2 times); 2:1, 4(2 times), 5(2 times), 6; 6:4, 5, 6, 11(2 times), 12(2 times), 13(2 times), 17(2 times); 7:3, 4, 6, 10, 12, 14, 17(2 times), 18, 19, 21(2 times), 23, 24; 8:1, 3, 7, 9, 11, 13, 14, 17, 19, 22; 9:1, 2, 7, 10(2 times), 11, 13, 14, 16, 17, 19. In connection with the rivers originating from the Garden of Eden, the specific geographic regions of Havilah and Cush are mentioned (Gen. 2:11-13).

3 Mathews, *Genesis 4:27-11:26*, 383; Waltke and Fredricks, *Genesis: A Commentary*, 128-129.

4 Waltke and Fredricks, *Genesis: A Commentary*, 128-129.

"raven," "dove," "the earth."

(5) Day 6. The creatures of heaven and earth were called forth. Gen. 1:24-25, "living creature," "cattle," "creeping thing," "beast of the earth" = Gen. 8:17-19, "living thing," "birds," "cattle," "creeping thing."

(6) Humanity. Re-emergence of the nuclear family (man and woman) bearing the image of God. Gen. 1:26-28, "man," "image of God," "man and woman" = Gen. 8:16, 18, Noah and his wife, 9:6, "man," "image of God."

(7) Blessings. God blessed mankind, assigned to them sustenance, and restored mankind's sovereignty over creation. Gen. 1:28, "blessed," "be fruitful," "multiply," "fill the earth," "have dominion over all living things" = Gen. 9:1-2, "blessed," "be fruitful," "multiply," "fill the earth," "fear of you...they are given into your hand."

Light, created on the first day, and celestial bodies, created on the fourth day, are not mentioned in the re-creation account (Gen. 8-9) because these elements did not need to be recreated.

(5) Comparison between Adam in the original creation and Noah in the re-creation

Genesis 6-9 portrays Noah as a new Adam, both reflecting the image of God (Gen. 1:26-28; 9:6) and having dominion over animals (Gen. 7:15). Like Adam, Noah received a blessing coupled with a promise (Gen. 1:28-30; 9:1-7) and had a close relationship with God, walking with Him (Gen. 2:15; 3:8; 6:9). Noah also engaged in cultivating the earth (Gen. 2:5; 3:17-19; 9:20). Just as Adam sinned (Gen. 3:21), Noah similarly experienced shame through sinful actions (Gen. 9:21) and faced the same outcome of shameful nakedness (Gen. 3:21; 9:23).

2. Theological correlation

In the execution of judgment, God manifests himself as the Sovereign Ruler, the Almighty Executor, and the Restorer, all of which are intricately connected to the act of creation.

(1) Ruler with absolute sovereignty

In Genesis 1-11, the absolute sovereignty of God is unquestionable. His dominion extends throughout the entire universe (Gen. 1:1). God alone holds the authority over the entire process of judgment. All of humanity, including Noah, is positioned to passively accept God's verdict. God alone speaks, commands, and takes action. During Noah's era, mankind had multiplied, as originally ordained in creation (Gen. 6:1; cf. Gen. 1:27-28). As the great men of ancient times became known for their wicked deeds, God intervened, halting humanity's headlong descent into destruction by proclaiming divine judgment (Gen. 6:4-5).

God is the creator and controller of time. Through his act of creating the heavens and the earth, He initiated human history. The luminaries he put in the sky serve as signs to mark hours, days, and years (Gen. 1:14). In the aftermath of the Flood, God renewed the cycles of time that govern sowing and harvesting, as well as the changing seasons of cold and heat, summer and winter, and the alternating periods of day and night (Gen. 8:22).

God, the master of time, orchestrates the unfolding of eschatological events, denoted through the term "ketz" ("end"). Rather than abruptly bringing an end to time, He graciously allowed for a 120-year grace period before the apocalyptic event of the Flood.

God exercises dominion over space. As the Creator, he could not abide the utter pollution of the earth, the chosen abode for humanity, through sin, and cleansed the earth through water (Gen. 6:7). The earth becomes a sanctuary for righteous individuals, as exemplified by Noah's presence (Gen. 6:7-8). God has the absolute authority to select the inhabitants of earth. Such sovereignty over time and space influences the destinies of humans and other creatures alike.

God possesses the power to render life nonexistent (Gen. 6:7, 13, 17), and to provide the path of salvation (Gen. 6:18-21). The universal scope of the Flood emphasizes that all living entities are sustained and provided for by the Creator's maintenance and providence.

(2) Almighty Executor

Genesis 7 serves as a testament to the Creator's exercise of power over time, space, and all creatures.

The "end," the eschatological time of Genesis 6:13, comprises the seven days of waiting in the ark (Gen. 7:4, 10), 40 days of continuous flood (Gen. 7:4, 17), and 150 days of the water covering the earth. God foretold the beginning of the Flood in Genesis 7:4, indicating that God had limited the duration of the Flood from the beginning.[5] Wenham posits that the Flood—the de-creation—commenced on Sunday, the first day of the week, paralleling the original creation

---

5 Terence E. Fretheim, 'The Book of Genesis', *The New Interpreter's Bible: General Articles & Introduction, Commentary, & Reflections for Each Book of the Bible, Including the Apocryphal/Deuterocanonical Books*, ed. Leander E. Keck et al. (Nashville, TN: Abingdon Press, 1994), 391.

week.[6] The seventh-day Sabbath was accorded eschatological significance by God the Creator. Sabbath observance was a sign of the righteousness God found in Noah (Gen. 7:1). The Sabbath calls upon mankind to remember God the Creator in order to be saved from God's judgment. Only the Almighty Creator God can provide a day of salvation from his judgment, which entails total destruction.

God's omnipotent power encompasses both heaven and earth. God brought about the destruction of the earth through the flood, which submerged even the highest mountains under at least 15 cubits of water (Gen. 7:20). Genesis 7:4 utilizes the terms "I" (in the emphatic form) and "cause it to rain" (participle of Hiphil), emphasizing Yahweh's role as the source of a supernatural downpour of rain that destroyed the whole world and his complete sovereignty over natural phenomena.

God broke open the "fountains of the great deep" and opened the "windows of heaven," so as to flood the whole earth (Gen. 7:11). The word "broken" ("split") may be used with a positive connotation to refer to the production of water, and the concept of creation underlies this term (Ps. 74:15; 78:15; Isa. 48:21; Prov. 3:20). In Genesis 7:11, this verb is used negatively to refer to a severe judgment emanating from God the Creator. Mankind's "great sin" ("wickedness was great," Gen. 6:5) encountered retribution through the bursting open of the fountains of the "great deep" (Gen. 7:11).[7] God's purpose of destroying all the wicked from the face of this earth was thoroughly attained (Gen. 7:23; cf. Gen. 6:7; 7:4). "Their memories were forgotten, because they left no heirs," and they were blotted out, not only in this life but also in the world to come.[8]

(3) Restorer

In Genesis chapters 8–9, God the Creator is depicted as the Restorer. The process of universal restoration commenced when God remembered Noah and all the living creatures aboard the ark with him (Gen. 8:1).

The weekly cycle in Genesis 8 reflects the week of the original creation. According to Wenham's calculations, the re-creation took place on Sunday and Wednesday.[9] These are the days on which the

---

6 Wenham, *Genesis 1-15*, 180-181. Wenham's theory was based on Jaubert's work, which presupposed that the 364-day calendar found in the Book of Jubilee (ca. 2 century BC) was used in the Genesis account of the great flood.

7 Sarna, 55.

8 Nachmanides, *Commentary on the Torah, trans*., Charles B. Chavel (New York: Shilo 1971), 119-120.

9 Wenham, *Genesis 1-15*, 180.

two pairs of three days respectively began in the original creation week.[10] Noah sent out a raven and dove over the course of three Sundays (Gen. 8:6, 10, 12). On Wednesday, which marks the half of the week, the mountain peaks appeared, and the waters dried up so that the earth's ecosystem began the process of restoration to a condition suitable to sustain life (cf. Gen. 1:14-31). Noah and all living things with him in the ark—in other words, the inhabitants of the new world—left the ark on the same day of the week (Gen. 8:5, 13, 14).

The Sabbath from the original creation having persisted, now the day served as the commemoration of both the initial and renewed creation. It stands as a reminder of the new life humanity enjoyed, as beings rescued from the tumultuous flood of uncreation and death. Despite being saved from the deluge, Noah eventually passed away at the age of 950, three and a half centuries after the Flood (Gen. 9:28-29). This world is not yet a paradise. Humanity resides in anticipation of an era characterized by ultimate rest and harmony, where the perfect communion between God and mankind, reminiscent of Eden, will be reinstated through the Final Judgment. In a world marred by sin and suffering, the Sabbath serves as a steppingstone towards an eternity of bliss.

Similar to the earth of the original creation, the post-Flood world emerged from the waters (Gen. 1:2, 9; 7:24; 8:1). This renewed earth was once again put under the dominion of humanity (Gen. 1:28; 9:1, 7). The act of cultivation also resumed (Gen. 2:5; 3:17-19; 9:20).

However, despite the restoration, the world following the Flood exhibited notable differences from its antediluvian state. Drastic changes in the climate changes compelled humans to inhabit physically challenging environments (Gen. 8:22). Furthermore, this world, now tainted by sin and unrighteousness, anticipates the fulfillment of the promise of "new heavens and a new earth in which righteousness dwells," a divine pledge that will be fulfilled through the ultimate judgment of God (2 Pet. 3:13). Until that prophesied event occurs, God continues to uphold his covenant with Noah, preserving the earth as stipulated in Genesis 9:1-17.

Just as animals emerged on earth during the midpoint of the original creation week, the creatures within the ark disembarked to their new dwelling place in the middle of the week (Gen. 8:14-18). Humanity retained dominion over the animal kingdom, and the sanctity of human life—rooted in humanity's status as beings created in the image of God—was recognized by God, echoing the order established in the original creation (Gen. 9:6; cf. Gen. 1:26-27). God reaffirmed the blessing to be fruitful and multiply and fill the earth (Gen. 8:17; 9:1, 7; cf. Gen. 1:28).

---

10 Waltke and Fredricks, *Genesis: A Commentary*, 130.

Yet, even though the survivors of the Flood emerged as stewards of the new world, their nature was different from Adam's pristine state. Their inclination towards evil persisted and such evil would spread alongside their population of the earth (Gen. 8:21; cf. Gen. 6:5). It was necessary for God to find a way to create a new heart in mankind. Unless human nature could be restored to the condition before the fall, the physical restoration of the earth would mean little. The prospect of humanity's redemption lies in God's ability to create anew through the agency of the Holy Spirit. By acknowledging their sinful nature, seeking forgiveness through the grace of Jesus Christ's sacrifice on the cross, and embracing renewal, individuals can experience a profound transformation and become new creations.

Upon exiting the ark, Noah's act of offering a burnt offering symbolized his commitment to eternal salvation. Likewise, God's people are called to dedicate themselves afresh each day to their Creator, the source of life.

Chapter 21 | Eschatology

The English word "eschatology" is a combination of the Greek words "eschatos" ("last, final") and "logos" ("word"). The word refers to words or doctrines concerning the last things.[1] Eschatology deals with the fates of individuals[2] and of history.[3] Traditionally, eschatology is primarily concerned with the fate of the individual. But in biblical eschatology, the fate of the individual must be understood in relation to the fate of history as a whole.[4] The Old Testament emphasizes the future of communal Israel, while the New Testament pays special attention to the fate of the individual.[5]

Because Genesis is the revelation of one who "declares the end from the beginning" (Isa. 46:10), it serves as a foundational source for comprehending both the destiny of individuals and the course of history.

1. Fate of the individual

Genesis teaches the following regarding the essence of the human existence.

Image of God. Human beings were created in God's image, unlike animals that were created "according to their kind" (Gen. 1:26-27; cf. Gen. 1:21, 24, 25).

Created from dust. Despite the inherent dignity and worth of human beings, they were created from dust just like other animals (Gen. 2:7, 19). Mankind's superiority over animals cannot be established based on their physical composition alone. Respecting on this aspect brings about humility, as in the example of Abraham, who confessed to God that he was but "dust and ashes" (Gen. 18:27). This confession stems from a creation faith that recognizes that humanity's essence is dust.[6]

---

1 Virgil H. Todd, 'Biblical Eschatology: An Overview,' *Cumberland Seminarian* 22 (1984): 3-4.

2 Death and resurrection

3 Day of the lord, end of the world, judgment, thousand years and end of sin, God's kingdom in the new world

4 G. E. Ladd, 'Eschatology', *ISBE* 2:130.

5 'Eschatology', *The Eerdmans Bible Dictionary*, (Grand Rapids, MI: Eerdmans, 1987), 347.

6 Through his creation faith, Abraham referred to God as "the Lord, God Most High, the Possessor of heaven and earth" (Gen. 14:22).

God is the source of life. Mankind received the gift of life from God. God "breathed into [man's] nostrils the breath of life; and man became a living being" (Gen. 2:7). It is God who gives life (Job 33:4).

Conditional immortality. Human beings are not immortal, but are conditionally immortal beings whose continued existence can be guaranteed only to the extent that they obey God's word. Man was to eat from the tree of life (Gen. 2:9) and commanded not to eat from the tree of the knowledge of good and evil. "[F]or in the day that you eat of it you shall surely die" (Gen. 2:17).

Death is an undoing of creation. The death of human beings is an undoing of creation. After the Fall, mankind was subject to the following sentence: "For dust you are, and to dust you shall return" (Gen. 3:19). Death is the taking away of the breath of life imparted by God. Mankind was created from the dust, and returns to the dust that is his origin (Job 34:15; Ps. 104:29; Eccles. 3:20).

All have sinned and deserve to die. Adam's death testifies that death is the penalty for sin. Indeed, the genealogy of the patriarchs in Genesis 5 and 11 shows that no one can escape the power of death. Adam lived nine hundred and thirty years and died (Gen. 5:5). His death, the first natural death in the Bible, surely inspired a deep awareness of human mortality in the people of his time.

Methuselah, from Adam's genealogy, is the person who enjoyed the longest recorded lifespan, living for a remarkable nine hundred and sixty-nine years (Gen. 5:27). Even for this man, whose life spanned near a millennium, the grip of death remains an inescapable reality. After the Flood, there was a marked decrease in life expectancy, as reflected in Shem's genealogy chronicled in Genesis 11.

The hope of eternal life remains. There is one in the Genesis genealogies whose story does not end in death. Adam's descendant Enoch was the exception. "And Enoch walked with God; and he was not, for God took him" (Gen. 5:24). A path to break the bonds of death was opened before mankind. This path was provided in the promise of the Savior, Jesus Christ, the seed of the woman (Gen. 3:15). In Christ alone, mankind meets God (John 14:6), is reconciled to God (Rom. 5:1-2) and enjoys eternal life (John 3:16; 5:24).

Jesus Christ brought an end to sin and death. When Adam sinned, all of humanity faced the end of the world, but God in his grace postponed the end.[7] Christ, the seed of the woman, interjected himself into both individual and collective history (Gen. 3:15). The genealogies of Genesis chapters 5 and 11 reveal that even as the list of the dead accumulated, God was at work in the lives of the

7 David J. A. Clines, 'Themes in Genesis 1-11', *Catholic Biblical Quarterly* 38 (1976): 490.

patriarchs to shape history and bring about the redemption of humanity. The words "the son of Adam, the son of God" in the genealogy of Jesus (Luke 3:38) amounts to a declaration that the Savior who would break the bonds of death and open a new era for mankind had finally arrived. Jesus imparts new life to humanity, hitherto bound by the chains of mortality, and ends the age of injustice and brings about an era of love and justice; hence, Jesus' first advent is essentially an eschatological event. It is for this reason that the author of Hebrews proclaimed that God "has in these last days spoken to us by His Son" (Heb. 1:2).

2. Fate of history

The Flood account shows that the end of the individual and of history can occur simultaneously. The mighty men of the antediluvian world and their achievements were completely wiped out by the Flood. Jesus pointed to the Flood as an example to teach what the condition of the world would be like during the end times (Matt. 24:37-38; Luke 17:26-27). The Flood account contains echoes that hint at the ultimate finale of history.

Eschatological predicate. The eschatological predicate "ketz" ("end") appears for the first time in the account of the Flood (Gen. 6:13). The term is used in rare instances to refer to "spatial boundaries" (Jer. 50:26), and usually refers to the end of time (eschaton). In Daniel in particular, it was used in the latter sense (Dan. 8:17, 19; 11:40; 12:4, 6). Within the context of the divine judgment, the term denotes the end of the antediluvian age and the ends of the nations of Israel and Judah (Gen. 6:13; Amos 8:2; cf. Ezek. 7:3).[8]

The phrase "while the earth remains" from Genesis 8:22 foresees a time when the earth will cease to exist. This is a "prophetic oracle" that envisions the "eschatological terminus"[9] and points to a time when the history of mankind will come to an end.[10]

The end of the pre-Flood era is a representation of the ultimate end of days where God's purpose for the created order will be finally achieved.[11] We see here the correlation between the primitive and

8 Andrew E. Hill and Gordon H. Matties, '*qetz*', *NIDOTTE* 3:955.

9 Gage, 8.

10 Claus Westermann, *Creation*, trans., John J. Scullion (London: S.P.C.K., 1974), 22.

11 Defining eschatology solely based on events rather than as a dynamic manifestation of God's activity is overly narrow. K.E. Brower broadened the scope of eschatology, defining it as the direction and purpose of God's active covenantal faithfulness within God's created order, thus connecting God and God's created world more expansively. Kent E. Brower, "Let the Reader Understand': Temple & Eschatology in Mark,' *Eschatology in*

the last ages.[12] Protology and eschatology go hand in hand.

3. Correlation between protology and eschatology

(1) Relationship between Genesis 1-3 and Genesis 6-9

As we have observed in the previous chapter, creation and the end times are closely intertwined. Genesis 1-3 and Genesis 6-9 correspond in God's blessing to "be fruitful and multiply." Just as Adam received blessings at the time of creation, so too Noah was blessed following the Flood. Genesis 5 is the fulfillment of God's blessing at creation, while Genesis 10 shows the fulfillment of the same blessing after the Flood.[13] Although Noah was a godly man, he was also beset by human frailties, as shown by his drunkenness and exposure to shame (Gen. 9:20-21). Man's sinful nature, which had brought about the Flood, was not corrected after the Flood, resulting in a dispersion of sin throughout the world. The raison d'être for the end of the world is rooted in human nature (Gen. 9:20-21; cf. Gen. 8:21).

(2) Relationship between Genesis 1-7 and Genesis 8-12

Drawing on a protological analysis of Genesis 1-7, W. A. Gage has presented the "eschatological structure of Genesis" covering Genesis 8-12. There are parallels between pre-Flood history (Gen. 1-7) and post-Flood history. Gage's inclusion of Genesis 12 is intended to connect the universal history of humanity with the history of Israel through the "seed" motif. He presents five eschatological structures in the respective accounts, as follows.

(1) Genesis 8: New creation

(2) Genesis 9: New Adam

(3) Genesis 9:20-27: Renewed apostasy

(4) Genesis 11-12: Renewal of the controversy involving the seed

(5) Eschatological Expectations: New judgment[14]

Because of mankind's evil nature, it is imperative for God to judge humanity; thus, the "eschaton"

Bible & Theology: Evangelical Essays at the Dawn of a New Millennium, (Downers Grove, IL: InterVarsity Press, 1997), 119.

12 Westermann, *Creation*, 22.

13 Ibid., 23-28.

14 Gage, 7-16.

through God's judgment is inevitable (Gen. 8:21). Genesis 1-11 deal with the universal history of mankind and Genesis 12 connects the creation of the world with the history of Israel; thus, the eschatological elements contained in the theological accounts of Genesis 1-11 are useful for understanding important characteristics of both the global eschaton and the national eschaton of Israel (see Jer. 4:23-26).[15]

A study of the correlation between the protological and eschatological themes in Genesis 1-11 provides a sound theological basis for applying a typological lens to the events in Noah's day to illuminate the events that will transpire in the last days of earth's history. Jesus (Matt. 24:36-39; Luke 17:26-27) and Peter (1 Pet. 3:19-21; 2 Pet. 3:6-7) used this approach, focusing our attention on the eschaton of human history at large.

4. Eschatological timeframes

Some believe that because God is omniscient, He can judge the world in an instant without the need for any separate period of judgment. Thus, the reasoning goes, the pre-Advent judgment, also termed the "investigative judgment," is unnecessary. However, the judgment is a distinct apocalyptic event, and the account of the Flood offers a crucial insight into gaining a proper understanding of the matter.

Genesis 6-9 forms an "eschatological unit," marked by the placement of the eschatological predicate "end" at the beginning of the Flood narrative (Gen. 6:13) and use of "while the earth remains" near its end (Gen. 8:22). This literary structure reveals that the eschaton is not a single point in time, but a period of time. This position is also supported by the New Testament. In Matthew 24:36-39, "the days of Noah" (Matt. 24:37) were described as encompassing the events before the flood narrated in Genesis 6-7, "the day that Noah entered the ark" (Matt. 24:38), and the point in time where "the flood came and took them all away" (Matt. 24:39). Similarly, Peter referred to Genesis 7-9 to remark that the "world" in Noah's day was destroyed by water and that God had protected Noah and seven members of his family from the flood (2 Pet. 2:5; 3:6).

The term "ketz" is not used to point to a single point in time as the eschaton. From the temporal perspective, "ketz" refers to a set term, the completion of a definite temporal period (Hab. 2:3; Ps.

15 The "eschaton" of Israel may be understood as the uncreation. See Jack W. Vancil, 'From Creation to Chaos: An Exegesis of Jeremiah 4:23-26,' *Biblical Interpretation: Principles and Practice*, ed. F. Furman Kearley et al. (Grand Rapids, MI: Baker Book House, 1986), 181-192.

39:5; Job 6:11), and may connote doom as in the instances of Amos 8:2 and Lamentations 4:18).[16] The "ketz" in Genesis 6:13, interpreted in context, refers to two eschatological realities. The first pertains to the immediate "destruction" of all living beings, as directly indicated in Genesis 6:13. The second holds a broader connotation, encompassing the 120-year period of divine forbearance, followed by the one-year period of implementation (Gen. 6:3; 7:11; 8:14-18),[17] and even includes the period of mitigation after the Flood.

The temporal elements of the Flood account show that the global eschaton comprises three phases of time in relation to the fate of mankind in the face of God's judgment: (i) the pre-judgment period; (ii) the judgment period; and (iii) the post-judgment period.

5. History of late Israel from an eschatological perspective

In the broad context of salvation history, Israel's history through the exile and the time of return is the same as the pattern of God's judgment. Gowan D.E. Kowan summed this up in the formula of death 722-587 BC—resurrection 538 BC and the late captivity. Since death includes the pre-judgment era and the judgment age, Israel's history can be divided into pre-judgment, judgment-age, and post-judgment according to this formula. The Age of Judgment includes the Assyrian threat and the death of Israel, Amos, Hosea, Micah, Isaiah 1-39, the threat of Neo-Babylon and the death of Judah Zephaniah, Nahum, Habakkuk, Jeremiah, Obadiah, Ezekiel, and Jonah. The prophetic books look to an ideal time when God's will shall be fully fulfilled in Escaton in the midst of destruction and restoration.

In the broader context of salvation history, Israel's trajectory, from its times of adversity and exile to its restoration, mirrors the pattern of God's judgment. D.E. Gowan articulated this pattern as a sequence of death (722-587 BC) followed by resurrection (538 BC and latter period of captivity).[18] Since the "death" phase encompasses both the pre-judgment era and the age of judgment, it is also possible to categorize Israel's history into pre-judgment, judgment, and post-judgment phases. The age of judgment encompassed significant events such as the Assyrian threat and Israel's

16 Sarna, 51.

17 The Flood began on the seventeenth day of the second month of the six hundredth year of Noah's life (Gen. 7:11), and Noah left the ark on the 27th day of the second month of his 601st year.

18 Donald E. Gowan, *Theology of the Prophetic Books: The Death & Resurrection of Israel* (Louisville, KY: Westminster John Knox Press, 1998).

downfall (covered in the prophetic books of Amos, Hosea, and Micah, as well as Isa. 1-39), the Neo-Babylonian threat, and the fall of Judah (covered in Zephaniah, Nahum, Habakkuk, Jeremiah, Obadiah, Ezekiel, and Jonah). The prophetic books are infused with yearning for an ideal future where God's will shall be fully realized within the context of the destruction and restoration cycle of the eschaton.

6. Eschatological periods within the book of Revelation

The book of Revelation delves deeply into eschatology, documenting the realization of God's eternal purpose through the lens of judgment. While much of the book isn't focused on historical accounts, it intricately explores the eschaton through a tripartite structure of pre-judgment, judgment, and post-judgment.

After the initial proclamation by the first angel that "the hour of his judgment has come" (Rev. 14:7), the subsequent chapters of Revelation depict the downfall of Babylon (Rev. 18) and the defeat of demonic forces (Rev. 20). This paves the way for a new world containing a new Jerusalem and the river of life (Rev. 21-22). These three aspects of the eschaton—pre-judgment, judgment, and post-judgment—are strikingly evident in the text. The ultimate realization of the new creation, envisioned through both the protological and eschatological aspects present in Genesis, finds its fulfillment through the agency of God's judgment in the book of Revelation.

The fulfillment of God's ultimate purpose is vividly depicted in Revelation 21-22, serving as a complementary counterpart to the themes presented in Genesis 8 within the context of new world. God "makes all things new" (Rev. 21:5), and within a new heaven and new earth (Rev. 21:1) where all that is corrupt has been banished forever (Rev. 21:8, 26; 22:15), God will dwell eternally with his holy people (Rev. 21:22-24; 22:3-5; cf. 22:11). The last two chapters of the Bible, Revelation 21-22, depict a complete restoration of the original creation, echoes of which are found in Genesis 8's poignant evocation of the initial creation order of Genesis 1-2.

Appendix

Bibliography

Kim Young-jin. *Introduction to the Torah-Pentateuch, Revised Supplementary Edition.* Handl Publishers, 2005.

________. *Reading the Old Testament*. Ereyseowon, 2006.

Antarctic airspace. *Genesis-Exodus*. Seventh-day Adventist Bible Commentary 1. Poetry, 2000.

Lloyd-Jones, Martin. *The joy of living before God*. Translated by Cho Cho Hwan. Words of Life, 1995.

Milton, John P. *Hebrew thinking and* Christianity. Moving the Divine Bell. Concordia, 1982.

Stone, Nathan J. *God's names in the Old Testament*. Moving the Trade. Evangelistic Publishers, 1992.

Wenham, Gordon. *Pentateuch*. Understanding the Bible, Vol. 3.' Translated by Dae-Young Park. Biblical Union Mission, 2007.

Lee Jong-keun. 'A Theological Examination of the Cultural Injunction to 'Be Fruitful and Multiplier' (Gen. 1:28; 2:15)." 舊約論壇 8 (2000): 9-31.

________. *Hebrew* Thought. Sahmyook University Press, 2007.

Lee Hee-seung, ed. *Korean Language Dictionary*. Seoul: Minjung Seorim, 2003.

Kaiser, Walter. *Old Testament Theology*. Final Move. Words of Life, 1982.

Ferguson, Sinclair B. 'The Image of God.' *Agape Theological Dictionary*, 1115-1118. Agape, 2001.

Hillier, P.N. Stewardship. Agape *Theological Dictionary*, 983-984. Agape, 2001.

Albertz, Rainer. 'Das Motiv für Die Sintflut im Atramhasis-Epos.' *Mythos im Alten Testament Und Seiner Umwelt: Festschrift für Hans-Peter Müller Zum 65 Geburtstag*, edited by Armin Lange, Hermann Lichtenberger and Diethard Romheld, 3-16. Berlin; New York: Walter de Gruyter, 1999.

Alexander, T. Desmond. 'nwyh,' *New International Dictionary of Old Testament Theology & Exegesis*, edited by Willem A. VanGemeren, 1, 834-835. Grand Rapids, MI: Zondervan, 1997.

________. *From Paradise to the Promised Land: An Introduction to the Pentateuch*. 2nd ed. Grand Rapids, MI: Baker Academic, 2002.

Anderson, Bernhard W. 'From Analysis to Synthesis: The Interpretation of Genesis 1-11.' *Journal of Biblical Literature 97* (1978): 23-39.

Arichea, Daniel C.; Hatton, Howard. *A Handbook on the Letter from Jude and the Second Letter from Peter*, UBS Handbook Series. New York: United Bible Societies, 1993.

Arnold, Bill T.; Bryan Beyer. *Encountering the Old Testament: A Christian Survey*. 2nd ed. Encountering Biblical Studies. Grand Rapids, MI: Baker Academic, 2008.

Astour, Michael C. 'Shaveh, Valley Of.' *The Anchor Bible Dictionary*, edited by David Noel Freedman, 5, 1168. New York: Doubleday, 1992.

Baer, D.A.; R. P. Gordon. 'hsd,' *New International Dictionary of Old Testament Theology & Exegesis*, edited by Willem A. VanGemeren, 2, 211-218. Grand Rapids, MI: Zondervan 1997.

Bandstra, Barry L. Genesis 1-11: *A Handbook on the Hebrew Text*. Waco, TX: Baylor University Press, 2007.

Bietenhard. 'ὄνομα, ὀνομάζω, ἐπονομάζω, ψευδώνυμος.' *Theological Dictionary of the New Testament*, edited by Gerhard Kittel, 5, 243-283. Grand Rapids, MI: Eerdmans, 1964-1976.

Birch, B. C. 'Number.' *The International Standard Bible Encyclopedia, Revised*, edited by Geoffrey W. Bromiley, 3, 556-561. Grand Rapids, MI: Wm. B. Eerdmans, 1986.

Blenkinsopp, Joseph. 'P and J in Genesis 1:1-11:26: An Alternative Hypothesis.' *Fortunate the Eyes That See: Essays in Honor of David Noel Freedman in Celebration of his Seventieth Birthday*, edited by Astrid B. Beck, Andrew H. Bartelt, Paul R. Raabe and Chris A. Franke, 1-15. Grand Rapids, MI: Eerdmans, 1995.

Bracke, John M. 'ryb.' *New International Dictionary of Old Testament Theology & Exegesis*, edited by Willem A. VanGemeren, 3, 1107-1108. Grand Rapids, MI: Zondervan, 1997.

Bromiley, Geoffrey W. 'Reveal; Revelation.' *The International Standard Bible Encyclopedia*, edited by Geoffrey W. Bromiley, Everett F. Harrison, Roland K. Harrison and William Sanford Lasor, 4, 161-171. Grand Rapids, MI: William B. Eerdmans Publishing Co., 1988.

Brower, Kent E. "Let the Reader Understand': Temple & Eschatology in Mark." E*schatology in Bible & Theology: Evangelical Essays at the Dawn of a New Millennium*, edited by K. E. Brower and M. W. Elliott, 119-144. Downers Grove, IL: InterVarsity Press, 1997.

Brown, Francis, S. R. Driver, and Charles A. Briggs. *A Hebrew and English Lexicon of the Old Testament, with an Appendix Containing the Biblical Aramaic Based on the Lexicon of William Gesenius*. Oxford: Clarendon Press, 1951.

Calvin, John. *Commentaries on the First Book of Moses Called Genesis*. Translated by John King. Vol. 1 Calvin's Old Testament Commentaries. Grand Rapids, MI.: Wm. B. Eerdmans, 1948.

Candlish, Robert S. *Studies in Genesis*. Grand Rapids, MI: Kregel, 1979.

Carpenter, E. E. 'Tithe.' *The International Standard Bible Encyclopedia, Revised*, edited by Geoffrey W. Bromiley, 861-864. Grand Rapids, MI: Wm. B. Eerdmans, 2002.

Carpenter, Eugene; Grisanti, Michael A. *New International Dictionary of Old Testament Theology & Exegesis*, edited by Willem A. VanGemeren, 3, 706-710. Grand Rapids, MI: Zondervan, 1997.

Cassuto, Umberto. *A Commentary on the Book of Genesis: Part 1, from Adam to Noah, a Commentary on Genesis I-Vi8*. Translated by Israel Abrahams. Jerusalem: Magnes, 1961.

________. *The Documentary Hypothesis and the Composition of the Pentateuch: Eight Lectures*. Translated by Israel Abrahams. Jerusalem: Magnes, 1961.

________. *A Commentary on the Book of Genesis: Part 2, from Noah to Abraham, Genesis Vi9-Xi32.* Translated by Israel Abrahams. Jerusalem: Magnes, 1964.

Clifford, Richard J. 'Review of Mythos im Alten Testament und Seiner Umwelt: Festschrift für Hans-Peter Müller Zum 65. Geburtstag by Hans-Peter Muller.' *Catholic Biblical Quarterly* 62 (2000): 781-783.

Clines, David J. A. 'Themes in Genesis 1-11.' *Catholic Biblical Quarterly* 38(1976): 483-507.

________. *The Theme of the Pentateuch.* Journal for the Study of the Old Testament, Supplement Series, vol. 10. Sheffield, Eng.: University of Sheffield. Dept. of Biblical Studies, 1978.

Cohen, A., ed. *The Soncino Chumash: The Five Books of Moses*, with Haphtaroth. Soncino Books of the Bible.' London/ Jerusalem/ New York: The Soncino Press, 1983.

Collins, F. Raymond. 'Commandment.' *The Anchor Bible Dictionary*, edited by David Noel Freedman, 1, 1097-1099. New York: Doubleday, 1992.

Collins, John C. *Genesis 1-4: A Linguistic, Literary, and Theological Commentary.* Phillipsburg, NJ: P&R Publishing Company, 2006.

Coppes, Leonard J. 'qwm.' *Theological Wordbook of the Old Testament*, edited by R. Laird Harris, Gleason L. Archer and Bruce K. Waltke, 2, 793-794. Chicago, IL: Moody, 1980.

Cornwall, Judson; Smith, Stelman. *The Exhaustive Dictionary of Bible Names.* North Brunswick, NJ: Bridge-Logos, 1998.

Davidson, Richard M. 'Biblical Interpretation.' *Handbook of Seventh-Day Adventist Theology*, edited by R. Dederen, 58-104. Hagerstown, MD: Review and Herald Publishing Association, 2001.

________. 'Flood, The.' *Baker Theological Dictionary of the Bible*, edited by Walter A. Elwell, 261-263. Grand Rapids, MI: Baker Books, 1996.

De Vries, Simon J. 'Sin, Sinners.' *The Interpreter's Dictionary of the Bible*, edited by G. A. Buttrick, 4, 361-376. New York/ Nashville: Abingdon Press, 1962.

Dorman, T.M. 'Steward.' *The International Standard Bible Encyclopedia, Revised*, edited by Geoffrey W. Bromiley, 4, 617-618. Grand Rapids, MI: Wm. B. Eerdmans, 2002.

Dumbrell, William J. *Covenant and Creation: A Theology of Old Testament Covenants.* Nashville, TN: Thomas Nelson, 1984.

Dyrness, William. *Themes in Old Testament Theology.* Downers Grove, IL; Carlisle, UK: InterVarsity Press, The Paternoster Press, 1977.

Eichrodt, Walther. *Theology of the Old Testament*, 2 vols. The Old Testament Library. Philadelphia, PA: Westminster Press, 1961.

Enns, Peter. 'mshpt.' *New International Dictionary of Old Testament Theology & Exegesis*, edited by Willem A. VanGemeren, 2, 1142-1144. Grand Rapids, MI: Zondervan, 1997.

Erickson, Millard J. *Christian Theology.* 2nd ed. Grand Rapids, MI: Baker Books, 1998.

'Eschatology.' *The Eerdmans Bible Dictionary*, edited by Allen C. Myers, 347-349. Grand Rapids, MI: Eerdmans, 1987.

Flint, V. Paul. *Strangers & Pilgrims: A Study of Genesis*. Neptune, NJ: Loizeaux Brothers, 1988.

Foster, Benjamin R. 'Atra-Hasis (1.130).' *The Context of Scripture: Canonical Compositions from the Biblical World*, edited by William W. Hallo and K. Lawson Younger, Jr., 1, 450-453. Leiden, New York: Brill, 1997.

________. 'Epic of Creation (1.111): Enuma Elish.' *The Context of Scripture: Canonical Compositions from the Biblical World*, edited by William W. Hallo and K. Lawson Younger, 1, 390-401. New York: Brill, 1997.

Fowler, John M. 'Sin.' *Handbook of Seventh-Day Adventist Theology*, edited by Raoul Dederen, 233-270. Hagerstown, MD: Review and Herald Publishing Association, 2000.

Freedman, D. N.; Lundbom, J. R. '*ḥānan*;* ḥēn; *ḥannûn*; *ḥanînâ*; *teḥinnâ*; *taḥanûn*' *Theological Dictionary of the Old Testament*, edited by G. Johannes Botterweck and Helmer Ringgren, 5, 22-36. Grand Rapids, MI: Eerdmans, 1986.

Fretheim, Terence E. *The Book of Genesis*. The New Interpreter's Bible: General Articles & Introduction, Commentary, & Reflections for Each Book of the Bible, Including the Apocryphal/ Deuterocanonical Books, edited by Leander E. Keck, David L. Petersen, Bruce C. Birch, John J. Collins and Katheryn Pfisterer Darr. Nashville, TN: Abingdon Press, 1994.

________. 'el.' *New International Dictionary of Old Testament Theology & Exegesis*, edited by Willem A. VanGemeren, 1, 400-401. Grand Rapids, MI: Zondervan 1997.

________. 'elohim.' *New International Dictionary of Old Testament Theology & Exegesis*, edited by Willem A. VanGemeren, 1, 405-406. Grand Rapids, MI: Zondervan 1997.

Fritsch, Charles T. *Genesis*, vol. 2. The Layman's Bible Commentary, edited by Balmer H. Kelly. Atlanta, GA: John Knox, 1959.

Fronmüller, G. F. C.; Mombert, Jacob Isidor. *The Epistle General of Jude*. New York: C. Scribner, & co., 1867.

Fruchtenbaum, A. G. *The Messianic Bible Study Collection*. Tustin, CA: Ariel Ministries, 1983.

Futato, Mark D. 'min.' *New International Dictionary of Old Testament Theology & Exegesis*, edited by Willem A. VanGemeren, 2, 934-935. Grand Rapids, MI: Zondervan, 1997.

Gage, Warren Austin. *The Gospel of Genesis: Studies in Protology and Eschatology*. Winona Lake, IN: Carpenter Books, 1984.

God, Names Of. *Tyndale Bible Dictionary*, edited by Walter A. Elwell and Philip Wesley Comfort, 539-543. Wheaton, IL: Tyndale House Publishers, 2001.

Goldingay, John. *Old Testament Theology: Israel's Gospel*, vol. 1. Downers Grove, IL: InterVarsity Press, 2003.

Gowan, Donald E. *Theology of the Prophetic Books: The Death & Resurrection of Israel*. Louisville, KY: Westminster John Knox Press, 1998.

Grimm, Carl Ludwig Wilibald. *A Greek-English Lexicon of the New Testament, Being Grimm's Wilke's*

Clavis Novi Testament. Translated by Joseph Henry Thayer. New York Cincinnati, OH; Chicago, IL: American Book Company, 1889.

Groningen, Gerard Van. 'Covenant.' *Baker Theological Dictionary of the Bible*, edited by Walter A. Elwell, 124-132. Grand Rapids, MI: Baker Books, 1996.

Hagan, G. Michael. 'Exodus, Theology Of.' *Baker Theological Dictionar of the Bible*, edited by Walter A. Elwell, 226-229. Grand Rapids, MI: Baker, 1996.

Hamilton, Victor P. *Theological Wordbook of the Old Testament*. Chicago, IL:Moody, 1980.

________. *The Book of Genesis: Chapters 1-17*. The New International Commentary on the Old Testament, edited by R. K. Harrison and Robert L.' Hubbard. Grand Rapids, MI: Eerdmans, 1990.

________. *Handbook on the Pentateuch*. 2nd ed. Grand Rapids, MI: Baker Academic, 2005.

Hamp, V., and G. J. Botterweck. 'dyn.' *Theological Dictionary of the Old Testament*, edited by G. Johannes Botterweck and Helmer Ringgren, 3, 187-194. Grand Rapids, MI: Eerdmans, 1965.

Harland, P. J. *The Value of Human Life: A Study of the Story of the Flood (Genesis 6-9)*. Supplements to Vetus Testamentum, vol. 64. . Leiden: Brill, 1996.

Harris, R. K. 'Law in the OT.' *The International Standard Bible Encyclopedia, Revised*, edited by Geoffrey W. Bromiley, 3, 76-85. Grand Rapids, MI: Wm. B. Eerdmans, 1988.

Harrison, R. K. 'Circumcision.' *Baker Theological Dictionar of the Bible*, edited by Walter A. Elwell, 98-99. Grand Rapids, MI: Baker, 1996.

Hart, Ian. 'Genesis 1:1-2:3 as a Prologue to the Book of Genesis.' *Tyndale Bulletin* 46 (1995): 315-336.

Hartley, John E. 'tswh.' *Theological Wordbook of the Old Testament*, edited by R. Laird Harris, 757-758. Chicago, IL: Moody Press, 1980.

________. 'hshb.' *New International Dictionary of Old Testament Theology & Exegesis*, edited by Willem A. VanGemeren, 2, 303-310. Grand Rapids, MI: Zondervan, 1997.

Hasel, Gerhard F. *The Remnant: The history and Theology of the Remnant Idea from Genesis to Isaiah*. Berrien Springs, MI: Andrews Univ Pr, 1972., 1972.

________. 'Some Issues Regarding the Nature and Universality of the Genesis Flood Narrative.' *Origins* 5 (1978): 83-98.

________. 'Genesis 5 and 11: Chronogenealogies in the Biblical history of Beginnings.' *Origins* 7 (1980): 23-37.

________. 'The Meaning of the Chronogenealogies of Genesis 5 and 11.' *Origins* 7 (1980): 53-70.

________. 'Remnant.' *The International Standard Bible Encyclopedia, Revised*, edited by Geoffrey W.; Harrison Bromiley, Everett F.; Harrison, Roland K.; Lasor, William Sanford, 4, 130-134. Grand Rapids, MI: William B. Eerdmans Publishing Co., 1988.

________. *Old Testament Theology: Basic Issues in the Current Debate*. Grand Rapids, MI: Eerdmans, 1991.

________. 'Divine Judgment.' *Handbook of Seventh-Day Adventist Theology*, edited by Raoul Dederen,

Nancy J. Vyhmeister and George W. Reid, 12, 815-856. Hagerstown, MD: Review and Herald Publishing Association, 2000.

Healey, Joseph P. 'Faith (Old Testament).' *The Anchor Bible Dictionary*, edited by David Noel Freedman, Gary A. Herion, David F. Graf and John David Pleins, 2, 744-749. New York: Doubleday, 1992.

Hendricksen, William. *The Covenant of Grace*. Rev. ed. Grand Rapids, MI: Baker, 1978.

Henry, Matthew. *Matthew Henry's Commentary on the Whole Bible: Complete and Unabridged in One Volume*. Peabody, MA: Hendrickson, 1991.

Hertz, J. H., ed. *The Pentateuch and Haftorahs Hebrew Text. English Translation and Commentary.* London: Soncino Press, 1960.

Hess, Richard S. *Studies in the Personal Names of Genesis 1-11*. Kevelaer: Verlag Butzon & Bercker, 1993.

Hill, Andrew E., and Gordon H. Matties. 'qtz.' *New International Dictionary of Old Testament Theology & Exegesis*, edited by Willem A. VanGemeren, 3, 955. Grand Rapids, MI: Zondervan, 1997.

Hodge, Charles, and Edward N. Gross. *Systematic Theology*. Abridged ed. Phillipsburg, N.J.: P&R Pub., 1997.

Hughes, R. J., III. 'Haran.' *The International Standard Bible Encyclopedia, Revised*, edited by Geoffrey W. Bromiley, 2, 614. Grand Rapids, MI: Wm. B. Eerdmans, 1986.

Hughes, R. Kent. *Genesis: Beginning and Blessing*. Preaching the Word. Wheaton, IL: Crossway Books, 2004.

Jacobsen, Thorkild. 'The Eridu Genesis (1.158).' *The Context of Scripture: Canonical Compositions from the Biblical World*, edited by William W. Hallo and K. Lawson Younger, 1, 513-515. New York: Brill, 1997.

Jamieson, Robert, A. R. Fausset, and David Brown. *A Commentary, Critical, Experimental and Explanatory, on the Old and New Testaments*. Oak Harbor, WA: Logos Research System, Inc, 1997.

Jaubert, Annie. 'Le Calendrier Des Jubilés Et Les Jours Liturgiques De La Semaine.' *Vetus testamentum* 7 (1957): 35-61.

Johnson, B. 'mspt.' *Theological Dictionary of the Old Testament*, edited by G. Johannes Botterweck, Helmer Ringgren and Heinz-Josef Fabry, 9, 86-98. Grand Rapids, MI: Eerdmans, 1998.

Köhler, Ludwig, Walter Baumgartner, M.E.J. Richardson, and Johann Jakob Stamm. *The Hebrew and Aramaic Lexicon of the Old Testament*. Leiden: Brill, 1994-2000.

________. *The Hebrew and Aramaic Lexicon of the Old Testament*. Leiden: Brill, 1994-2000.

Kaiser, Walter C. 'sm.' *Theological Wordbook of the Old Testament*, edited by R. Laird Harris, Gleason L. Archer and Bruce K. Waltke, 934-935. Chicago, IL: Moody, 1980.

Kaiser, Walter C., Jr. 'The Theology of the Old Testament.' *The Expositor's Bible Commentary: Introductory Articles*, edited by Frank E. Gaebelein, 1, 285-305. Grand Rapids, MI: Zondervan Publishing House, 1979.

Keil, Carl Friedrich, and Franz Delitzsch. *Pentateuch*, vol. 1. Translated by James Martin. Grand Rapids, MI: Eerdmans, 1949.

________. *Biblical Commentary on the Old Testament*. Peabody, MA: Hendrickson, 2002.

Kittel, Gerhard; Friedrich, Gerhard; Bromiley, Geoffrey W., eds. *Theological Dictionary of the New Testament (Abridged)*. Grand Rapids, MI: William B. Eerdmans Publishing Company, 1985.

Kline, Meredith G. *The Structure of Biblical Authority*. Grand Rapids, Mich.,: Eerdmans, 1972.

Knierim, R. 'hatah.' *Theological Lexicon of the Old Testament*, edited by Ernst Jenni and Claus Westermann, 1, 406-411. Peabody, MA: Hendrickson, 1997.

________. 'pesha, Crime.' *Theological Lexicon of the Old Testament*, edited by Ernst Jenni and Claus Westermann, 2, 1033-1037. Peabody, MA: Hendrickson, 1997.

Knutson, F. B. 'Flesh.' *The International Standard Bible Encyclopedia, Revised*, edited by Geoffrey W. Bromiley, 313-315. Grand Rapids, MI: Wm. B. Eerdmans, 2002.

Kok, Johnson Lim Teng. *Grace in the Midst of Judgment: Grappling with Genesis 1-11*. Berlin: W. de Gruyter, 2002.

Konkel, A. H. 'ytsr.' *New International Dictionary of Old Testament Theology & Exegesis*, edited by Willem A. VanGemeren, 2, 503-506. Grand Rapids, MI: Zondervan, 1997.

Kselman, John S. 'Forgiveness (Old Testament).' *The Anchor Bible Dictionary*, edited by David Noel Freedman, Gary A. Herion, David F. Graf and John David Pleins, 2, 831-833. New York: Doubleday, 1992.

Kutsch, E. 'bryt.' *Theological Lexicon of the Old Testament*, edited by Ernst Jenni and Claus Westermann, 1, 256-266. Peabody, MA: Hendrickson, 1997.

Ladd, G. E. 'Eschatology.' *The International Standard Bible Encyclopedia*, edited by Geoffrey W. Bromiley, Everett F. Harrison, Roland K. Harrison and William Sanford Lasor, 2, 130-143. Grand Rapids, MI: Eerdmans, 1982.

Ladd, George E. 'Flesh.' *Baker Encyclopedia of the Bible*, edited by Walter A. Elwell, 1, 793-796. Grand Rapids, MI: Baker, 1988.

Lambert, W. G. 'Enuma Elish.' *The Anchor Bible Dictionary*, edited by David Noel Freedman, 2, 526-528. New York: Doubleday, 1992.

Lange, Johann Peter, Tayler Lewis, and Abraham Gosman. *Genesis, or the First Book of Moses, Together with a General Theological and Homiletical Introduction to the Old Testament*. New York: C. Scribner & co., 1868.

________. *A Commentary on the Holy Scriptures*. Translated by Tayler; Gosman Lewis, A. Bellingham, WA: Logos Research Systems, Inc., 2008.

LaSor, William Sanford; Hubbard, David Allan; Bush, Frederic WM. *Old Testament Survey: The Message, Form, and Background of the Old Testament*. Grand Rapids, MI: Eerdmans, 1982. Reprint, May 1991.

Leuwen, Raymond C. Van. 'Form, Image.' *New International Dictionary of Old Testament Theology & Exegesis*, edited by Willem A. VanGemeren, 4, 643-648. Grand Rapids, MI: Zondervan 1997.

Liedke, G. 'spt.' *Theological Lexicon of the Old Testament,* edited by Ernst Jenni and Claus Westermann, 3, 1392-1399. Peabody, MA: Hendrickson, 1997.

Longacre, Robert E. 'The Discourse Structure of the Flood Narrative.' *Annual Meeting Seminar Papers, Society of Biblical Literature*, edited by George MacRae, 235-262. Missoula, MT: Scholars Press, 1976.

Luc, Alex. 'awon.' *New International Dictionary of Old Testament Theology & Exegesis*, edited by Willem A. VanGemeren, 3, 351. Grand Rapids, MI: Zondervan, 1997.

________. 'pesha.' *New International Dictionary of Old Testament Theology & Exegesis*, edited by Willem A. VanGemeren, 3, 706. Grand Rapids, MI: Zondervan, 1997.

Müller, Hans P. 'Das Motiv für Die Sintflut: Die Hermeneutische Funktion des Mythos und Seiner Analyse.' *Zeitschrift für die Alttestamentliche Wissenschaft* 97 (1985): 295-316.

Manley, G. T.; Bruce, F. F. 'God, Names Of.' *New Bible Dictionary*, edited by D. R. W. Wood, 420-422. Leicester: Inter-Varsity Press, 1996.

Manor, Dale W. 'Kadesh-Barnea.' *The Anchor Bible Dictionary*, edited by David Noel Freedman, Gary A. Herion, David F. Graf and John David Pleins, 4, 1-3. New York: Doubleday, 1992.

Mathews, Kenneth A. *Genesis 1-4:26*, vol. 1A. The New American Commentary, edited by E. Ray Clendenen. Nashville, TN: Broadman & Holman Publishers, 1996.

________. *Genesis 4:27-11:26, vol. 1B*. The New American Commentary, Edited by E. Ray Clendenen. Nashville, TN: Broadman & Holman Publishers, 1996.

________. *Genesis 11:27-50:26* The New American Commentary, Edited by E. Ray Clendenen. Nashville, TN: Broadman & Holman Publishers, 2005.

Mauch, T.M. 'Shephatiah.' *The Interpreter's Dictionary of the Bible*, edited by G. A. Buttrick, 4, 323-324. New York/ Nashville: Abingdon Press, 1962.

Mauldin, Frank L. 'Singularity and a Pattern of Sin, Punishment, and Forgiveness: [Tower of Babel; Gen 3-11].' *Perspectives in Religious Studies* 10 (1983): 41-50.

McComiskey, Thomas, E. *Theological Wordbook of the Old Testament*, edited by R. Laird Harris, 127-128. Chicago, IL: Moody Press, 1980.

________. 'asa.' *Theological Wordbook of the Old Testament*, edited by R. Laird Harris, 701-702. Chicago, IL: Moody Press, 1980.

________. *The Covenants of Promise: A Theology of the Old Testament Covenants*. Grand Rapids, MI: Baker Book House, 1985.

McConville, Gordon J. 'Abraham and Melchizedek: Horizons in Genesis 14.' *He Swore an Oath, Second Edition*, edited by R.S.; Wenham Hess, G.J.; Satterthwaite, P.E., 93-118. Grand Rapids, MI: Baker Book House, 1994.

________. 'bryt.' *New International Dictionary of Old Testament Theology & Exegesis*, edited by Willem A. VanGemeren, 1, 747-755. Grand Rapids, MI: Zondervan, 1997.

McGrath, Alister E. *Christian Theology: An Introduction.* 3rd ed. Malden, MA: Blackwell Publishers Inc., 2001.

Merrill, Eugene H. 'Covenant and the Kingdom: Genesis 1-3 as Foundation for Biblical Theology.' *Criswell Theological Review* 1 (1987): 295-308.

Meyer, Lester V. 'Remnant.' *The Anchor Bible Dictionary*, edited by David Noel Freedman, Gary A. Herion, David F. Graf and John David Pleins, 5, 669-671. New York: Doubleday, 1992.

Milgrom, Jacob. *Leviticus 1-16: A New Translation with Introduction and Commentary.* 1st ed. New York: Doubleday, 1991.

Moran, William L. *The Amarna Letters*. English-language ed. Baltimore: Johns Hopkins University Press, 1992.

Mounce, Robert H. *Romans*. The New American Commentary. Nashville, TN: Broadman & Holman, 1995.

Mulzac, Kenneth D. *The Remnant Motif in the Context of Judgment and Salvation in the Book of Jeremiah.* Ph.D. diss, Andrews University, Seventh-day Adventist Theological Seminary, 1995.

Nachmanides. *Commentary on the Torah.* Translated by Charles B. Chavel. New York: Shilo 1971.

Nel, Philip J. 'ndh.' *New International Dictionary of Old Testament Theology & Exegesis*, edited by Willem A. VanGemeren, 3, 1055-1056. Grand Rapids, MI: Zondervan, 1997.

Neusner, Jacob. *The Mishnah: A New Translation.* New Haven/London: Yale University Press, 1988.

Neusner, Jacob, Alan J. Avery-Peck, William Scott Green, and Museum of Jewish Heritage (New York N. Y.). *The Encyclopedia of Judaism*. 5 vols. New York: Continuum, 1999.

Nichol, Francis D. ed. *Philippians to Revelation.* The Seventh-day Adventist Bible Commentary: The Holy Bible with exegetical and expository commentary, vol. 7. Washington, D.C.: Review and Herald Publishing Association, 1957.

Ogden, Graham S.; Zogbo, Lynell. *A Handbook on Ecclesiastes*. UBS Handbook Series; Helps for Translators. New York, NY: United Bible Societies, 1998.

Oswalt, John N. 'baqa.' *Theological Wordbook of the Old Testament*, edited by R. Laird Harris, Gleason L. Archer and Bruce K. Waltke, 1, 123-124. Chicago, IL: Moody, 1980.

Packer, J. I. 'Revelation.' *New Bible Dictionary*, edited by D. R. W. Wood and I. Howard Marshall, 1014-1016. Leicester, England; Downers Grove, IL: InterVarsity Press, 1996.

Park, Sang Hoon. *New International Dictionary of Old Testament Theology & Exegesis*, edited by Willem A. VanGemeren, 4, 11-17. Grand Rapids, MI: Zondervan 1997.

Perdue, Leo G. 'Names of God in the Old Testament.' *Harper's Bible Dictionary*, edited by Paul J. Achtemeier, 685-687. San Francisco: Harper & Row, 1985.

Pfeiffer, E. 'Glaube Im Alten Testament.' *Zeitschrift für die alttestamentliche Wissenschaft* 71 (1959): 151-

164.

Plaut, W. Gunther. *Genesis: Commentary*. New York: Union of American Hebrew Congregations, 1974.

Preuss, Horst Dietrich. *Old Testament Theology*, vol. 1. Translated by Leo G. perdue. The Old Testament Library, edited by James L.; Newsom Mays, Carol A.; Petersen, David L. Louisville, KY: Westminster John Knox Press, 1995.

Purkiser, W. T. *Exploring Christian Holiness: The Biblical Foundations*, vol. 1. Kansas City, MS: Beacon Hill Press of Kansas City, 1983.

Rad, G. von. *Genesis: A Commentary*. The Old Testament Library, Edited by Peter Ackroyd, James Barr, Bernhard W. Anderson and James L. Mays. Philadelphia, PA: Westminster Press, 1972.

Rendtorff, Rolf. 'Noah, Abraham and Moses: God's Covenant Partners.' *In Search of True Wisdom: Essays in Old Testament Interpretation in Honour of Ronald E.* Clements, edited by Edward Ball, 127-136. Sheffield, England: Sheffield Academic Press, 1999.

Reventlow, Henning. *Problems of Old Testament Theology in the Twentieth Century*, 1st ed. Philadelphia: Fortress Press, 1985.

Reyburn, William David; Fry, Euan McG. *A Handbook on Genesis*. UBS Handbook Series. New York: United Bible Societies, 1997.

Richards, Lawrence O. *The Bible Reader's Companion*. Wheaton, IL: Victor Books, 1991.

Ross, Allen P. *Creation and Blessing: A Guide to the Study and Exposition of the Book of Genesis*. Grand Rapids, MI: Baker, 1988.

Ryken, Leland, James C. Wilhoit, Tremper Longman, eds. *Dictionary of Biblical Imagery*. Downers Grove, IL: InterVarsity Press, 1998.

Sailhamer, John H. 'Genesis.' *Genesis-Numbers*, edited by Frank E. Gaebelein, 2, 1-284. Grand Rapids, MI: Zondervan, 1990.

________. *The Pentateuch as Narrative: A Biblical-Theological Commentary*. Library of Biblical Interpretation. Grand Rapids, MI: Zondervan Publishing House, 1992.

Sarna, Nahum M. *Genesis*, vol. 1. The JPS Torah Commentary, edited by Nahum M. Sarna. Philadelphia, PA: The Jewish Publication Society, 1989.

Schmid, H. H. 'amr.' *Theological Lexicon of the Old Testament*, edited by Ernst Jenni and Claus Westermann, 1, 159-162. Peabody, MA: Hendrickson, 1997.

Schultz, Carl. 'awh.' *Theological Wordbook of the Old Testament*, edited by R. Laird Harris, 650-652. Chicago, IL: Moody Press, 1980.

Schultz, Richard. 'dyn.' *New International Dictionary of Old Testament Theology & Exegesis*, edited by Willem A. VanGemeren, 1, 938-942. Grand Rapids, MI: Zondervan, 1997.

________. 'spt.' *New International Dictionary of Old Testament Theology & Exegesis*, edited by Willem A. VanGemeren, 4, 213-220. Grand Rapids, MI: Zondervan, 1997.

Selman, M.J. 'Law.' *Dictionary of the Old Testament: Pentateuch*, edited by T. Desmond; Baker Alexander,

David W., 497-515. Downers Grove, IL: InterVarsity Press, 2003.

Shea, William H. 'The Structure of the Genesis Flood Narrative and Its Implications.' *Origins* 6 (1979): 8-29.

Skinner, John. *A Critical and Exegetical Commentary on Genesis*, vol. 1. 2nd ed. The International Critical Commentary on the Holy Scriptures of the Old and New Testaments. Edinburgh: T. & T. Clark, 1930.

Smith, Gary V. 'Structure and Purpose in Genesis 1-11.' *Journal of the Evangelical Theological Society* 20 (1977): 307-319.

Speiser, E. A. *Genesis*, vol. 1. Anchor Bible. Garden City: Doubleday & Co., 1964.

Stoebe, H. J. 'hnn.' *Theological Lexicon of the Old Testament*, edited by Ernst Jenni and Claus Westermann, 1, 439-447. Peabody, MA: Hendrickson, 1997.

Stolper, Pinchas. 'The Man-Woman Dynamic of Ha-Adam: A Jewish Paradigm of Marriage.' *Tradition* 27, (1992): 34-41.

Stone, Nathan J. *Names of God in the Old Testament*. Chicago, IL: Moody Press, 1944.

Thompson, Henry O. 'Yahweh (Deity).' *The Anchor Bible Dictionary*, edited by David Noel Freedman, 6, 1012. New York: Doubleday, 1992.

Thompson, J. Arthur. 'Covenant (OT).' *The International Standard Bible Encyclopedia*, edited by Geoffrey W. Bromiley, Everett F. Harrison, Ronald K. Harrison and William Sanford Lasor, 1, 790-793. Grand Rapids, MI: Eerdmans 1979.

Todd, Virgil H. 'Biblical Eschatology: An Overview.' *Cumberland Seminarian* 22 (1984): 3-16.

Turner, Laurence A. *Genesis*. Readings: A New Biblical Commentary, Edited by John Jarick. Sheffield, England: Sheffield Academic Press, 2000.

________. *Announcements of Plot in Genesis*. Journal for the Study of the Old Testament. Supplement Series, vol. 96, edited by David J. A. Clines and Philip R. Davies. Sheffield, England: JSOT Press, 1990.

van Bemmelen, Peter M. 'Revelation and Inspiration.' *Handbook of Seventh-Day Adventist Theology*, edited by Raoul Dederen, 22-57. Hagerstown, MD: Review and Herald Publishing Association, 2000.

Vancil, Jack W. 'From Creation to Chaos: An Exegesis of Jer. 4:23-26.' *Biblical Interpretation: Principles and Practice*, edited by F. Furman Kearley, Edward P. Myers and Timothy D. Hadley, 181-192. Grand Rapids, MI: Baker Book House, 1986.

Vollmer, J. 'asa.' *Theological Lexicon of the Old Testament*, edited by Ernst Jenni and Claus Westermann, 2, 944-951. Peabody, MA: Hendrickson, 1997.

Vos, G. 'Omniscience.' *The International Standard Bible Encyclopedia, Revised*, edited by Geoffrey W. Bromiley, 598-600. Grand Rapids, MI: Wm. B. Eerdmans, 2002.

Waltke, Bruce K., and Cathi J. Fredricks. *Genesis: A Commentary*. Grand Rapids, MI: Zondervan, 2001.

Waltke, Bruce K., and M. O'Connor. *An Introduction to Biblical Hebrew Syntax*. Winona Lake, IN: Eisenbrauns, 1990.

Waltke, Bruce K., and Charles Yu. *An Old Testament Theology: An Exegetical, Canonical, and Thematic Approach*. 1st ed. Grand Rapids, MI: Zondervan, 2007.

Wenham, Gordon J. 'Coherence of the Flood Narrative.' *Vetus Testamentum* 28 (1978): 336-348.

________. 'Sanctuary Symbolism in the Garden of Eden Story.' *Proceedings, 9th World Congress of Jewish Studies*, 19-25. Jerusalem: World Union of Jewish Studies, 1986.

________. *Genesis 1-15*, vol. 1. Word Biblical Commentary. Waco, TX: Word Books, 2002.

Westermann, Claus. *Creation*. Translated by John J. Scullion, S.J. London: S.P.C.K., 1974.

________. *Genesis 1-11: A Commentary*. Translated by John J. Scullion. Minneapolis, MN: Augsburg 1984.

________. *Genesis: A Practical Commentary*. Text and Interpretation. Grand Rapids, MI: Eerdmans, 1987.

Whitelaw, Thomas; Farrar, Frederic William, Cotterill, Henry. *Genesis*. The Pulpit Commentary, edited by H. D. M. Spence-Jones. New York, Toronto: Funk & Wagnalls Company, 1913.

Wiersbe, Warren W. *Wiersbe's Expository Outlines on the Old Testament*. Wheaton, IL: Victor Books, 1993.

________. *Be Obedient*. Wheaton, IL: Victor Books, 1996.

Williams, Stephen N. 'Revelation.' *Dictionary for Theological Interpretation of the Bible*, edited by Kevin J.; Bartholomew Vanhoozer, Craig G.; Treier, Daniel J.; Wright, N. T., 678-680. London; Grand Rapids, MI: SPCK; Baker Academic, 2005.

Williamson, P.R. 'Abraham.' *Dictionary of the Old Testament: Pentateuch*, edited by T. Desmond; Baker Alexander, David W., 8-17. Downers Grove, Ill.: InterVarsity Press, 2003.

Wolf, Herbert. *An Introduction to the Old Testament Pentateuch*. Chicago, IL: Moody, 1991.

Wright, Christopher J. H. 'God, Names Of.' *The International Standard Bible Encyclopedia, Revised*, edited by Geoffrey W. Bromiley, 504-508. Grand Rapids, MI: Wm. B. Eerdmans, 2002.

Wyatt, Robert J. 'God, Names Of.' *The International Standard Bible Encyclopedia*, edited by Geoffrey W. Bromiley, Everett F. Harrison, Ronald K. Harrison and William Sanford Lasor, 2, 504-509. Grand Rapids, MI: Eerdmans, 1982.

Young, Edward J. *Genesis 3: A Devotional & Expository Study*. London: Banner of Truth Trust, 1966.

Youngblood, Ronald F. *The Book of Genesis: An Introductory Commentary*. 2nd ed. Grand Rapids, MI: Baker, 1991.

Zerafa, P. 'La Retribuzione Nella Bibbia.' *Angelicum* 74 (1997): 145-170.

Everlasting Gospel Series:

Genesis

1판 1쇄 2025년 11월 20일

편저자 Chunsik Park · Juhyun Park
발행인 이경화

발행처 디자인21
주소 04560 서울특별시 중구 퇴계로 293-1(쌍림동 원진프라자 3층)
전화 02-2269-6561(대)
팩스 02-2269-6568
이메일 21publish@naver.com
블로그 https://blog.naver.com/publish21
인스타 https://www.instagram.com/21publish.co.kr
홈페이지 https://21publish.co.kr

등록번호 제1-1128호
등록일자 1991. 2. 12

ISBN 978-89-6131-197-7 93230

정가 25,000원